**Elementary
Statistical
Procedures**

Elementary Statistical Procedures

Clinton I. Chase

Associate Director
Bureau of Educational Studies and Testing
Associate Professor of Education
Indiana University

McGraw-Hill Book Company

New York   St. Louis   San Francisco
Toronto   London   Sydney

To Pat and Steven—
a nonrandom sample from a
population toward which I
am decidedly biased.

Elementary
Statistical
Procedures

Library of Congress Catalog Card Number 67-11453

10680

4567891011 HDMM 754321069

Preface	This is a textbook in introductory statistical methods, designed for use primarily by students in the social sciences. The emphasis is on deriving procedures out of the logical structures that underlie the methods of analyzing data. Therefore, the initial step in all presentations is the rationale that is the foundation of the computational procedure.

Statistical methods are merely tools for bringing order into accumulated data and for helping us to make reasonable decisions in the face of uncertainty. To this end statistics may be thought of as a kind of language —a mode of communication. Words are symbols for things and ideas; statistical methods also involve symbols that stand for things and ideas. Words, arranged in a given order, provide the structure for greater, more expansive concepts.   Similarly, statistical symbols, arranged in various orders, become "sentences" that communicate to us expansive information. The job in statistics, then, is to become familiar with the ideas represented by symbols and how these ideas are arranged into broader concepts.   Then, just as words and sentences make up an exposition, so do statistical symbols.

Many students of beginning statistics become so involved with the mathematics of fitting numbers into formulas and solving equations that the basic logic of the procedure either is not grasped in the first place or becomes lost in the maze of formula solutions.   In this book the rationale is presented first and then computations are introduced.   The step-by-step procedures are provided only as an adjunct to the basic concepts and are designed to elaborate these concepts, not to be taken in place of them.

It is believed that learning progresses most efficiently when the application of information is most contiguous with its presentation.   Therefore problems are interspersed throughout the chapters to provide the student with a chance to apply information immediately after a given topic is discussed.   Since review is often an important element in learning, a general set of problems dealing with the topics of a chapter are provided at its close.

This book is constructed to be meaningful to students who have a minimum of mathematical skill, but it also provides for students who may be more sophisticated in mathematics.   The topics of each chapter are presented in such a way as to be meaningful to students who have had only simple work in algebra, and for a review of these basic operations a list of rules with examples is provided in Appendix A.   However, for the more advanced and more curious student complete mathematical developments of many procedures are provided in Appendix B.   Therefore, students who need a review of various topics in algebra may well profit from the use of this book, since references in the body of the text are often made to basic mathematical procedures in Appendix A, while the more advanced student may spend his time acquiring additional foundational information from Appendix B.   However, the basic logic of the procedures described in the text is for everyone.

In several sections of the text some procedures are presented which are more adaptable to hand calculations, whereas other procedures are more adaptable to calculator operations.   In these days when calculating machines are increasingly available, one may wish to concentrate on the procedures more likely to be used with such machines.   However, it is the experience of the author that in many practical situations calculators are not available. Therefore, hand techniques, such as grouped-data methods, are presented along with other procedures.   In this way the student may select the method that is most expeditious for his setting.

The writing of a textbook such as this is rarely the effort of a single person, although one person claims authorship. To this text Richard Pugh, Assistant Director of the Bureau of Educational Studies and Testing at Indiana University, has contributed a number of appealing suggestions. Also, the author's orientation has been significantly influenced by his own instructors. Therefore, a debt of gratitude is due Prof. William H. Boyer, Chairman Emeritus, the Department of Psychology, University of Idaho, who projected an atmosphere of excitement into the author's first course in statistics, and to Prof. Guy T. Buswell and Prof. William A. Brownell, both Emeritus of the University of California, who repeatedly emphasized the need for meaning and communication in research methodology.

But the most significant contributors to the author's knowledge and point of view have been his students who have asked questions, posed problems, and suggested alternative procedures and who have translated into simple language the tasks that often look forbidding in symbols. These are the people who have forced this writer to explore new areas and new modes of presentation, to look for more effective ways to communicate various procedures, and to integrate his knowledge in many areas so as to focus it upon a single question. The efforts of these students, often unwittingly in this writer's behalf, are of inestimable value. From this collection of experiences the author presents this textbook in the hope that the topic will become an exciting body of useful, logical, and meaningful material for all future students.

Clinton I. Chase

Contents

Preface v

1 Definitions and Concepts, 1
2 Frequency Distributions and Graphic Representation of Data, 7
3 Measures of Central Tendency, 26
4 Indicators of Relative Position in a Distribution, 46
5 Variability, 57
6 The Normal Curve and Its Applications, 75
7 Correlation and Regression, 91
8 Probability and Statistical Inference, 117
9 Testing Differences between Means, 140
10 Introduction to Analysis of Variance, 161
11 Chi Square and Other Nonparametric Procedures, 173
Appendix A Review of Arithmetic and Algebraic Processes, 195
Appendix B Mathematical Developments of Procedures, 205
Appendix C Tables, 212
Appendix D Answers to Practice Problems, 236
Index, 243

ix

1

Definitions and Concepts

When the man on the street uses the term *statistics*, he is usually referring to items of quantitative information, which are typically submitted as support for a given point of view. In the newspaper we read the statistics on automobile accidents, divorce, crime, high school dropouts. (The ill in society attracts the attention of counters, while the good often goes untabulated.) Numbers are poured upon a public that drinks them in with an insatiable thirst.

This popular idea of statistics is not, however, the topic of this book. Quantitative observations are indeed important in all sectors of our society, but they are only useful if order can be put into the masses of numbers collected by scientific and domestic agencies. It is these methods that put order into data

1

which make up the topics of the chapters ahead.   Thus, this is a book not on statistics but on statistical methods.

The techniques described in successive chapters will do one of only two things.   They will describe a set of data, or they will provide a basis for making a generalization about a large group of individuals when only a selected portion of such a group has been observed.   Certain procedures, then, are called *descriptive methods* because they point up a characteristic of the group being observed.   Other techniques are called *inferential procedures*, because they make inferences about large numbers of individuals when only a small sample from the larger group has been observed.

At this point we need to identify the terms *statistic* and *parameter*, but to do this we first must talk about samples and populations.

A population is any group of individuals all of whom have at least one characteristic in common.   We typically think of populations in terms of census data, such as the population of a nation, a state, a city.   Certainly these concepts fit our definition, since they each describe a group of people who have a common characteristic—locality of residence.   But populations can be defined on bases other than residence.   For example, all women with naturally red hair or all men with beards or all people with annual incomes above $100,000 are populations, and the defining characteristic has nothing to do with residence.   Populations may be large—such as all persons within the city limits of New York on a given day—or they may be small—such as all persons who man forest lookout stations in Clearwater County, Idaho, or all persons over one hundred years of age in California.

In research in the social sciences, as well as in other disciplines, it is often impossible to study entire populations.   Instead we select smaller portions of the population and from these make inferences as to what the population is like.   These smaller portions of a population we call *samples*.

In choosing samples our hope is to get a segment of the population which looks just like—is representative of—the entire population.   There are several techniques for selecting representative samples, but the one on which the inferential techniques in successive chapters rely is randomization.   For a sample to be truly random, all individuals in the population must have an equal chance to be selected each time a selection is made.   In this way the selection of one individual has nothing to do with determining who else will be selected in the sample.

In actual practice the individuals we observe are often not truly random samples from the parent population.   Therefore, we go to some length to compare the characteristics of the sample with known characteristics of the population so that we may decide whether our sample looks sufficiently like the population to venture on with further assessments.   For example we cannot observe all the six-year-old children in Detroit, so we go to five public schools dispersed across the city and observe children from 1 first-grade class in each school. This is not a method for selecting a random sample. However, we know something about the expected varieties of IQs for all six-year-olds, we know something about the numbers of people in various socioeconomic levels, we know something about the numbers of various races in the city. With this type of information we could look at our sample to see how closely it fits the known traits of the population. If the sample seems to fit the population on several traits, we often hypothesize that it also will look like the population in other ways. This assumption may be in error; but when populations are large, truly random selection techniques are next to impossible to implement, and the above alternative is often the next resort.

When we have selected a sample from a population, we usually compute certain characteristics of that sample, e.g., an average for some trait. Characteristics of samples are called *statistics*. However, when we are dealing with populations, characteristics, such as averages, are then called *parameters*. Thus, if we define our population as all people taking elementary statistics at Eks University, the average height of these people would be a parameter. But if we put all the names of these students into a barrel, stir them well, and blindfolded, draw out 10 names (replacing each name once it was drawn out—why?), the average height of this group of 10 people would be a statistic. Statistics tell us something about samples taken from given populations; parameters tell us something about populations.

Statistical workers deal with many kinds of variables, but all these kinds can be sorted into about two categories. In the first category we have data obtained by counting indivisible units, such as children in a classroom or errors on a true-false test. We call a succession of these units a *discrete* series. The data are always collections of whole numbers, since at no time do we have a part of a unit. If we are going from house to house tabulating the number of children in the family, each report is of a whole number of children. There is no such thing as a fractional part of a child. Families are made up of two, three, four, etc., children, never three and a fraction or two and a fraction. If there are two children in a family and another child is born, the number of children changes from two to three without passing through a series of fractional parts between those two numbers. The series is a discrete one.

However, many kinds of data come in units which are divisible into an infinite number of fractional parts. This is the second category of data. To expand an observation from one unit to the next, we must pass through a large number of fractional parts of that next unit. For example, when a child grows from 43 to 44 inches in height he passes through all fractions of that forty-fourth inch before he actually acquires the fine height of a full 44 inches. Numbers which are obtained from a succession of units, each of which can be divided an infinitely large number of times, are called a *continuous* series. If we have driven 2 miles, to go 3 we must pass through all fractional parts of that next mile; if we walk a block, we must walk through all fractional parts of that segment of the street. All such measurement kinds of data represent a continuous series.

We may wish at times to visualize discrete and continuous data which progress together. For example, a mile race may mean that the runners must go around the race track four times. The actual distance of a mile represents a continuous variable; however, if we count the runner's progress by laps around the track, we are in the realm of discrete data. Either the runner has completed one, two, three laps, or he has not.

But what if a runner has completed 2.67 laps? Shall we count him as having completed only two laps? But he is really nearer to completing three laps than two. When we are counting events in a discrete series which is paralleled by a continuous one, we typically mark off units at the halfway point between two successive numbers. For example, if we are counting inches, the unit labeled 4 inches would run from 3.5 to 4.5. The unit labeled 2 would run from 1.5 to 2.5, and so on, as shown in Fig. 1.1. In

Figure 1.1

other words we shall think of any given number in a continuous series as the midpoint of a unit. The unit may be small ($\frac{1}{8}$ inch, an ounce) or it may be large (a mile, a decade), size being a relative matter. In any case, the numbers we use to label the units will represent the midpoint of the unit. Thus, if our unit is $\frac{1}{2}$ inch, the number 3 would represent the third half inch in a series of $\frac{1}{2}$-inch units, and it would be the midpoint of that segment of length that runs from $\frac{1}{4}$ inch below the third half inch to $\frac{1}{4}$ inch above it. If our unit is the mile, 3 would represent the distance from 2.5 to 3.5 miles, etc.

Thus, in statistical methods we often have occasions to deal with a discrete series of units which is paralleled by a continuous series. When this occurs, the units in the discrete series label the midpoints of units in the continuous series, and the units in the continuous series are thought of as beginning a half unit below the labeled point and extending a half unit beyond it.

Summary

Not everyone today is a statistician, but everyone, almost without choice, must be a consumer of statistics. In either case knowledge of basic methods of manipulating data is saliently important to intelligent behavior in a quantitative world.

This is a book about methods of dealing with data—statistical methods. Some of these methods tell us how to describe a body of data. These are called descriptive statistics. Other techniques allow us to make judgments about a large group of individuals when we have only observed a carefully chosen segment of the total group. These techniques are categorized under the term statistical inference.

All individuals who have one or more characteristics in common can be defined as a population. Characteristics of a population are called parameters. A collection of individuals who represent a portion of a given population is called a sample. Characteristics of samples are called statistics.

Conditions observed by social scientists provide numbers. These numbers represent a discrete series, in which each unit is an indivisible whole, or a continuous series, in which case a given unit may be divided an infinite number of times. A discrete series is reported only in whole numbers, such as the number of students in a class, whereas a continuous series may involve combinations of whole numbers and fractions.

PROBLEMS

1 List four populations other than those tied to geographical boundaries, such as city limits or state lines.
2 Label each of the following conditions as a parameter or a statistic, and state why you have so labeled them.
   a The average age of all red-haired children in the sixth grade in Centerville Public School
   b The proportion of all employees of the Ford Motor Company who are left-handed
   c The average weight of 10 boys whose names have been drawn from a hat containing names of all boys in the senior class at Centerville High School
   d The first five numbers selected by a roulette wheel out of all the numbers around the wheel
3 Decide whether the following variables represent discrete or continuous series.

    a The number of dogs caught by the dogcatcher in a given city
       on December 12, 1960
    b The time it takes a rat to run through a T maze
    c The number of children whose fathers are college professors
       at Eks University
    d The amount of change in height of 10 children during a period
       of six months
    e The number of birthdays 10 children in grade 6 have had
4 List five situations where we have a parallel discrete and continuous
   series.
5 State how you would select a random sample of:
    a 20 six-year-olds from all those enrolled in the first grade in
       Centertown city schools
    b 100 persons who are unemployed from the population of those
       on unemployment compensation rolls in the city of Lewiston,
       Idaho
    c 30 registered Democrats in Harlan County, Kentucky

2

Frequency Distributions and Graphic Representation of Data

The collection of research data results in an accumulation of numbers which stand for various amounts of some observed condition. If we wish to know if drug X has an influence on the number of errors rats make in running a maze, the numbers that we collect in our research could represent errors made by rats. If we want to know the effect of instructional method A, compared with method B, on the learning of arithmetic in grade 5, the numbers we collect here might represent the numbers of correct answers on an arithmetic achievement test given to students who were taught A and students who were taught B. In any case, researchers are collectors of numbers, and they seek out ways to put order into the masses of numbers they collect.

7

Frequency Distributions

One of the most fundamental techniques for putting order into a disarray of data is the frequency distribution. Basically it is a systematic procedure for arranging individuals from least to most in relation to some quantifiable characteristic. If we are observing intelligence, we could better see what our data tell us if we record the individual IQ scores in a column with the lowest IQ appearing at the bottom, the next lowest IQ second from the bottom, and so on until we have the highest IQ at the top of the column. Since we probably will have several individuals with the same IQ at many points in our arrangement, we usually make two columns for our data. In the one column we show the list of possible scores (or amounts of the condition observed), and beside this a second column shows how many people got that score. An example using the weights of 20 children will illustrate this procedure. It is shown in Table 2.1.

Table 2.1 Fictitious Weights of 20 Children

Unordered Weights	Frequency Distribution	
	Ordered weights	Frequency of occurrence
97, 108, 102,	110	1
103, 106, 104,	109	0
105, 110, 101,	108	1
103, 105, 104,	107	0
106, 102, 102,	106	3
99, 103, 104,	105	2
106, 103	104	3
	103	4
	102	3
	101	1
	100	0
	99	1
	98	0
	97	1

Tabulations of data, such as Table 2.1, in which score values (or other quantitative characteristics) are arranged from low to high in one column and the number of individuals who achieved each score is shown in an adjacent column are called frequency distributions.

Frequency distributions are constructed primarily for two reasons: First, they put the data into order so that a visual analysis can be made of the results of the measurements which have been made; and secondly, they provide a convenient structure for simple computations, as we shall see in later chapters. Look back at Table 2.1. By scanning this frequency distribution, we see that most of the weights, three-fourths of them in fact, lie between 102 and 106 pounds and that half of them fall between 102 and 104. We could not quickly observe these simple facts—and others like them—from the unordered data. However, when the unordered IQs are arranged into a frequency distribution, many interesting results can be quickly seen simply by scanning the distribution.

In building frequency distributions, we go through three basic stages:

1   We choose a given step to represent points on our scale. The step represents a specified quantity of the condition being observed. In Table 2.1 the step was 1 pound. But we could have made our measurements to the nearest $\frac{1}{2}$ pound and arranged our scale in $\frac{1}{2}$-pound steps, we could have even gone to an ounce scale, or we could have made our scale in 2-pound steps. Steps should not be confused with units of measurement. For example, we could use a pound as our step but measure to the nearest ounce. The pound would be the step, the ounce the unit of measurement.

2   We then arrange our score values from the lowest to the highest in terms of the selected step.

3   We tabulate the number of individuals whose scores come within each step on the scale.

As an example, let us take height as the characteristic being observed and make a frequency distribution following the three stages described above. We might (1) prescribe 1-inch steps, although we could measure to the nearest $\frac{1}{4}$ inch. We would then (2) arrange our scale units, and if we are observing height among 30 high school senior boys, a scanning of the data could show the scale might begin at 60 inches and run—inch by inch— through 79 inches. We would then (3) tabulate the number of boys whose height fell within the range of each of the inch units between 60 and 79. The result would be a frequency distribution for height for this group of individuals. It might look like Table 2.2.

In Table 2.2 we have the steps on our scale in the left-hand column, and the number of boys who came at each step are listed in the right-hand column. A step in the scale, in this case 1 inch, is called a *step interval* or

Table 2.2 A Frequency Distribution of Height for a Sample of 30 High School Senior Boys

Scale in Inch Units	Number of Boys (frequency)
79	1
78	0
77	1
76	0
75	2
74	1
73	0
72	2
71	2
70	4
69	5
68	3
67	0
66	3
65	2
64	0
63	1
62	2
61	0
60	1

simply an *interval;* the number of individuals at a given step interval is called the *frequency* for that interval.

Several decisions must be made, however, before we can construct such a frequency distribution.   One of these decisions deals with how to classify persons whose measurements involve fractions of steps.   Where do I tabulate the boy who might be 68.75 inches tall?   Where do I include the one who is 71.25?   Before I begin to construct a frequency distribution, I need a few basic rules that will tell me how to classify these cases so that I shall be consistent in my classifications of all persons whose measurements involve fractions of units.

When the frequency distribution is based on a scale with a defined unit of measurement and individuals are measured in fractional parts of the defined units, we usually handle them in the following manner.   If for any individual the measurement contains a fraction which is less than half a unit, it is included in the table under the last whole unit in the scale *before* the fraction. Thus, a boy who was 68.25 inches tall would be tabulated at 68 inches in the frequency distribution of Table 2.2; a boy 72.38 inches would be tabulated at 72. However, fractional parts that are equal to or more than half a unit represent amounts which are nearer to the next larger unit on the scale than to the previous unit and are, therefore, tabulated under that next larger unit. Thus, a boy who was 68.75 inches tall would appear in Table 2.2 under the unit labeled 69 inches.

This leads us to determining the *real limits* of a given step interval. For a given point on a scale the real limits begin a half unit prior to that point, and they extend up to a half unit beyond that point. Therefore, in Table 2.2, the real limits of the unit listed as 70 are actually from 69.5 to 70.5, as shown in Fig. 2.1. Any measurement which falls from 69.5 to 70.5 would

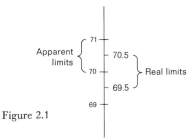

Figure 2.1

be tabulated within the class interval of 70. Thus, in Table 2.2 the four cases that are in the interval labeled 70 may range anywhere within the real limits of the interval 69.5 up to 70.5.

A second decision that must be made in regard to frequency distributions is the number of measurement units that will be included within a step interval. In Table 2.2 our unit was 1 inch, and we included only one unit per step interval. However, suppose we had decided to use $\frac{1}{4}$ inch as our unit. Then by using 1 inch as our step interval, we would have been including four measurement units within each interval ($\frac{4}{4}$ inch equals 1 inch, the step interval width). Many measurement units are made up of smaller parts, so when we use these units, we are in effect using groups of the smaller parts that make up the unit. For example, the unit used in measuring a football field is the yard. But 1 yard is a group of 3 feet, or it is a group of 36 inches. Now agreeing that 3 feet would make up 1 yard is pretty much an arbitrary arrangement. We might do as well if we all agreed to use, say, 2 feet or 4 feet instead. The point is that measurement units are often made up of smaller parts, and the way that we group those parts into larger units is pretty much an arbitrary matter, workable only as long as we all agree to the grouping method.

With this thought in mind, let us again go to Table 2.2.   There are quite a few class intervals in which we have no frequencies, making an unevenness in our distribution.   Suppose instead of using 1 inch for our step interval, we all decided to use 2 inches per interval, just as we could decide (if everybody agreed) to use 2 feet for a yard.   In the table this would not spoil the integrity of our inch as the basic unit of measurement.   It only influences our method of grouping the inches, just as grouping feet into a yard does not disturb the adequacy of the foot as a unit of measurement.   Now using our 2-inch interval, let us make up a second frequency distribution from the same data as before.   Our new frequency distribution would look like Table 2.3.

Table 2.3   A Second Frequency Distribution of Height for a Sample of 30 Fictitious High School Senior Boys

Intervals Based on Inch Units	Number of Boys (*f*)
78–79	1
76–77	1
74–75	3
72–73	2
70–71	6
68–69	8
66–67	3
64–65	2
62–63	3
60–61	1

The data in Table 2.3 are listed in 10 step intervals, instead of the 20 in Table 2.2, but the distribution has no breaks in it as it did before when six intervals contained no frequencies.   This scheme of compressing distributions by including several measurement units per interval is known as *grouping data* and is especially helpful when the range of scores is wide, wider than is true even of Table 2.2.   The method reduces the number of intervals so that we can reasonably handle them in subsequent computations and so that they are meaningful in terms of the number of cases that come within each interval.

The question now arises concerning how many intervals are a "good" number with which to work. As a rule of thumb something near 15 intervals is usually quite satisfactory, but we would certainly not want less than 10, and usually not more than 20. If we use too few intervals, the shape of the distribution may become distorted, while too many intervals may not compress the data enough to be of advantage in subsequent manipulations.

The number of intervals to be used also provides us with the basic information we need for estimating how many measurement units will go into each interval. The procedure goes like this: First, we subtract the smallest quantity from the largest and add 1 to that difference. This gives us the total range of scores. Then we divide the result by 15 and round the answer, whenever possible, in the direction that will make the number of units in an interval an odd number. (The reason for this will become evident later; it should suffice to say now that we shall want to find the midpoint of an interval, and if the intervals have an odd number of units in them, the midpoint will always be a whole number. If the interval width is an even number of units, the midpoint of an interval will always end in a fraction.)

Suppose in a group of 30 six-year-olds the highest IQ is 125 and the lowest is 90. How many IQ points should go into each interval? First, we subtract 90 from 125 and add 1. This comes out to be 36. Dividing this by 15, we find an answer of 2.4 units. An interval two units long would result in 18 intervals; three units per interval would result in 12 intervals. Since we agreed to go with an odd number of units in an interval, we choose the latter width, three units of IQ per interval.

Another question has pushed its way into focus as a result of our grouping more than one measurement unit into a step interval. What are the real limits of intervals that contain more than one unit?

Nothing is changed when we decide to group several units into one interval. We still are measuring in terms of the basic unit, even though we have grouped several of these units into a single interval. Therefore, the *real limits* are based on fractions of the *unit of measurement,* not upon fractions of the step interval. For example, let us take the first interval in Table 2.3. The interval is 60–61. Its real limits begin one-half of a unit before the designated beginning point of the interval and end a half unit beyond the designated ending of the interval. Thus, the real limits of the interval designated 60–61 are from 59.5 to 61.5. The real limits of the next interval begin at 61.5 and go on to 63.5, etc. A graphic representation would look like Fig. 2.2.

It is well to remember in working with frequency distributions such as

Table 2.3, where measurement units have been grouped within intervals, that by so grouping we do not abandon our unit of measurement. In measuring a football field in yards, we do not abandon the use of feet to determine yards, and to make a first down the team must still move ahead 30 feet. Twenty-eight feet will not suffice, even though it is within the last

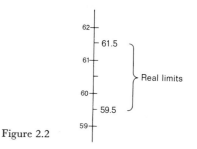

Figure 2.2

step interval (yards) of the 10 intervals needed. Thus in determining real limits of an interval, the basic unit of measurement still is used regardless of how many units are grouped into a single step interval.

PROBLEMS

1   We have IQ scores on a group of 50 ten-year-old children. The highest IQ is 144; the lowest is 78. What will be our scale *unit?* How many units will be used in an interval? How many intervals will this make? What are the apparent limits of the first interval? What are its real limits?

2   We have the weights of 75 high school freshmen. The heaviest is 192 lb, 8 oz; the lightest is 89 lb, 14 oz. If our scale unit is 1 lb, how many units should we include in an interval? How many intervals will this make? If the unit is 1 oz, how many units will be included in each interval if we have 15 intervals?

3   Given the following IQ data, construct a frequency distribution according to prescribed procedures: 144, 116, 97, 111, 112, 85, 132, 128, 123, 106, 80, 93, 118, 113, 104, 121, 101, 117, 138, 122, 118, 112, 109, 114, 105, 125, 129, 133, 103.

4   Using the data given in Prob. 3, construct a frequency distribution using five intervals. Now compare the shape of this distribution with the one you constructed in Prob. 3. Does this give you some idea why too few intervals is not desirable? (Be on the lookout for more on this topic later.)

Graphic Representations of Data

There are many opportunities to present frequency distributions in graphic form, and several standard procedures for graphing data have emerged. The choice of procedure depends upon what characteristic we wish to emphasize.

One way that frequency distributions might be presented is in the form of a *histogram*.*   The procedure here is first to construct a frequency distribution and then within the *real limits* of the first interval to construct a bar, the length of which represents the frequencies in that interval. The same procedure is repeated for each succeeding interval until all intervals are depicted as bar graphs adjacent to one another. A histogram of the data in Table 2.3 would look like Fig. 2.3.

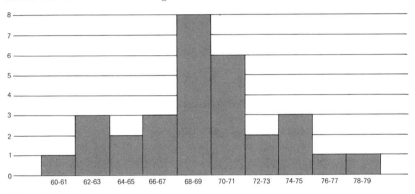

Figure 2.3

In Fig. 2.3 the frequencies in a given interval can be interpreted either by the height of the various bars or by their areas. At this point we probably do well to think of the frequencies in terms of the height of the bars, but later on we shall have occasions to interpret a distribution in terms of relative areas of the histogram that are associated with given segments on the base line of the distribution. So if for a moment we can think of a given interval in terms of the area of its bar, and the relationship of the frequencies in, say, two intervals as the relative magnitude of the two areas, we shall then be prepared for a topic in a later chapter, when in a graph the area which is cut off between a given segment of scores assumes primary importance.

* The Greek word *histos* referred to the warp in weaving, that is, the lengthwise threads in the loom.   Karl Pearson, the English statistician who is said to have originated the term *histogram*, supposedly saw in it a pattern similar to that of a loom loaded with its warp.

The histogram represents the data in terms of distinct and discrete segments (intervals) and emphasizes the relative magnitude of each of these segments.   If this is the characteristic of the data we wish to illustrate, then the histogram is the technique to use.

Oftentimes, however, we wish to reflect the continuous nature of our data.   In this case we would like to illustrate differences in frequencies from interval to interval as they occur in a steady incremental fashion.   We could do this by placing a point at the center of the top of each bar in Fig. 2.3, and connecting these points with lines.   The resulting figure is called a *frequency polygon,* which for our data would look like Fig. 2.4.

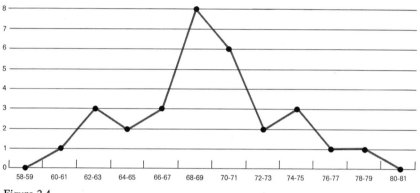

Figure 2.4

Oftentimes we graph data from a sample of people who are supposedly typical of the population from which the sample came.   For example, we may wish to show the distribution of IQ scores for ten-year-old children, but we have scores on only 100 cases.   If we were to put these data into a frequency polygon like Fig. 2.4, we would probably see irregular peaks in the graph owing to the fact that our sample does not amply represent the entire population.   Such irregularity might very well diminish if we could graph data from the entire population, that is, the graph may well show a minimum of irregularity, or, as we say, become "smooth."

Luckily, there is a very simple technique for smoothing frequency polygons. We do a kind of averaging among adjacent intervals in the distribution. The smoothed frequency for a given interval is the average of the frequencies of that interval and the intervals on each side of the one being considered.

From Fig. 2.4 let us determine the smoothed frequency for the interval 62–63.   We work with the frequency of that interval, 3, and the frequencies of the interval below and the one above the 62–63 interval.   These frequencies are 1 and 2. The sum of the three frequencies is 6, divided by 3 is 2. The smoothed frequency for the 62–63 interval is therefore 2. This procedure is repeated for all intervals, and the smoothed frequencies are then graphed.

Sometimes students are uncertain about handling the first and last intervals in a distribution, since the first interval contains no frequency below it, and the last no frequency above. The answer lies in the same process as was used in constructing the histogram. The interval below the first one in which we had frequencies is certainly there, but it simply has no cases falling within it. Its frequency is zero, and so is the frequency of the interval beyond the highest one in which we have cases. Therefore, in smoothing our first interval 60–61 as it appeared in Table 2.3, we begin with the frequency of that interval, 1, add the frequencies of the interval below, 0, and the one above, 3, and divide by 3. The smoothed frequency for the interval 60–61 is 1.3.

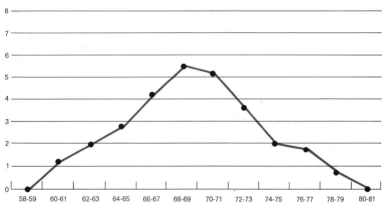

Figure 2.5

Figure 2.5 shows the same data as Fig. 2.4, except that smoothing has been applied to the data, reducing the irregularities seen in Fig. 2.4. Since marked irregularities in graphs are often due to properties of the sample upon which the frequency polygon is based, not due to characteristics of the population from which the sample comes, smoothing usually gives us the best picture of what the population distribution might look like. Therefore, if we are using a sample of cases to represent the entire population, it is advisable to use the smoothing procedure. For example, where IQ scores were available for 100 ten-year-olds, if we are attempting to illustrate the shape of the distribution of IQs for all ten-year-olds, smoothing would be advised for these data.

The frequencies in Fig. 2.5 pile up in the intervals in the center of the distribution but are rather sparse at either extreme.   However, data are not always so evenly distributed.   Sometimes frequencies pile up near one end or the other of a distribution and stretch out in rather small numbers through the rest of the intervals.   Such an outcome would look like one of the graphs in Fig. 2.6.   These distributions are said to be *skewed*.   Graph *A* is positively skewed; graph *B* is negatively skewed.

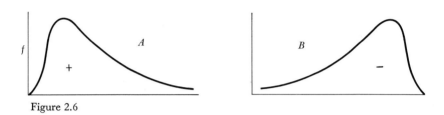

Figure 2.6

Occasionally we see a distribution which has two nonadjacent intervals both of which contain a large number of frequencies.   This produces two high points in our frequency polygon, as is the case in Fig. 2.7.   We call such a distribution *bimodal*.*

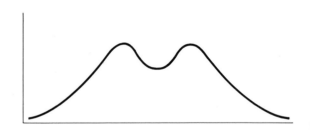

Figure 2.7

As previously noted, the data in Fig. 2.5 piled up near the center of the distribution, with few cases appearing at either extreme of the scoring range. This is characteristic of many kinds of data collected in the social sciences; in fact, if enough cases are included, this type of graph, even without smoothing, begins to look bell-shaped.   This bell-shaped curve is called the *normal curve* and can be plotted by use of a specific formula which will appear in a later

---

* In Chap. 3 we shall run across the topic of the *mode*.   The term *bimodal* will become more meaningful at that point.

chapter when we have seen how to compute and use the elements that go into the formula.

Grouping Errors

Arranging data into intervals which are larger than the unit of measurement has some conveniences but is not without its problems. We assume that within a given interval the frequencies are equally distributed across the interval. For example, suppose we have an interval of 60–64, a five-point width, and this interval contains 10 cases. We hypothesize that the data look like Fig. 2.8, with two frequencies in each of the five units in the interval.

Figure 2.8   60   61   62   63   64

Now this is often not the case. It is very likely that one unit in the interval will have more frequencies than another, e.g., six persons having a score of 61 and only one person getting each of the rest of the scores in the interval, thus putting an "imbalance" of frequencies at one end of the interval. We are not especially concerned with this problem, however, because across many intervals the effects of the imbalances tend to average out.

However, there is a problem in grouping scores into intervals which is tied to the assumption of frequencies being equally distributed throughout the interval.   Looking at most distributions of scores, we see that beginning at one end of the distribution and moving toward the middle of the score range, the frequencies tend to increase, as is shown in Fig. 2.5.   Now let us chop out the rather wide interval 62–65 from Fig. 2.5 and see what that portion of the curve would look like.   Clearly in Fig. 2.9 the frequencies in the lower half

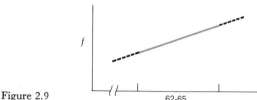

Figure 2.9

of the interval are not equal in number to those in the upper half, nor would we expect this condition to be averaged out in the next interval because Fig. 2.5 shows the frequencies in successive intervals steadily increasing as we approach the center of the distribution.   Our assumption of equal spread of frequencies within an interval probably is not entirely correct and does in fact lead to some small errors in computations, especially if the intervals are wide.   This is one reason we hesitate to have too few intervals, since the fewer the intervals, the wider they must be and the greater will be our grouping error.

Cumulative Frequencies

Occasionally, we wish to describe a given interval in a distribution in terms of the total number of cases that have appeared up to and including that interval.   What we are saying about our distribution is that from interval X down, so many people have appeared.   For this purpose, we illustrate our data by using a cumulative frequency graph, that is, each interval includes not only its own frequency but also the sum of all frequencies below it.

The data which we first saw in Table 2.2, and which have been converted into the graphs in Figs. 2.3 to 2.5, are here incorporated into the cumulative frequencies in Table 2.4.   Here the first interval is composed of all the cases below and included in that interval.   Since no cases came in the interval below, we include only the frequencies of the 60–61 interval, or one case. The next interval is tabulated as containing its own frequencies plus all those below it, or 3 plus the 1 in the first interval, or 4 cases.   We proceed in this

Table 2.4   Construction of Cumulative Frequencies Based on
the Heights of 30 High School Senior Boys

Intervals Based on Inch Units	Number of Boys in Each Interval	Cumulative Frequency	Cumulative Per Cent
78–79	1	30	100
76–77	1	29	97
74–75	3	28	93
72–73	2	25	83
70–71	6	23	77
68–69	8	17	57
66–67	3	9	30
64–65	2	6	20
62–63	3	4	13
60–61	1	1	3

manner through the last interval, 78–79, where there is only one case, which
is added to the frequencies of all intervals below, becoming 30 cases.

Frequencies themselves are often not as informative as percentages of the
total cases.   Therefore, we often see cumulative frequencies converted into
cumulative percentages, as is the case of the data in Table 2.4.   It is probably more meaningful to say that 57 per cent of the boys were 69 inches tall
or shorter than it is to say that 17 boys were in this range.   The value of 17
is relative to the total number, and this relationship is reflected in the per cent.

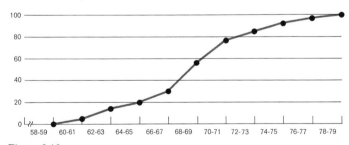

Figure 2.10

Cumulative frequencies and percentages can also be graphed to provide a
pictorial representation of the distribution.   The data in Table 2.4 are
graphed in Fig. 2.10 as cumulative percentages.   Here the data appear to
have a "lazy" S shape.   This characteristic shape of cumulative percentage
data is often referred to as an *ogive*.

Bivariate Graph

Sometimes we want a graph to show the relationship between two conditions which we have observed. For example, how do height and weight
change together?   How does student achievement change with changes in
amounts of training for teachers?   When two variables are plotted together,
the result is called a *bivariate graph*.   In this type of graph two measurements
must be made for each individual observed.   One variable is scaled along
the ordinate (the vertical axis), and the other along the abscissa (the horizontal axis).   A point is placed on the graph where a given person's ordinate
value intersects his abscissa value.   This point is called the *coordinate*.   An
example will illustrate this procedure.

The following fictitious data represent hours studied and number of items
correct on an arithmetic test for 4 sixth-grade boys.

Hours studied: 1,   1.5, 2,   2.5
Test score: 10, 14, 18, 22

A bivariate graph of these data, with hours studied recorded on the abscissa
and test scores on the ordinate, would look like Fig. 2.11.   Here the graph
shows how one variable is expected to change when there is a change in the
other one.   The data in Fig. 2.11 show that for each hour studied after the
first hour, the test score is expected to increase eight points.   From the graph
we could also determine expected test scores for various fractional parts of
hours.   For example, $1\frac{3}{4}$ hours of study should produce a test score of 16.

As presented in Fig. 2.11, test scores are said to be a mathematical function
of hours of study; as one condition changes, a predictable change occurs in
the other.*   However, in most human traits, relationships are not as precise
as those in Fig. 2.11, partly because our measuring tools are imprecise and
partly because variables do not change together with complete regularity.
Nevertheless, we utilize a functional relationship between two variables to
predict one from the other, realizing that a margin of error comes into our
predictions.   Suppose the points in Fig. 2.11 turned out to be like those in

---

* The student who is unfamiliar with the idea of functions should consult Appendix A,
   IV.

Fig. 2.12. We could still plot our line through the dots, coming as close to each as a straight line can, and from this line predict test scores from hours studied. Our predictions would not be as exact as they were in Fig. 2.11, but from these data we could determine the range of our error. If this

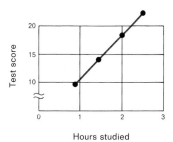

Figure 2.11

device will prove predictions more reliable than mere chance, even with our range of error it will serve a purpose for us. In a later chapter this idea will again appear under the topic of Correlation. At that point the prediction of one variable from another will be referred to as *regression* and our plotted line will be a regression line, but for now Figs. 2.11 and 2.12 are bivariate graphs.

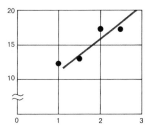

Figure 2.12

In Figs. 2.11 and 2.12 the data fit a straight line. We say the variables show a *rectilinear* relationship. But sometimes the straight line does not fit the data as well as a curve does, in which case we say the relationship is *curvilinear*.

Summary

Several simple techniques for bringing order into data are tied to the frequency distribution. We have seen that data can be grouped into segments (class intervals) that are longer than the unit of measurement without distorting the basic character of the score distribution. By arranging class intervals from the lowest score value to the highest and tabulating the number of cases in each interval, we construct a frequency distribution.

Frequency distributions can be graphed in several ways.   The bar graph, with adjacent bars representing intervals and their frequencies, is called a histogram.   If the midpoints of the upper end of each bar on the histogram are located and a continuous line is drawn to connect these points, the resulting figure is called a frequency polygon.   Frequency polygons are often rather irregular (saw-toothed) in shape.   Smoothing techniques can be applied to the data, however, to reduce this irregularity.

Sometimes we want to know, not how many individuals fell at a given point on our frequency distribution but rather how many people came below a given point.   For this purpose the cumulative frequency table is used; it is constructed by adding the number of cases in an interval to the total number of cases that have preceded this interval.   A typical graph of cumulative percentages takes an S shape and is called an ogive.

The relationship between two variables can also be shown graphically by placing the scale of one variable on the ordinate, the other on the abscissa, and locating the coordinate points.   With this method we show the change in one variable that is expected with a given change in the other variable, a procedure which provides a basis for prediction of one condition from another.

PROBLEMS

1   What are the real limits of the following intervals?

   a 1–4   b 56–58
   c 3.5–4.0   d 1.25–1.50

2   Give the width of the interval and the number of intervals for each of the situations in the following table.

	Highest Score	Lowest Score	Interval Width	No. of Intervals
Example	40	11	2 points	15
a	56	27		
b	101	32		
c	17	−5		
d	6.25	1.75		

3   The following data, collected by a school psychologist, represent raw
    scores on a clerical aptitude test.

    20, 25, 26, 48, 44,   43, 40, 42, 29, 39,
    23, 26, 24, 47, 45,   28, 29, 41, 38, 36,
    27, 44, 42, 43, 29,   37, 34, 31, 33, 30,
    42, 43, 28, 41, 29   36, 35, 30, 32, 31

    a   Make a frequency distribution beginning with the interval
        20–21.
    b   Make a frequency polygon from these data.
    c   How would you describe this distribution?
    d   Construct a smoothed curve from the frequency polygon.
    e   From the frequency distribution construct cumulative percent-
        ages. What per cent of the group fall below a score of 36?
        Below 34?

4   Five children made the following scores on two spelling tests.

Child	Test 1	Test 2
A	8	6
B	7	5
C	6	3
D	4	2
E	2	1

    a   Construct a bivariate graph from these data.
    b   If a pupil had a score of 5 on test 1, what would you predict as
        his score for test 2?

3

Measures of
Central
Tendency

Probably the most striking thing about people is that they are all different from each other. In the typical social gathering no two people are likely to be exactly the same height and weight, nor are they apt to be identical on any other common measurement. Yet differences among them in a given trait are not without limits. For example, we rarely find a person who is as tall as 7 feet, or as short as 4 feet. No, the height of most people ranges around a point located centrally between these extremes. And since so large a portion of the group approaches this central level, we think of that point as representing typical height for the group. This most typical point is what we compute when we find an average.

We are often faced with problems which

demand knowledge of typical conditions.   If I am going to buy a set of read-ing books for my fifth grade, I need to know the reading skills of the typical—or average—fifth-grade child; if I am going to estimate my team's chances in the spring relays, I need to know the average speed of my runners compared with the average speed of my opponents.   If I am going to buy food for three troops of boy scouts on a weekend trip, I can estimate the necessary amounts if I know the average consumption of food for boys in one of the troops. These examples point up the principal uses of averages: (1) they indicate the amount of a given condition which is typical for a defined group of indi-viduals; (2) they provide a basis for comparing a condition in one group with the same condition in a second group; and (3) they allow us to estimate a typical condition for many individuals when we have measurements on only a portion of the total number of those individuals.

We often think of "average" as being the result of a single arithmetic procedure, but there are several averages which we find useful, each being found by a process different from the others.   These averages are the *mode*, the *median*, and the *mean*.   Since each of them is based on a slightly different definition of average, we shall deal with each separately.   Keep in mind, however, that each of the three procedures is an attempt to identify a typical condition for a given group of individuals.

PROBLEMS

1   List five specific situations in which you have been involved where knowledge of the typical—or average—condition was important in describing a group of people.

2   List three specific situations in which you have been involved where averages were useful as a basis for comparing groups of people.

3   List three specific situations where we may wish to estimate an aver-age condition for a large group of people when we know the average of a sample from that large group.

The Mode

Suppose we wanted to find the central point in a distribution of scores around which the bulk of the data seems to congregate.   A quick scan of the distribu-tion shows that several scores near the center of the range have relatively high frequencies.   From these we might select the most frequently appearing score as the one which is most typical.   We call this point the *mode*, and it is defined as that scale value which occurs most frequently* in a distribution. Since scores usually pile up around a central point, it may be assumed that the point of central tendency is that value that accumulates the greatest frequency of cases. This is the point we call the mode.

Because the score which is designated as the mode depends upon only a fraction of the total cases for this designation, the mode of one sample is likely to be quite different from another within a population. Therefore, we say that it is an unstable figure. Its primary value lies in its ease of computation and, consequently, in its use as a quick indicator of the central value in a distribution. Beyond this its statistical uses are extremely limited.

The Median

If research data tend to cluster around a value centrally located between the extreme values, why not locate the exact central point and label it as most typical for the characteristic being observed? We could begin at the lower end of the distribution and count up until we find the point below which exactly 50 per cent of the cases fall. This would be our central point. And it would also be the *median*. The median is simply that point in the distribution which divides the total observations into two parts which are equal in number. It is not influenced by how far extreme scores may range in a given direction, because the range of these scores does not change the point that divides the distribution into two equal-sized groups. For example, the median in the following two sets of scores is the same.

Sample I: 1, 3, 5, 6, 7, 9, 10
Sample II: 1, 3, 5, 6, 7, 15, 21

The fact that the second distribution has two scores that deviate widely in a given direction has no influence on the median, which is 6 in both samples. The performance of Sample I is not identical to that of Sample II, but the median is not sensitive to the difference, since widely deviating scores do not influence the midpoint in a distribution.

The data that researchers collect are not always additive, because the distance between points is not the same length on all segments of the scale. For example, the same number of seconds does not elapse between the runners who are first, second, third, fourth, and fifth in a race. Such data only provide us with a basis for ranking individuals; we cannot add the quantities involved since each step on the scale is not equal to all other steps. The median, because it is determined simply by a counting procedure, is appro-

---

* Mathematicians may wish to call this the *crude mode.*

priately used with these data. Other techniques involving even the simple arithmetical process of addition are not so appropriate.

The median is a more stable figure than the mode; that is, two random samples from a population are more likely to agree on medians than on modes. It is, however, a less stable characteristic than the mean, as we shall soon see.

Locating the median in a distribution of scores is a relatively simple procedure, although not as simple as finding the mode. If ungrouped data are arranged in order of magnitude, as in Samples I and II, the median can be found by counting up to the point below which there are $(N + 1)/2$ cases. For example, if the ordered scores are 1, 3, 4, 5, 7, then $N + 1$ is 6, and 6 divided by 2 is 3. The third score, 4, is therefore the median. But data only rarely come in such neat order, with only one case at each score value. Usually a frequency distribution will appear with a number of cases at each interval, especially in the central portion of the distribution. Therefore, the following more detailed procedure for identifying the median must be employed.

Suppose we have the income data in Table 3.1 for a group of laborers who

Table 3.1 Fictitious Incomes for Store Patrons

Weekly Wage in $	f
80–84	4
75–79	6
70–74	9
65–69	12
60–64	11
55–59	9
50–54	8
45–49	8
40–44	4
35–39	1
	N = 72

patronized a given department store on Saturday afternoon, and we want to know the median weekly wage of these patrons. Our first step is to find the number of cases that will make up half of the group, since the median is the point that divides the distribution so that 50 per cent of the cases fall above it and 50 per cent fall below it. The median will then be the income that corresponds with that dividing point. We therefore divide N by 2. In the distribution of Table 3.1, that number is $\frac{72}{2}$ or 36 cases. Now we count up the distribution until we find the median interval, the one containing the thirty-sixth case. This is the interval 60–64 (from 59.5 to 64.5). There are 30 cases below this interval, and so to make up the 36 cases we need 6 more, which must come from the 11 in the interval. In other words, we need $\frac{6}{11}$ of the cases in the interval to add on to our 30 cases.

We now assume that the cases in the 60–64 interval are equally distributed throughout this interval. So if we take $\frac{6}{11}$ of the cases in the interval, we will also be taking $\frac{6}{11}$ of the total width of the interval or $\frac{6}{11}$ of 5, each interval in our distribution being five points wide. Figure 3.1 illustrates this process.

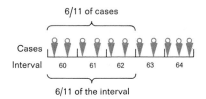

Figure 3.1

Well, $\frac{6}{11}$ of 5 is 2.73 score points. We added the 6 cases on to 30 to make up 50 per cent of the group; so we also add the 2.73 on to the score range below the interval in order to find the scale value that cuts the distribution into two groups of 50 per cent each. The top of the last interval below 60–64 is 59.5; we add our 2.73 on to 59.5 and find the median value to be 62.23.

Now in Table 3.2 we see what we have done to the distribution shown in Table 3.1. We are looking for the point that divides the total number of cases into two equal parts. We found that this point comes within the interval 60–64, but we need a portion more of the interval in order to have 50 per cent of the cases below the chosen point. In Table 3.2, segment A of the distribution is short of the 50 per cent point by 6 cases, or $\frac{6}{11}$ of the next interval. This needed additional amount is segment C. Since we need segments A and C to make 50 per cent of the cases, we also need scale-value segments B and D in order to identify that scale point which gives us the 50 per cent split in cases. If we take a given fraction of the cases in interval C, we also take a similar fraction of the width of the interval D. This fraction of the interval added to the top of the preceding interval (59.5 in Table 3.2) will identify the median point for us (59.5 plus 2.73, or 62.23).

Table 3.2 Reproduction of the Data in Table 3.1

	Weekly Wage in $	f	
	80–84	4	
	75–79	6	
	70–74	9	
	65–69	12	
D	60–64	11	C
	55–59	9	
	50–54	8	
B	45–49	8	A
	40–44	4	
	35–39	1	
		N = 72	

A second example with a different kind of data may be helpful as an illustration. In Table 3.3 the necessary steps for finding the median are:

Table 3.3 Fictitious Distribution of IQs for a Fourth-Grade Class

IQ	f	
130–139	3	
120–129	5	
110–119	2	
100–109	8	
90–99	4	
80–89	2	7
70–79	0	
60–69	1	
	N = 25	

1 We find $N/2$, $\frac{25}{2}$, is 12.5 cases. The score point below which 12.5 cases comes is the median. The next steps will identify that score point.

2   We find the interval containing case 12.5; it is the interval 100–109. This interval will contain the median score.   We have 7 cases up to that interval.

3   We find the portion of the interval needed to complete 12.5 cases. This is 5.5 cases.   We have 7 cases up to that interval; adding 5.5 to this, we get 12.5.

4   We need 5.5/8 of the cases in the interval to complete our 50 per cent of the cases; therefore, we will also take 5.5/8 of the score width of the interval to identify the score point which cuts off that 50 per cent.

5   The value 5.5/8 of 10 (this interval width) is 6.88, and we add this on to the range already accounted for below the interval, or 99.5 plus 6.88.   The median, then, is 106.38.

PROBLEM

1   A teacher-rating form is given to students in Introduction to Psychology classes.   The score is the number of favorable points checked by a student in reference to his instructor.   Instructor X received the following rating scores:

    7, 12, 11, 9, 18,   20, 9, 15, 16, 13,
    7, 6, 8, 9, 12,   16, 13, 12, 13, 18,
    19, 17, 15, 12, 21   14, 13, 14, 15, 10

Instructor Y received the following ratings:

    13, 5, 6, 16, 7,   15, 15, 10, 11, 8,
    8, 15, 9, 8, 15,   15, 8, 9, 9, 12,
    14, 13, 9, 13, 14   15, 13, 14, 9, 14

a   Compute a median for each instructor.
b   In scanning the distributions of ratings for each instructor, do you believe the medians would be a good basis for comparison of X and Y?   Why?

The Mean

Most upper-elementary school children can give you the average amount of money for three persons who have among them $3, $5, and $2.   A sixth-grade child would add up the amounts of money and divide by the number of persons who have that money. The result is the average known as the *arithmetic mean*, or just the *mean*. It is simply found by adding together the values of the quantities we have and then dividing this sum by the number of quantities which were so added.

This process can be simply written in shorthand by using a few symbols to represent the quantities and the arithmetical processes involved. If we let X stand for the quantity of a given trait as measured for one individual, then $\bar{X}$ will represent the mean, the typical quantity for the group. The letter N will represent the number of individuals on whom we have the quantities designated X, and the Greek letter Σ (sigma)* will tell us that the quantities (X) are to be summed. Our shorthand designation for computing the mean is found in Table 3.4.

Table 3.4   Computing the Mean from Ungrouped Raw Scores

Formula 3.1	What It Says to Do
$\bar{X} = \dfrac{\Sigma X}{N}$ where $\bar{X}$ = mean X = raw score of a given individual N = number of individuals on whom we have scores	Add together individual scores and divide by the total number of individuals thusly: $\bar{X} = \dfrac{X_1 + X_2 + X_3 + \cdots + X_N}{N}$

Example   Find the mean, $\bar{X}$, IQ for the five persons whose individual IQs are 100, 105, 90, 115, 110.

$$\bar{X} = \frac{100 + 105 + 90 + 115 + 110}{5}$$
$$= \frac{520}{5}$$
$$= 104$$

This procedure does not require that the raw data be put into any kind of order, such as a frequency distribution. Computations can be made directly

* If the Greek letter Σ is an unfamiliar symbol, turn to Appendix A, 7c for an explanation and exercises.

from the raw scores as they are observed. This procedure is especially recommended when a desk calculator is available. However, if computations must be made without such mechanical assistance and a considerable number of scores are involved, a technique to be noted later will somewhat reduce the total amount of arithmetic.

PROBLEMS

1   Ten children ran the 50-yard dash in the following times in seconds: 8, 11, 14, 10, 9, 7, 11, 13, 10, 12. What is their mean time?
2   Mary and Elizabeth are studying typing. In six speed tests Mary has typed the following number of words per minute: 32, 76, 54, 60, 45, 51, while Elizabeth has typed 46, 60, 54, 58, 52, 48. Compare the two girls' mean performances.
3   Suppose Mary and Elizabeth had been selected randomly from a class of 20 girls. What might be a good estimate of the class's average typing speed?

The mean, in contrast with the median and mode, represents a balance point in the distribution of scores. As an illustration of this fact, let us imagine individuals as blocks and their scores as inches on a 10-inch ruler. The score values, let us suppose, are 3, 4, 4, 8, 8, and 9. The mean for this set of scores would be $3 + 4 + 4 + 8 + 8 + 9$ divided by 6, or $\frac{36}{6}$, which equals 6. In Fig. 3.2 we discover an important idea about the mean.

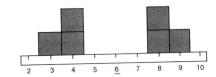

Figure 3.2

There are two blocks a distance of 2 inches below the mean and one block a distance of 3 inches below the mean. There are also two blocks 2 inches above the mean and one which is 3 inches above it. Now we see that the total blocks-times-distance-from-the-mean arrangement below the balance point equals the total blocks-times-distance arrangement above it. This finding illustrates a fact about the mean as a balance point. Its position must be influenced by the number of scores at any point in a distribution in relationship to the *location* of that point in the distribution. This frequency-times-distance-from-the-mean arrangement on one side of the mean will always be equal to the frequency-times-distance arrangement on the opposite side of the mean; thus the position of scores in a frequency distribution is important in computing and interpreting the mean.

Figure 3.3 also illustrates this point. Again we use blocks to represent individuals and the ruler to represent a continuum of scores for these indi-

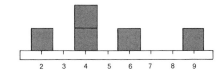

Figure 3.3

viduals. Now suppose we have scores of 2, 4, 4, 6, and 9. The mean will be 5. Now computing the frequency-times-distance values for scores on both sides of the mean we find:

Below the Mean		Above the Mean	
Distance	*Frequency*	*Distance*	*Frequency*
$(4 - 5) \times 2$ blocks $= -2$		$(6 - 5) \times 1$ block $=$	1
$(2 - 5) \times 1$ block $= -3$		$(9 - 5) \times 1$ block $=$	4
Total	-5	Total	$+5$

Algebraic total for all scores $= 0$

If the position of any block on the ruler were changed, the balance point would also be changed. Likewise, in a frequency distribution the magnitude of each of the scores influences the location of the mean. In other words, the position of every score in a distribution plays a part in determining the location of the mean and does so to the extent to which a score deviates from the central area of the distribution. This condition is not true of the median or mode, as we shall soon see.

When the number of scores in a distribution is large, it is difficult to add them all up one at a time without the aid of an adding machine. We can, however, shorten the adding process by two methods.* One way is illustrated by the data below. First, using the procedure described in Table 3.4,

---

* The student who is uncertain of his basic algebra may wish to consult Appendix A, I and III before proceeding.

we find

$$
\begin{array}{c}
X \\
10 \\
8 \\
8 \\
10 \\
8 \\
6 \\
6 \\
\hline
\Sigma X = 56
\end{array}
\qquad
\frac{\Sigma X}{N} = \frac{56}{7} = 8
$$

Now if these data were arranged in a frequency distribution, we would have

X	f	fX
10	2	20
9	0	0
8	3	24
7	0	0
6	2	12

$$
\Sigma fX = 56 \qquad \frac{\Sigma fX}{N} = \frac{56}{7} = 8
$$

Multiplying each score by the number of times it appears, fX, and then adding these values, ΣfX, produces the same result as ΣX above, and dividing ΣfX by N gives us the same value for the mean as does $\Sigma X/N$, and we added only three numbers instead of seven.   Therefore, this procedure is one approach to reducing slightly the extensive addition necessary in computing the mean without the aid of a calculator.

A second method for reducing the amount of arithmetic is also based on the frequency distribution, and this time grouped data can be used.   Its basic principles can be illustrated by once more going to the ruler and blocks for an illustration.   Suppose we have a distribution of scores as in Fig. 3.4.   The blocks in Fig. 3.4A are not in a symmetrical arrangement, and so we are not sure where the balance point is.   We can begin by guessing it is at about 6. We try this (B) and find we are in error.   Now we must correct for the fact that our guessed balance point was too high, and we move the balance (C) slightly in the direction of the "heavy" end; thus the distribution balances.

What we have just now done to find the balance point with the blocks on the ruler, we can also do with scores in a distribution.   First we guess where the mean will fall, note the error in our guess, and correct that guess.

But how do we correct the guess?   You will recall from the discussion of Figs. 3.2 and 3.3 that if we find the distance (or deviation) each score is from the mean and multiply this distance by the number of individuals at that distance, the sum of these products for cases above the mean will equal the sum of these products below the mean. We may also figure these sums below

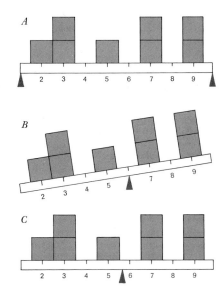

Figure 3.4

and above the guessed mean. If the sum of distance-times-frequency products on one side of the guessed mean is larger than the sum for the other side of the guessed mean, our guess has missed the true mean and must be adjusted in the direction of the larger sum.

Let us take an example:

	X	f	d	fd
	10	1	4	4
	9	2	3	6
	8	2	2	4
	7	4	1	4
Guessed mean	6	7		$\Sigma fd = 18$
	5	6	-1	-6
	4	6	-2	-12
	3	2	-3	-6
	2	1	-4	-4
	1	1	-5	-5
		$N = 32$		$\Sigma fd = -33$
				Total -15

We guess the mean to be the midpoint of the interval 5.5–6.5, or 6. The letter d represents the distance (or deviation) of each of the other intervals from the interval containing our guessed mean. We next get the distance-times-frequency product for each interval and add these up for all intervals above the mean and for all intervals below the mean (Σfd). The sum of the fd values above our guessed mean interval is 18, whereas the sum of the fd values below the guessed mean interval is -33. Since -33 has a greater absolute value than 18, we now see that our guess was too high. In order to make Σfd above the mean equal Σfd below it, we must move our point down a little.

How do we make this correction? Well, Σfd for our total distribution (the algebraic sum of all fd values) is -15, that is, 18 plus -33.* Since each score in the distribution played a part in creating that Σfd value, each score must also be involved in the correction. We therefore find how much our guess is in error *on the average* for all scores in the distribution. We find averages by adding the values and dividing by their number. We have already added the values and have come up with -15. Now dividing by the number of values involved (N), we have the average amount each score played in creating the error of our guess. This figure ($-15/32$) becomes $-.47$; it is the amount our guess is in error. But notice that our deviations from the guessed mean were based on distances of the class intervals from the interval containing our guessed mean. Deviations were therefore in terms of intervals, not in terms of score points, and so our correction, $-.47$, is in terms of intervals and must be converted to score points by multiplying the correction by the number of score points in an interval. Since in the above data we have only one score point per interval, this is not a problem. But if our intervals were 1–3, 4–6, etc., we would have to multiply our interval correction by 3 to convert it to a score-point correction.

Now computing our mean, we multiply the interval correction, $-.47$, by the score width of our interval, 1, and add algebraically this amount to our guessed mean, 6. The true mean then is found to be 6 plus $-.47$ times 1, or 5.53.

The process we have just gone through is the arithmetic equivalent of what we did in Fig. 3.4. First, we guessed the balance point (the mean interval), found that we were in error, Σfd, and corrected our guess by the proper amount, $(\Sigma fd/N)i$. This procedure is written in mathematical shorthand in Table 3.5.

In summary of this procedure, we see that the position of the mean, like a balance point, is influenced by the cases in a distribution in relation to where

---

* For rules of adding negative and positive values, see Appendix A, 8.

Table 3.5 Computing the Mean from Grouped Data

Formula 3.2a, b, c	What It Says to Do

a. $\bar{X} = GM + C$
 	
 b. $C = \left(\dfrac{\Sigma fd}{N}\right) i$
 	
 c. $\bar{X} = GM + \left(\dfrac{\Sigma fd}{N}\right) i$
 	
 where GM = guessed mean
 f = frequency of a given class interval
 d = deviation of a class interval from the interval containing the GM
 N = number of scores
 i = score width of the intervals
 $\bar{X}$ = mean
 GM = guessed balance point
 C = correction in guess
	1. Guess where the mean will be. (This is the midpoint of the selected interval.)
	 2. To determine the accuracy of this guess:
	    a. Find the distance or deviation d each interval is from the one containing the GM.
	    b. Multiply the number of cases in each interval by its deviation (fd), and then add these values algebraically (Σfd).
	 3. If this value is not zero, to make the correction:
	    a. Find the average of fd for all the intervals in the distribution $(\Sigma fd/N)$. This is the correction in terms of intervals.
	    b. To change interval corrections to corrections in terms of score values, multiply $(\Sigma fd/N)i$.
	    c. Add this amount to the guessed mean. This is the corrected mean.

Example A 60-item test in arithmetic was given to 3 fifth-grade groups. The tests were scored and arranged into the following distribution. Compute the mean

X	f	d	fd
47–49	4	5	20
44–46	3	4	12
41–43	7	3	21
38–40	9	2	18
35–37	13	1	13
32–34	16*		84
29–31	10	−1	−10
26–28	7	−2	−14
23–25	7	−3	−21
20–22	3	−4	−12
	79		−57
		$\Sigma fd =$	27

Steps (numbered as above)

1. GM = 33 (midpoint of 32–34)
2. (a) and (b) = Σfd = 27

3a. $\dfrac{\Sigma fd}{N} = .34$

 b. $\left(\dfrac{\Sigma fd}{N}\right) i = 1.02$

 c. $33 + 1.02 = 34.02$

$$\bar{X} = GM + \left(\frac{\Sigma fd}{N}\right) i$$
$$= 33 + \tfrac{27}{79} \times 3$$
$$= 34.02$$

those cases are situated in that distribution. We can apply this idea to grouped data by first estimating where the mean is and then noting the sum of the deviations-times-frequency products for intervals above and below that estimated point. If the algebraic sum of all of these products is zero ($\Sigma fd = 0$), we have guessed correctly; if it is other than zero, an adjustment of the guessed mean must be made. In so doing we convert the idea of the mean as a balance point into a computational procedure. This approach is especially useful in that it reduces the arithmetic when N is large or when the scores we are working with are of two digits or larger. In these cases adding all the scores to find $\Sigma X/N$ is extremely laborious without machine assistance. In such cases, the procedure described in Table 3.5 will help reduce the labor involved in computing.

PROBLEMS

1 Given the following grouped data representing the height in inches of 70 junior high school students, compute the mean.

X	f
72–73	3
70–71	5
68–69	7
66–67	10
64–65	9
62–63	12
60–61	8
58–59	7
56–57	6
54–55	3
	70

2 Now for each interval in the distribution of Prob. 1 find the midpoint and multiply it by its frequency ($f \times$ M.P.), and then add these products (Σf M.P.) and divide by N. Compare your result with your answer to Prob. 1.

One additional point about the mean—sometimes we have means on several different samples and would like to know the mean for the total, combined group. For example, I have the mean IQ for children in each of the 10 sixth-grade classes in my city. What is the average IQ for all sixth-graders in the city? Or I have the average number of dates co-eds have in a month in each of seven sorority houses. What is the mean number of dates for all these sorority girls combined?

When means of several samples are being combined into a grand mean for the total of all the samples, we must take into account the fact that each sample mean was probably based on a different number of cases. Therefore, in combining groups we weight each mean relative to the number of cases from which it has been computed. The procedure for this weighting is shown in Table 3.6.

Table 3.6 Procedure for Computing a Grand Mean from Several Group Means

Formula 3.3	What It Says to Do
$$\bar{X}_t = \frac{N_1\bar{X}_1 + N_2\bar{X}_2 + \cdots + N_k\bar{X}_k}{N_1 + N_2 + \cdots + N_k}$$ where $\bar{X}_t$ = mean for combined groups N_1, N_2, N_k = number of cases in samples 1, 2, and k $\bar{X}_1, \bar{X}_2, \bar{X}_k$ = means of samples 1, 2, k	1. The number of cases in first sample times its mean is added to the number of cases in second sample times its mean, and the number of cases in each successive sample times their respective means are successively added until all k samples are included. 2. This sum is then divided by the total number of cases represented by all samples combined. The result is the mean of the combined groups.

Example We have mean IQs for the 3 third grades in Centerville. What is the mean third-grade IQ for Centerville?

	$\bar{X}$	N
Class 1	101	30
Class 2	107	35
Class 3	95	26

$$\bar{X}_t = \frac{30(101) + 35(107) + 26(95)}{30 + 35 + 26} = 101.6$$

So if we have several sample means, we cannot simply add up these means and divide by the number of them to find the grand mean for the combined groups.   We must weight each sample mean in proportion to the number of cases involved in the computation of that mean.

Which Average to Use

We have noticed several characteristics of each of the indicators of central tendency.   These characteristics should help us choose the one of the three indicators which best suits the data with which we are dealing.   The mean is tied to the positions of the scores and as such is dependent upon each observation in the distribution for its location.   To this end it is the best indicator of the total group's performance, unless the distribution is conspicuously skewed.   Widely deviating scores in one direction from the center of the distribution tend to pull the mean toward them.   This is not true, however, of the median, and for this reason the median may be more nearly central to the bulk of the scores in markedly skewed distributions than the mean.   For example, the following extreme situation shows the mean, 7, entirely out of range of the majority of the scores, but the median, 5, is centrally located in the greater portion of the data:

2, 3, 3, 4, 5, 6, 6, 6, 28

Therefore, the fact that the median is not influenced by widely deviating scores makes it preferable to the mean when one wishes to describe typical behavior in a distribution that contains a few cases whose scores range in one direction far beyond the rest of the cases.   The mode, like the median, is also insensitive to widely deviating scores, but its instability makes it last choice even in markedly skewed data.   Figure 3.5 indicates the relative position of the three indicators of central tendency in a skewed distribution.

Stability of the indicator is an especially important consideration when choosing among averages.   From sample to sample in a population the means are expected to be more nearly alike than medians, and medians more

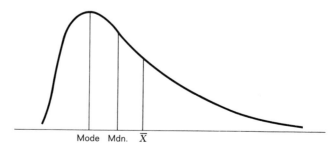

Figure 3.5   Mode Mdn. $\overline{X}$

alike than modes.   Therefore, if we are using a sample as a basis for estimating the typical performance for the population, we would choose the
mean because of its stability.   This is also true if we are comparing the performance of two groups.   But to use the mean, we must have additive scale
units; simple rankings with unequal units between them will not do.   And,
of course, if the distribution should be markedly skewed, the mean may not
describe the group as precisely as the median.

The purpose to which we are applying the descriptive data may also be a
consideration in choosing between the mean, the median, and the mode.
It has often been said that "figures don't lie, but liars can figure."   It therefore is to our advantage to know the figuring that liars use in order to catch
them in their ruses.   One trick of deceit lies in the use of averages.   How
one's purpose influences the choice of an average may be illustrated by a
devious example.

We have seen in Fig. 3.5 that it is entirely possible for the three indicators
of central tendency to give completely different values in a distribution of
scores.   Now those persons who use statistics to promote their own objectives
feel free to choose the average which best suits their ends rather than the one
which best fits the data.   For example, consider the following teachers'
salaries.   For simplicity suppose we have only six teachers and a teaching
principal, whom we shall include as a teacher also.   Their salaries are:

$9,000
5,150
5,100
5,000
4,800
4,800

The chairman of the teacher salary committee declares to the PTA that the
average teacher's salary is $4,800—the mode.   The chairman of the school
board later reports to the chamber of commerce that the teachers' salaries
average $5,642—the mean.   Now neither person has really departed from
the truth.   Both have used a bona fide average; but the statistical tool has
been employed that best suited the reporter's objective rather than the one
that best described the data—in this case the median.   So beware of persons
who argue with averages, unless you know what average is being used and
how well it fits the data it represents.

Summary

There are three indicators of typical—or average—status that are used rather
widely.   These indicators of central tendency are the mean, the median, and

the mode. The mean is simply the arithmetic average. Of the three statistics, it is the most stable from sample to sample. The median is the point that divides the distribution into two equal-sized parts, that is, the point that has 50 per cent of the cases above it and 50 per cent below it. It is not influenced by widely deviating scores in a given direction and is more stable than the mode. The mode is the one scale value that occurs most often in a distribution. It is a quickly found indicator of central tendency but is unstable from sample to sample.

PROBLEMS

1   An admissions officer at Eks University wanted to compare high schools on the basis of the college entrance test scores. Test scores for Pine Crossing High School and for Wolf Run High School were as follows:

Scores	Pine Crossing	Wolf Run
65–69	1	1
60–64	1	2
55–59	2	8
50–54	11	10
45–49	9	0
40–44	16	9
35–39	12	6
30–34	1	2
25–29	1	0
20–24	1	2

   a   Compute a mean and median for each school.
   b   Are the means or the medians more alike for the two schools? How do you account for this?
   c   What is the mean for the combined groups from the two schools?
2   Take four coins and toss them up and let them settle on the desk. Count and record the number of heads. Repeat this procedure 10 times so that you have 10 figures, each representing the number of heads found in one toss of the four coins.

a Find the mean number of heads for the 10 tosses.

b Imagine each toss of the four coins is a separate "experiment." Will each experiment provide us with the same result as the other experiments? Will each experiment produce the same result as the average for the group? Are separate experiments good estimates of the average for the total for all experiments?

3 Suppose you are an instructor and you wish to increase the *median* performance for your class. Which group would you want to work with the most and why?

a Those who are now scoring the highest

b Those who are now just above the median

c Those who are now just below the median

d Those who are now at the lowest end of the scale

4 Suppose you wished to increase the *mean* performance of your class. Which of the alternatives in Prob. 3 would you wish to work with most? Why?

5 In the following groups of data, tell whether the mean or median best describes the data.

a 6, 4, 2, 12, 3

b 45, 51, 47, 65, 36

c 21, 28, 24, 9, 23

6 $\Sigma X/N$ is the mean of all X scores, that is, X's are our basic data. In your own words state what the basic data are for each of the following formulas:

a $\dfrac{\Sigma Y^2}{N}$

b $\dfrac{\Sigma(X - \bar{X})^2}{N}$

c $\dfrac{\Sigma XY}{N}$

d $\dfrac{\Sigma(X - \bar{X})(Y - \bar{Y})}{N}$

4

Indicators of Relative Position in a Distribution

A given test score, or other measurement, assumes greatest meaning only when it can be compared with similar scores. Suppose you have taken an arithmetic test and you have been given a score of 30. What does this mean? Well, if we could determine that you have the highest score in a group of 50 graduate ichthyology students, or the lowest score, or the tenth-highest score in a group of 110 high school freshmen, the score of 30 then could be interpreted in terms of your position in a reference group, bringing considerable meaning to the score. But without a "landmark" of some kind, your score of 30 is next to uninterpretable.

Now if we know that a child is 3 feet tall and his father is 6 feet tall, we could interpret the child's height as a fractional portion of the father's height.   Here we know where true zero is, and our measurement begins at that point.   But with many measuring devices used by behavioral scientists true zero is not known.   The zero on their scale is an arbitrary one, and we do not know how far below this point the observed condition actually may extend.   For example, intelligence test results conceivably could be zero.   But even angleworms have been observed to learn.   How far below test zero is the angleworm's intelligence?   Well, when we do not know where true zero is, we cannot describe one measurement as a fraction of another.

Although some problems arise from using scales that begin at an arbitrary zero, much information can be collected by using these devices.   And even if we did know where true zero was, we would still want to apply many of the same techniques to data analysis that we use with scales which begin at an arbitrary point.   We still get the greatest meaning from a measurement if we know how that measurement ranks with other similar marks, no matter whether we start from true zero or an arbitrary zero.

It therefore appears that methods of bringing order and meaning into a disarray of data must include techniques for identifying the relative position of a given score among other scores.   The purpose of this chapter is to present some of the more common techniques for doing just this.   Specifically, we shall deal with (1) percentile ranks, (2) quartiles, and (3) deciles. These are by no means all the procedures available for showing relative position; however, they are among the most common.

Percentile Ranks

A person's position in a group with reference to a given trait can be shown by pointing out what per cent of the group has less of the trait than the person being considered.   We have all sat tensely fumbling our test papers in our moist hands while the instructor puts the distribution of scores on the blackboard.   Now suppose that on your test you have 23 questions correct.   We see from the instructor's distribution of scores that 30 of the 37 in the class have scores lower than yours.   Thus, 81 per cent of the group did less well than you did.   A statistician may say you were at the 81st *percentile rank*, or that your score of 23 is the 81st *percentile*.   Out of the corner of your eye you notice that your neighbor's score is 26, and the class distribution shows that 91 per cent of the group scored below 26.   Your neighbor is at the 91st percentile rank, or his score of 26 is the 91st percentile.

It now appears that *a percentile is a score point in a distribution, and the percentile rank with which we label a score reveals the per cent of the group that falls below that score.*   Therefore, the percentile rank tells us, in terms of percentage, the

relative position of a given person in the group in reference to the trait measured. If 25 per cent of the distribution falls below a score of 110, then 110
has a percentile rank of 25. If 80 per cent of the group appears below 130,
130 has a percentile rank of 80. However, the score value of 110 is the 25th
percentile, and 130 the 80th percentile.

The first steps in computing percentiles have already been completed in
building cumulative percentages. Let us look at an example. Table 4.1

Table 4.1   Fictitious Heights of 30 Girls on
Their Twelfth Birthdays

Height in Inches	f	cf	cp
67–69	1	30	100.0
64–65	3	29	96.7
61–63	5	26	86.7
58–60	9	21	70.0
55–57	6	12	40.0
52–54	2	6	20.0
49–51	2	4	13.3
46–48	1	2	6.6
43–45	1	1	3.3

shows cumulative percentages for the heights of 30 girls on their twelfth
birthdays. In a way this is a percentile table; the cumulative percentage
tells us what proportion of the group appears below a given interval. But
the table only gives us a few percentile ranks, and we often want the whole
range from 1 to 99. Moreover, this table yields fractional ranks, whereas we
usually deal with percentile ranks in whole numbers.

We could plot these data on a cumulative percentage graph and read any
point we wanted off the graph. The data given in Table 4.1 are, therefore,
graphed in Fig. 4.1. (Why are the plots in this graph placed at the upper
limits of each interval?) Now we can read the percentiles, at least to esti-
mable points within an interval. The 50th percentile rank appears to be
at about midway in the interval 58–60, or about equivalent to a score of 59.
The 75th percentile rank is about equivalent to a score of 62, and so on.

This procedure too lacks the precision we would like to see in a method for
finding percentiles, but it is fast and especially efficient when we have only
one score unit per interval, a condition which increases the accuracy of our
estimations of points within various intervals.

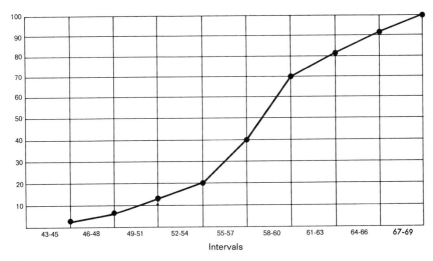

Figure 4.1

Percentiles can be computed directly, and indeed we have already learned how. You recall that the median was the point in the distribution tha-divided the group into equal numbers of cases. This means that 50 per cent of the cases were marked off below the median, placing it at the 50th pert

Table 4.2   The Number of Letter
Cancellations Made in a
3-Minute Cancellation
Test by 90 College
Freshmen

Cancellations	f	cf
37–39	2	90
34–36	10	88
31–33	15	78
28–30	19	63
25–27	16	44
22–24	8	28
19–21	9	20
16–18	7	11
13–15	3	4
10–12	1	1

centile rank.   The procedure applied to computing the median just needs to be generalized now so that we may find, not just that midpoint, but any point we wish to on the distribution.   The procedure to be used requires only a slight modification of the method we already know for computing the median.

You remember that our first step in computing the median was to find the number of cases that made up exactly half of the total group.   We then proceeded to locate the point on the raw-score scale that corresponded to the point below which 50 per cent of the group was cut off.   Now suppose we want to find, not the point below which there are 50 per cent of the cases, but the point below which there is 20 per cent of the group (the 20th percentile).   In locating the median (the 50th percentile), we divided N by 2, or took .50 of N.   In locating the 20th percentile, we begin by taking .20 of N.   Otherwise the basic steps are not really different.   An example will bear out this fact.

Let us begin by finding the 50th percentile (the median, or P_{50}) in Table 4.2. First we find 50 per cent of the group, or $.5N$, which is 45 cases.   We count up to find the interval that contains the forty-fifth case, and we find it to be 28–30.   We need one case from that interval (44 up to that interval, plus 1 makes 45 cases).   There are 19 cases in the interval, and so we need $\frac{1}{19}$ of those cases to add on to our 44.   We also then take $\frac{1}{19}$ of the interval width to add on to the range of scores below it, or $\frac{1}{19}$ of 3, which is .15.   Now, .15 added to 27.5 (the real upper limit of the last interval below 28–30) gives us 27.65, which is the median and the 50th percentile.

Now suppose we wanted again to find the score equivalent to the 20th percentile rank (P_{20}).   We begin as before by finding how many cases are cut off by that figure (20 per cent) and then proceed to find the point on the raw-score scale that matches with that number of cases.   In our 90 cases, 20 per cent is 18 cases.   We find the interval in which the eighteenth case comes and proceed to find its corresponding point on the raw-score scale. The interval is 19–21, and we need 7 of its cases to make up the 18.   This is $\frac{7}{9}$ of the width of the interval, or $\frac{7}{9}$ of 3, or 2.33 score points, which when added to the upper limit of the last interval, 18.5, becomes 20.83, the raw score which is the 20th percentile.

The generalized procedure for finding percentiles is given in Table 4.3.

Occasionally a zero frequency appears in an interval of a distribution of scores, and this complicates the calculation of percentiles.   For example, look at the data in Table 4.4.   Here the interval 140–149 contains no frequency.

What is the weight below which 20 per cent of the boys (six cases) appeared?   Any weight in the range from 139.5 to 149.5 could be considered

Table 4.3   Procedure for Finding Values Corresponding to Given Percentile Ranks

1. Where P_X is the desired percentile, we multiply the corresponding proportion (.X) times N (for example, for P_{38} and 150 cases, we multiply .38 times 150). This tells us how many cases will fall below the desired score.
2. Then we find the point on the raw-score scale that corresponds with that portion of the cases, thusly:
   a. We locate the interval that contains the desired number of cases (X times N).
   b. We determine the proportion of cases needed from that interval and find the corresponding portion of the width of the interval.
   c. We add this portion of the interval to the upper limit of the last interval below the one we have just divided. This gives us the raw-score point (the percentile) which corresponds with the desired percentile rank.

Example

X	f	cf
27–29	1	57
24–26	3	56
21–23	6	53
18–20	10	47
15–17	9	37
12–14	11	28
9–11	10	17
6–8	3	7
3–5	3	4
0–2	1	1
N = 57		

Problem   Locate the 80th percentile.
(Step numbers correspond to above procedural description.)

1. $.80 \times 57 = 45.6$ cases. These make up 80 per cent of N.
2a. 45.6th case falls in the interval 18–20.
   b. $45.6 - 37 = 8.6$ cases needed from the interval. The corresponding portion of the interval width is 8.6/10 of 3 score points (the interval width), or 2.58.
   c. 2.58 added to the upper limits of the interval below gives $17.5 + 2.58 = 20.08$, the score corresponding to the 80th percentile rank.

PROBLEMS

1   Fill in the following blanks:
   a   In a distribution of 1,000 IQs of six-year-old children, 16 per cent fall below an IQ of 85. An IQ of 85 is the _____, and 16 is the _____.
   b   In a survey of high school girls, 32 per cent had had their first formal date by fourteen years of age. Age 14 is the _____, and 32 is the _____.

2　From the data in Table 4.2 compute the raw score (percentile) that corresponds with

a　The 81st percentile rank

b　The 36th percentile rank

3　The freshmen in Centertown High School take a reading comprehension test, and the school counselor wishes to develop local norms for the test.　He decides to compute percentiles.　The scores are as follows:

10, 11, 32, 26, 18,	24, 27, 22, 26, 25,
31, 28, 27, 31, 30,	13, 16, 26, 18, 24,
23, 26, 19, 21, 26,	18, 26, 22, 24, 34,
15, 20, 30, 24, 24,	34, 23, 26, 20, 27,
19, 23, 20, 26, 25,	19, 22, 28, 19, 29

a　Begin with the score of 10 and make a distribution using intervals two scores wide, and find the raw score which is the 25th percentile.

b　Find the score which is the 50th percentile.

c　Find the score equivalent to the 75th percentile rank.

4　Joe Smith, a freshman at Centertown High School, had a raw score on the reading test of 28.　What is his percentile rank?　(Hint: The procedure is essentially the reverse of that which has been used in the examples of Prob. 3.　Begin by finding the score interval in which 28 appears, then find the portion of that score interval that falls below a score of 28, then locate the corresponding proportion of cases within the interval, etc.)

as the answer.　However, each score of this range being the same percentile seems to be leading us into problems that complicate rather than simplify our description of the data.　Therefore, in such instances where we have intervals with zero frequencies, we agree to follow a standard practice, that is, to define the midpoint of the interval as the point we are seeking.　Thus, in Table 4.4 a weight of 144.5 is the 20th percentile.

Frequency distributions with zero frequency in an interval usually occur when N's are small.　In these distributions the computations of percentiles may not be worth the effort.　In fact, the rank with which we identify a given score begins to be most stable only when the number of cases involved is several hundred.　In practice we probably would not bother to compute percentiles on less than 100 cases in a given distribution, although we have

Table 4.4 Weight of 30
Freshmen Boys
in High School

X	f	cf
210–219	1	30
200–209	1	29
190–199	2	28
180–189	6	26
170–179	5	20
160–169	6	15
150–159	3	9
140–149	0	6
130–139	3	6
120–129	2	3
110–119	1	1

done so for illustrative purposes in this chapter.   Although as N's get larger, the intervals with zero frequency become rare, they do not become extinct, and so some plan for dealing with them is necessary.

Another characteristic of percentile ranks that is important to note is the shape of the histogram plotted with percentile ranks on the base line.   Sup-

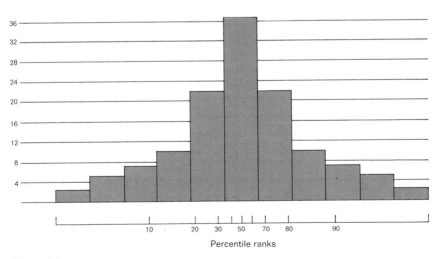

Percentile ranks

Figure 4.2

pose we tabulated our frequency distributions in intervals of percentile ranks instead of raw scores, and suppose our intervals were 10 ranks wide. What per cent of the cases would fall within the first interval 1–10? What per cent would fall in the second interval 11–20? The fifth interval 41–50? The answer to each of these questions is 10 per cent. Now we have seen that most raw-score distributions have few frequencies in the extremes, more frequencies near the center of the score range. This means that in a typical distribution it must take more raw-score points to achieve the desired 10 per cent of the cases at the extremes of a distribution than it would near the center of the distribution. This fact is illustrated in Fig. 4.2. The raw-score scale is presented in equal-sized units, but the corresponding percentile ranks are broad at the ends of the distribution compared with those at the center. In other words, the percentile ranks are not equal-sized units along our base line. This fact is very important; it means that we cannot add or subtract percentile ranks. If we want to do arithmetic computations with percentile ranks, we must first convert them to their raw-score equivalents, do the computations, then convert the results back to percentile ranks.

Deciles and Quartiles

Two kinds of figures, besides percentiles, are also frequently used to show relative standing in a group. These are *deciles* and *quartiles*, both of which are similar to, and indeed can be read from, percentile tables. Deciles are points that divide the distribution of raw scores into segments of 10 per cent each. Thus, the 1st decile D_1 would be that point on the distribution below which 10 per cent of the cases fell, D_2 the point below which 20 per cent of the cases fell, etc. Deciles can be computed in the same manner as percentiles, since D_1 is P_{10}, D_2 is P_{20}, etc.

Quartiles divide the distribution of raw scores into segments of 25 per cent each. Thus, the 1st quartile Q_1 is the point that cuts off the lowest 25 per cent, Q_2 the lowest 50 per cent of the group (what is another name for this point?), and Q_3 the lowest 75 per cent of the distribution.

It should be emphasized, however, that deciles and quartiles, like percentiles, are *points* along the scale. They are not *segments* of that scale. Many statistics instructors have felt a twinge upon hearing a student report that case X *is in the 3d decile*, or something similar. This clearly is in error, since the 3d decile is only a point on the scale.

However, we do want oftentimes to refer to an individual's status in the group in terms of the deciles, quartiles, etc., between which he falls. We therefore need a name to distinguish between the point (the decile, quartile, etc.) and the segments of the distribution between the points.   Let us retain the prefix of the terms that designate points, and to this prefix let us apply the suffix -*oid* to name the segments.   Thus, the segment between two deciles would be a *decoid*, between two quartile ranks a *quartoid*, between two percentiles a *percentoid*.   Although it is incorrect to say John is in the 6th decile, we can describe John's status as being in the 6th decoid.

Summary

One way to bring meaning into a collection of measurements is to show where given individuals rank among the group.   Thus, several procedures have been devised to locate relative position of various raw-score values.   Principal among the devices is the percentile rank which identifies the score below which given percentages of the group fall.   For example, if 30 per cent of the group achieved scores less than X, then X is the 30th percentile of the distribution (P_{30}), or has a percentile rank of 30.   Percentile-rank units are much wider at the extremes of a typical distribution than near the center. For this reason percentile ranks cannot be used in arithmetical computations.

Deciles and quartiles are like percentiles in that they show relative status in a group by indicating portions of the group that come below given points. The decile divides the distribution by segments of 10 per cent, D_1 cutting off the lowest ranking 10 per cent, D_2 the lowest ranking 20 per cent, etc. Quartiles divide the distribution by 25 per cent segments, Q_1 cutting off the lowest 25 per cent, Q_2 the lowest 50 per cent, etc.

Percentiles, deciles, and quartiles are dividing points in the distribution of scores; they are not the segments of scores between these points.   We have used percentoid, decoid, and quartoid, respectively, to refer to the segments between points.   Thus, it is correct to say that a student scored within X decoid; it is not correct to say that he scored within X decile.

PROBLEMS

1   Fifty psychology students took a clerical aptitude test.   Their scores were as follows:

31, 38, 26, 50, 42,	47, 39, 28, 61, 33,
27, 48, 60, 58, 53,	41, 36, 57, 51, 66,
43, 56, 59, 41, 35,	43, 49, 32, 58, 53,
47, 43, 68, 43, 31,	48, 34, 47, 59, 36,
32, 52, 60, 59, 41	65, 71, 62, 60, 45

Construct a frequency distribution beginning with the score of 26, with an interval width of three score points, and locate the following points in the distribution:

a   The 3d decile

b   The 2d quartile (What is another name for this point?)

c   The following percentiles: P_{20}, P_{67}, P_{90}

2   Using the data in Prob. 1, find the percentile rank for a score of 49; find the decile rank for a score of 60.

5

Variability

We have just seen that one way to describe a group of scores or other observations is to compute an average. This tells us what typical performance is, and it identifies the point around which the group of observations centers. But to know the typical condition alone is not enough to describe a set of data. We need to know how widely dispersed the scores are around that central point.

An example will illustrate this fact. Miss Jones has a class of fourth-grade pupils whose mean IQ is 105. Several students in her class, however, have IQs in the 70's and 80's, while others range up into the 130's. Miss Smith's fourth-graders also have a mean IQ of 105, but the lowest IQ is 89 and the highest is 115. The two classes have the same mean, but obviously the abilities represented in one class are quite different from those in the other class.   Figure 5.1 shows the difference graphically.

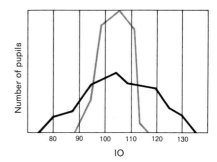

Figure 5.1

The teaching methods, the materials used, and the expected achievement of students in Miss Jones's class would be quite different from those in Miss Smith's room.   In making decisions about these two groups, it is not enough to know what the average ability is.   We must also know the dispersion of ability around that average.

A second situation shows another reason why we need an indicator of dispersion of scores.   Joe and Bill are throwing darts at a target.   They throw 20 darts each and record the scores noted in Table 5.1.   Their mean scores are identical, but the quality of Bill's performance is clearly different from Joe's.   We can see that the mean alone does not adequately describe

Table 5.1 Fictitious Scores Made
by Two Boys on 20
Trials Each

Scores	Joe (f)	Bill (f)
10	1	
9	2	
8	4	5
7	6	8
6	2	5
5	3	2
4	1	
3	1	
	$\bar{X} = 6.8$	$\bar{X} = 6.8$

the characteristic being observed; we must also know the extent to which scores are spread out around that average.

The following situation represents even a third example in which more than an average is needed to describe the observed condition. Suppose that the towns of Centerville and Unionville each have 15 fifth-grade classes, each class containing 25 students (an unusual condition, but pretend it is true). The mean IQs for the classes in each town are computed. If we combined the classes in Centerville, the mean would be equal to 100, and so would be the grand mean for Unionville. Are the fifth grades essentially comparable groups in intelligence? A plot of the distributions of class averages may help us decide. This plot is in Table 5.2.

Table 5.2 Fictitious Mean IQs for
15 Classes in Two Towns

IQ Means	Unionville (f)	Centerville (f)
130–139	1	
120–129	2	
110–119	3	4
100–109	3	7
90–99	3	4
80–89	2	
70–79	1	

Clearly the educational policies and procedures in Centerville are different from those in Unionville. The typical ability of a given group may be vastly different from class to class in Unionville, but typical ability varies little among classes in Centerville.

Several terms have been used to describe this tendency for data to be dispersed around the average. Of course, *dispersion* is one name often given this property, *spread* is another, and so is *scatter*. But probably the term most widely used by statisticians when they are referring to this condition is *variability*. The data in Fig. 5.1 represent variability within a group of individuals; Table 5.1 shows variability *within* individuals themselves; and the figures in Table 5.2, where the tabulated data are class means rather than IQs for individuals, represent *among-groups variability*.

People are different from each other on any given trait. What is the expected range of such differences above and below the average? This is what variability within a group of individuals tells us. For example, the average height of a sample of college students was 5 feet, 10 inches, but many of the group were shorter than this, and a like number was taller. Each person has a single measurement, and its value often ranges above or below the group average. Since the differences in height are among the separate members of a specific group, the variability reflected by these differences is known as *within-group variability*.

But the data in Table 5.1 show several observations on a single person. The variability in Joe's scores is due to conditions within him, not due to differences between Joe and other people. This is therefore called *within-individuals variability*. The computation of within-individuals variability does not differ from the computations of among-individuals variability, but the decisions to which the two types of dispersion apply are different. Shall the manager of the Yankees send "Slugger" Slayton in as a pinch hitter? His average is .320, but in some games he gets a hit every time he bats; in some games he strikes out every time. "Fingers" Fletcher has an average of .300, but he got this average by hitting twice in every game he played. Here within-individuals variability is important to know in deciding who should be selected as a pinch hitter.

On the other hand, how shall the Yankees arrange their batting order, and how shall the opponents arrange their fielding strategy? These decisions are tied primarily to the variability within the group of Yankee batters. Some are good hitters, some not so good. The essential differences are among the members of the team.

Occasionally we deal with several samples from a common population. The means of these samples, no matter how carefully selected, will not be the same from sample to sample. How will this variation between group means be useful in decision making? Let us look at an example. Suppose Sudsy Soap Company is making a survey of sales potential in Machineville. They first wish to know how much soap the typical Machinevillian uses a month; so they randomly select from the telephone book five samples of 25 persons each. They next find out what the average soap usage is for each of the five samples. Now the five group means are not identical, but they do cluster somewhat together. It is very likely that the means of other samples of this town's citizens, as well as the mean for the entire population of Machineville, will fall somewhere within the range of the sample means already observed, and Sudsy may proceed with fair confidence in their estimate of soap usage typical for Machinevillians without having surveyed the whole population in the town.

PROBLEMS

1   List five situations where an indication of variability within a group of individuals will help us describe the data.
2   List five situations where within-individuals variability will be important in making decisions.
3   List three situations where variability among groups may be an important characteristic to know.

If we now agree that variability is an important property of a group of observations because it helps us (1) to describe those observations and (2) to make better decisions based upon the available data, we are then ready to look at statistical ways to determine variability.

Range

A very simple approach in determining the dispersion of scores is to note how many scale points are included from the lowest value to the highest, inclusive. This statistic is called the *range*.   It is simply computed by subtracting the smallest score from the largest and adding one point.   For example, in Table 5.1 Joe's scores begin at 3 and run through 10.   The range is 10 − 3 + 1, which is 8; that is, from 3 to 10 there are 8 scale points.

As a measure of variability the range is less reliable than some other indicators.   Its numerical value rests upon two, and only two, scores in a distribution—the most extreme scores.   These two values may or may not be representative of the range of the bulk of the scores.   A wide gap may exist between the lowest score and the next lowest one, in which case that lowest score would not reflect the spread of the greater portion of the data.   An example of this point is given in Table 5.3.   In this case the scores progress continuously from 16 to 21, a range of 6; however, the actual range for the distribution is 10.   The one person who got a score of 12 determines this broader range compared with the narrower range within which the bulk of the data is dispersed.

For this reason the range as an indicator of variability falls into the same category as does the mode as an indicator of central tendency.   They are both simple to compute and are quickly obtained descriptive data; however, they are unreliable from sample to sample, especially when the number of observations in each sample is small.   For this reason we shall look for other methods of describing data whenever possible.

Table 5.3   Data Illustrating Problems
in Use of the Range

X	f
21	3
20	4
19	7
18	9
17	8
15	5
16	0
14	0
13	0
12	1

Quartile Deviation

We noticed that a problem with the range was the fact that it depended only on the capricious location of the extreme observations in a distribution, a condition which lends instability to the size of the range.   Now if we could choose our upper and lower points a given distance from the upper and lower ends of the distribution, we could avoid the problem illustrated in Table 5.3.   The inset points usually chosen are those points that cut off the highest scoring 25 per cent and the lowest scoring 25 per cent of the observations.   These points are called the *1st quartile* (cutting off the lower 25 per cent of the group) and *3d quartile* (cutting off the upper 25 per cent of the group).   Table 5.4 illustrates these points.   You may now notice

Table 5.4   Data Illustrating
Quartile Points

X	f	
15	1	
14	2	
		Q_3
13	3	
		Mdn
12	3	Q_1
11	2	
10	1	

that the median becomes the 2d quartile point since it cuts off two quarters, or 50 per cent of the number of cases in the distribution.

Variability of a group of scores can now be indicated by use of the two points, Q_1 and Q_3. In a perfectly symmetrical distribution, the distance in scores from the median to Q_1 will be the same as the score distance from the median to Q_3. Therefore, taking the median as a central point and thinking of the scores being dispersed above and below the median, we can get an indication of the extent of this dispersion by noting the deviation of the quartile points from the median. This indicator is the *quartile deviation*, and examples of this are given in Fig. 5.2*A* and *B*. The data in Fig. 5.2*A* show a distribution with very slight scatter, whereas Fig. 5.2*B* shows a considerable spread of scores. Similarly, the distance from the median to either quartile point in *A* is much less than it is in *B*.

But not all distributions of scores or other observations are symmetrical. Some are skewed. And when we have skewness, the median-to-Q_1 distance will not equal the median-to-Q_3 distance, as shown in Fig. 5.3. Therefore,

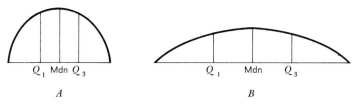

Q_1 Mdn Q_3 Q_1 Mdn Q_3

A   *B*

Figure 5.2

we do not compute the quartile deviation by finding the deviation of the quartile points from the median. Instead we find half the distance between Q_1 and Q_3, and this is our quartile deviation. In a symmetrical distribution this value will be the median-to-quartile distance. In a skewed distribution

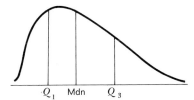

Figure 5.3 Q_1 Mdn Q_3

it will be an average of the median-to-Q_1 and median-to-Q_3 distances. The quartile deviation is, therefore, defined in symbols as

$$QD = \frac{Q_3 - Q_1}{2}$$

How do we find the quartile points?   The basic procedure is the one used to find the median with one small variation.*   The first step in computing the median was to find $N/2$, since half of the scores come below our median. The first step in obtaining Q_1 is to find $N/4$ since only one-fourth of the scores fall below the 1st quartile.   Similarly, to find Q_3 we begin by finding $\frac{3}{4}$ of N, since three-fourths of the group will fall below the 3d quartile. With this exception, the procedure for computing quartiles is the same as that for finding the median.

The quartile deviation is a more stable statistic from sample to sample than is the range, but like the range, it is not an algebraic function of all the scores in the distribution; however, because it is dependent upon a larger portion of scores than the range, it tends to be a more reliable indicator of spread.

Standard Deviation

The best indicator of dispersion of scores would be one which takes into account the location of every score in a distribution.   Since variability indicates spread of scores, and since scores in distributions tend to be dispersed around a central point, a very reliable indicator of variability would begin at the mean, the most stable average from sample to sample, and calculate distances of scores above and below that central point.   We could then compute the average distance all the scores range from the mean.   Figure 5.4

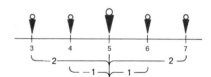

Figure 5.4

illustrates this procedure.   Here are children standing at points on a foot scale representing distances broad-jumped from a standing position.   The mean is 5 feet.   How widely dispersed are the marks around the mean?   We could compute the distances from each observation to the mean, a value called a *deviation*, and average these deviations.   But in a symmetrical distribution the average of the deviations would be zero, since we have as many with a minus value as we have with a plus value.   For example, in Fig. 5.4 our deviations are as follows:

* Chapter 4 provides more detail on this procedure.

Below the Mean	Above the Mean
3 − 5 = −2	7 − 5 = +2
4 − 5 = −1	6 − 5 = +1
Total = −3	Total = +3

A value of zero as an indicator tells us very little about spread of scores around the mean. Therefore, a method of eliminating the minus signs appears to be appropriate here. We find that method in *squaring* the deviations, averaging them, and then "unsquaring" them. The resulting value is called a *standard deviation*. Specifically, it is the *root-mean-squared deviation*. This definition is simplified by taking it apart and looking at its segments.

First, we are dealing with deviations. A deviation is merely the distance, in score points, a given observation is from the mean of the distribution, that is, $X_1 - \bar{X}$ is the deviation for X_1; $X_2 - \bar{X}$ is the deviation for X_2; etc. (We shall abbreviate these deviations by using the small x as their symbol, for example, $X_1 - \bar{X} = x_1$.) As we saw above, the deviations here must be squared, however, to avoid ending up with a total of zero. Now we have the deviation-"squared" portion of our definition.

Now let us add another term from the above definition—*mean-squared*

Table 5.5 Computation of the Standard Deviation

Formula 5.1	What It Says to Do
$\sigma = \sqrt{\dfrac{\Sigma(X - \bar{X})^2}{N}}$ $= \sqrt{\dfrac{\Sigma x^2}{N}}$	1. Subtract the mean from each score and square each of these differences: $(X_1 - \bar{X})^2, (X_2 - \bar{X})^2, \ldots, (X_n - \bar{X})^2$. 2. Add together all these squared deviations. 3. Divide by the number of deviations, which gives us the mean-squared deviation, or variance. 4. Take the square root of this value.

Example Given the following scores, compute the standard deviation: 6, 10, 5, 8, 6, and 7. $\bar{X} = 7$.

1. $(6 - 7)^2 = 1$
   $(10 - 7)^2 = 9$
   $(5 - 7)^2 = 4$
   $(8 - 7)^2 = 1$
   $(6 - 7)^2 = 1$
   $(7 - 7)^2 = 0$

2. $\Sigma(X - \bar{X})^2 = 16$

3. $\dfrac{\Sigma(X - \bar{X})^2}{N} = \dfrac{16}{6} = 2.67$

4. $\sqrt{2.67} = 1.63$

deviation. The mean of anything is simply the sum of the values (here squared deviations) divided by the number of values that were summed. Thus, we compute the $X_1 - \bar{X}$ value, square it, $(X_1 - \bar{X})^2$, then find $(X_2 - \bar{X})^2$ and add this value to $(X_1 - \bar{X})^2$, etc., until we have summed all the squared deviations of our scores from the mean. Then we divide this sum by the number of deviations we have, that is, $(X_1 - \bar{X})^2 + (X_2 - \bar{X})^2 + \cdots + (X_n - \bar{X})^2$ divided by N. The result is the mean-squared deviation. This value is often referred to as the *variance,* σ^2, and we shall deal with it more later.

Now the last term in our definition completes the picture—*root-mean-squared deviation.* This merely says that we shall now take the square root of that mean-squared deviation just computed. The result is the *standard deviation,* σ; it is symbolically written in Table 5.5.

PROBLEMS

1   Ten children have taken a test in maze tracing. They have made the following number of errors: 10, 7, 9, 5, 6, 13, 8, 4, 7, 9. Compute the standard deviation of errors for this group of children.

2   A runner has posted the following times in the 100-yard dash during time trials in the past week: 10, 12, 11.2, 11, 10.7, 10.5, 11.6 seconds. What is the standard deviation of his times?

3   Compare the effort in computing the standard deviation in Prob. 1 with that in Prob. 2. Which is easier and why?

In computing the standard deviation, we have little difficulty using the technique described in Table 5.5 when the mean is an even value. But if the mean is an uneven number, such as 7.438, or if score values are uneven, then computations are somewhat more complicated. We can get around this problem, though, by doing some algebraic manipulation of formula (5.1).*

The heart of the standard-deviation formula is $\Sigma(X - \bar{X})^2$. What would happen if we actually squared the portion within the parentheses? We would get $\Sigma(X^2 - 2X\bar{X} + \bar{X}^2)$. We can remove the parentheses now by summing each term before doing the internal calculations. We would get $\Sigma X^2 - 2\Sigma X\bar{X} + \Sigma \bar{X}^2$.

---

* If the student is unfamiliar with the procedure for squaring a binomial, he should consult Appendix A, 11a. Appendix A, 1, 2, and 7c will also be of use in understanding the above procedures.

Now if we recall that $\bar{X} = \Sigma X/N$, we see that the end of the second term, $-2\Sigma X\bar{X}$, is really equal to $\Sigma X/N$, and so the second term becomes $-2\Sigma X(\Sigma X/N)$, or $-2(\Sigma X)^2/N$. The third term can stand some scrutiny, too. Recall that $\bar{X}$ is a constant value for a given distribution of scores and to add the mean, a constant, to itself N times is the same as to multiply the mean by N. For example, suppose the mean of a group of scores is 12 and we have four scores for which we are computing the standard deviation. We would find $\Sigma\bar{X}^2$ by adding $12^2 + 12^2 + 12^2 + 12^2$. We would get the same value by multiplying $4(12^2)$, or $N\bar{X}^2$. So let us substitute $N\bar{X}^2$ for $\Sigma\bar{X}^2$ in the formula.

Now also let us substitute $\Sigma X/N$ for $\bar{X}$ in that term for which we have just written $N\bar{X}^2$. That gives us $N(\Sigma X/N)^2$, and squaring we have $N(\Sigma X)^2/N^2$, and canceling N's, $(\Sigma X)^2/N$. Now the entire equation with all our substitutions reads:

$$\Sigma(X - \bar{X})^2 = \Sigma X^2 - 2\frac{(\Sigma X)^2}{N} + \frac{(\Sigma X)^2}{N}$$
$$= \Sigma X^2 - \frac{(\Sigma X)^2}{N}$$

We may now substitute this value in formula (5.1) for the standard deviation according to the procedure in Table 5.6.

If a desk calculator is available, the procedure of Table 5.6 is by far the more simple. Since most calculators provide ΣX^2 and ΣX in a single operation, we come out with the basic data for computing both the mean and the standard deviation at the same time.

Now that we have computed a standard deviation, let us see what it looks like applied to a frequency distribution. Remember that σ begins at the mean and measures deviations above $(+)$ and below $(-)$ that point. The resulting application will look like Fig. 5.5. The normal range of a distribution of scores rarely runs beyond plus and minus three standard deviations, although theoretically scores in a given population may range beyond these values. In a normal distribution approximately two-thirds (68 per cent) of the observations will fall between plus one and minus one standard deviation.

Now let us apply our skill on an example. Suppose we have IQ data with the mean of 100 and σ of 15 IQ points. Since we begin at the mean and add or subtract σ, $+1\sigma$ would be an IQ of 115, $+2\sigma$ would be 130, and $+3\sigma$ would be 145. Similar values below the mean would be 85, 70, and 55. About two-thirds of the population, then, is expected to fall between IQs of 85 and 115. Also, we can now intuitively verify our previous statement about the range of values rarely running beyond plus and minus three stand-

Table 5.6 A Variation on the Original Standard-Deviation Procedure

Formula 5.2	What It Tells Us to Do
$$\sigma = \sqrt{\dfrac{\Sigma X^2 - \dfrac{(\Sigma X)^2}{N}}{N}}$$	1. Using the raw scores, we (a) square each value and summate these squared values, yielding ΣX^2, and (b) summate the values *without* squaring, yielding ΣX, which we then square, $(\Sigma X)^2$, (c) which when divided by N yields $(\Sigma X)^2/N$. 2. Subtracting $\Sigma X^2 - (\Sigma X)^2/N$, and then dividing this result by N, yields the variance, or σ^2. 3. Find the square root. This is σ.

Example   Using the data from the example in Table 5.5 (6, 10, 5, 8, 6, and 7), compute the standard deviation.

1a. $X_1^2 = 36$
　　$X_2^2 = 100$
　　$X_3^2 = 25$
　　$X_4^2 = 64$
　　$X_5^2 = 36$
　　$X_6^2 = 49$
　　$\overline{\Sigma X^2 = 310}$

b. $\Sigma X = 42, (\Sigma X)^2 = 1{,}764$

c. $\dfrac{(\Sigma X)^2}{N} = \dfrac{1{,}764}{6} = 294$

2. $\Sigma X^2 - \dfrac{(\Sigma X)^2}{N} = 310 - 294 = 16$

3. $\frac{16}{6} = 2.66$

4. $\sqrt{2.66} = 1.63 = \sigma$

ard deviations.   IQs beyond 145 and below 55 are indeed rare, although they do exist in the total population.

And speaking of populations, we have to this point been computing variability of scores by means of the standard-deviation procedures which apply

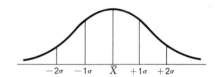

Figure 5.5

to data based on the entire population as limited by definition.   But very often we are working with samples from a population, estimating the population properties (parameters) from the sample properties (statistics).   When we compute a standard deviation on a sample from a population and wish to use this statistic as an estimate of the population value, a slight change must be made in our procedure. We change our formulas and symbols as follows:

$$\sigma = \sqrt{\frac{\Sigma(X - \bar{X})^2}{N}}$$

for the population value becomes

$$s = \sqrt{\frac{\Sigma(X - \bar{X})^2}{N - 1}}$$

for the sample estimate of the population, and

$$\sigma = \sqrt{\frac{\Sigma X^2 - \frac{(\Sigma X)^2}{N}}{N}}$$

for the population becomes

$$s = \sqrt{\frac{\Sigma X^2 - \frac{(\Sigma X)^2}{N}}{N - 1}}$$

for the sample estimate of the population. Here we have labeled the sample value s to distinguish it from the population value σ. The use of $N - 1$ in the denominator is especially important when a sample is small in size, say 30 or less, but should be used every time that we are estimating a population standard deviation from a sample from that population.

This kind of situation often occurs. For example, I want to know what the distribution of height looks like for all ten-year-old children in Chicago. I cannot measure all of them, and so I take a sample, carefully planned, and from it I estimate the characteristics of the population. We frequently do this kind of thing in studying all phases of human development. Also, in conducting experiments we may wish to make conclusions about the effect of a treatment on all adults in a given category or all children of a defined group or all rats of a given strain. We find it impossible to test them all, and so we resort to estimating population characteristics from carefully selected samples of the population. When we do make such estimates, we should use $N - 1$ in the denominator of the formula for standard deviation.

PROBLEM

1 We have a sample of 10 high school senior boys, selected at random from Localville High School. We have given them a clerical test

which involves cancelling as many as possible of the letters *a* and *o* in script in 1 minute's time. The numbers of letters canceled by the 10 boys are 9, 11, 8, 18, 12, 15, 7, 16, 14, 10.

a   Suppose we define our population as all boys who were selected to take the test. Compute the standard deviation for this population.

b   Suppose we define the population as all boys in Localville's senior class. Now compute the standard deviation for our sample as an estimate of the population.

c   Compare the two figures you have computed. What kind of error would we make if we used a sample standard deviation as an estimate of the population parameter without using $N - 1$ in the denominator? Can you think of a possible reason why this would be true? Would this error be greater for samples whose N is 100 or for samples with N of 15?

As mentioned earlier, the above procedures are most appropriate for computing the standard deviation when a desk calculator is available. Certainly these procedures can be used without a calculator, but if the number of observations is large, or if the scale values are large, the arithmetic becomes burdensome to calculate by hand. A grouped-data procedure, which slightly reduces the weight of computations when calculators are not available, has been developed, however.

The grouped-data procedure begins just as it did in deriving the mean. We guess the interval in which we expect to find the mean, count off interval deviations from that central point, and as in other procedures for standard deviation, we square each of those interval deviations. If we let I stand for a given interval, then the interval deviation would be $I - $ GM, a value which we labeled d when we were computing the mean. Then $(I - $ GM$)^2$ would be d^2. Each squared interval deviation is then multiplied by the frequency in that interval, and these fd^2 values are summed to yield a figure analogous to $\Sigma(X - \bar{X})^2$. The $X - \bar{X}$, or x, values, however, are score deviations from the actual mean, whereas d is an interval deviation and is computed from a guessed mean. However, the analogy between the methods should be clear.

But we recall from Chap. 3 that the guessed mean had to be corrected for error in our guess. If deviations are calculated from the guessed mean, they too will need correcting in proportion to the error in the guessed mean. The total procedure is described in Table 5.7.

Table 5.7 Calculation of the Standard Deviation with Grouped Data

Formula 5.3	What It Says to Do

$$\sigma = \sqrt{\dfrac{i^2\left[\Sigma fd^2 - \dfrac{(\Sigma fd)^2}{N}\right]}{N}}$$ where i = interval width in grouped data
 	
f = number of cases in a given interval
 	
d = deviation of an interval from the guessed mean interval
 	
N = total number of observations or scores
	1. With data in a frequency distribution:
	  a. Guess a mean interval, and count off interval deviations d from that guessed mean interval.
	  b. Square these interval deviations, d^2, and multiply each by the frequency in its interval, fd^2; summate to find Σfd^2.
	2. The d values, being from a guessed mean, require correction. This correction is the same one used in computing the mean, but d values are here squared, and so the correction must also be squared. We then subtract $\Sigma fd^2 - (\Sigma fd)^2/N$ and multiply the difference by i^2. This gives us a figure equal to $\Sigma(X - \bar{X})^2$, except for grouping errors.
	3. Divide the value found in step 2 by N (or $N - 1$), find the square root; this is the standard deviation.

Example Given the following IQ scores in a frequency distribution, compute the standard deviation.

IQ	f	d	fd	fd²
125–129	1	4	4	16
120–124	5	3	15	45
115–119	7	2	14	28
110–114	6	1	6	6
105–109	9			
100–104	9	−1	−9	9
95– 99	6	−2	−12	24
90– 94	4	−3	−12	36
85– 89	1	−4	−4	16
80– 84	1	−5	−5	25
	49		$\Sigma fd = -3$	$\Sigma fd^2 = 205$
	Computations completed to find $\bar{X}$			Additional work needed to find σ

$$\sigma = \sqrt{\dfrac{i^2\left[\Sigma fd^2 - \dfrac{(\Sigma fd)^2}{N}\right]}{N}}$$

Steps

1. $\Sigma fd^2 = 205$

2. $\dfrac{(\Sigma fd)^2}{N} = \dfrac{(-3)^2}{49} = .18$

  $i^2\left[\Sigma fd^2 - \dfrac{(\Sigma fd)^2}{N}\right] = 25(205 - .18) = 25(204.82) = 5,120.5$

3. $\sqrt{5,120.5/49} = \sqrt{104.50} = 10.2$

Again, the grouped-data procedure is useful only when a desk calculator is not available. Otherwise it is unnecessarily laborious and provides many opportunities for arithmetical and grouping errors. However, when used with care, the technique is very serviceable in computing the standard deviation in the absence of mechanical assistance.

PROBLEM

1   The data below represent raw scores on a statistics test taken by a class of 30 college students.

32, 36, 38, 40, 42,	52, 52, 53, 54, 51,
44, 45, 46, 47, 47,	62, 62, 63, 65, 66,
48, 49, 50, 51, 51	68, 69, 71, 73, 77

a   Arrange the scores into a frequency distribution with intervals five points wide, beginning with 30–34, and compute a standard deviation for the group.

b   Now, using the ungrouped-data method [formula (5.2)], again compute the standard deviation.

c   Does $i^2[\Sigma fd^2 - (\Sigma fd)^2/N]$ from (a) equal $\Sigma X^2 - (\Sigma X)^2/N$ from (b)? Which procedure do you feel is the least laborious in terms of the arithmetic involved?

The Standard Error

Let us for a moment imagine that we are studying height of fifth-grade boys in the city of San Diego. We have measured boys in 20 randomly selected classrooms in the city and have computed means for each of the 20 classrooms. We now see that all means are not just alike; in fact they seem to disperse themselves much like a bell-shaped curve in form around a central point. Can we compute a standard deviation for this distribution of means? Yes we can. This would be an among-groups figure. Now let us suppose we took many, many such samples, plotted their means in a distribution, and found the standard deviation for that distribution. The resulting figure would be called the *standard error* of the mean, to distinguish it from a standard deviation based on raw scores.

Thus, the standard error is simply a standard deviation, and it shows variability like other standard deviations, except its variability is among means many samples from a population, not among raw scores. Our example)ve will illustrate one application. Suppose I have a sample of San Diego boys about whom I know nothing except their mean height. I could ask, "Is it likely that these boys could be fifth-graders?" Now if their mean height is within the range of the standard error of our fifth-grade boys, we could answer this question affirmatively; but if their mean is beyond the expected range of among-samples variability within the fifth grade, we would have to say that it is unlikely that the unknown boys are fifth-graders. In other words, once we know the range within which means of random samples from a population will fall, we can hypothesize whether or not some specific sample has come from our population by seeing if its mean falls within this range.

The topic of the standard error will be taken up in detail in a later chapter, but since it is a special application of the idea of the standard deviation, it seemed appropriate to mention it here.

Summary

In describing a set of scores it is not enough to know the central point around which scores pile up. We must also know how spread out, or how dispersed, the scores are. Therefore, we need an indicator of variability. Several such indicators are readily computed. The range is merely the number of points from the highest to the lowest score, inclusive. It is dependent only on the position of these two extreme points and as such is not a reliable, although it is an easily determined, indicator of variability.

The quartile deviation is the difference between Q_3 and Q_1, divided by 2, and in a symmetrical distribution the median plus and minus the quartile deviation indicates the spread of the middle 50 per cent of the scores. The quartile deviation is more stable than the range, but it is not a function of the position of all the scores and does not have the reliability of the standard deviation.

The standard deviation is the square root of the arithmetic average of the squared deviations of scores from the mean of the distribution. It divides the score range (but not the frequencies) into about three equal units above the mean and about three below the mean. Thus in a distribution with a narrow scatter of scores these units cannot be large, whereas in a distribution with wide scatter these units must be large. This fact reveals the manner in which the standard deviation is an indicator of variability.

PROBLEMS

1   The counselor in Wolf Crossing High School wishes to do some analysis of aptitude-test scores. He found the following results on 40 senior boys:

31, 38, 26, 50, 42,   42, 39, 28, 61, 33,
27, 48, 60, 58, 53,   41, 36, 55, 51, 66,
43, 56, 57, 40, 35,   43, 48, 32, 58, 53,
47, 43, 68, 43, 31   44, 34, 47, 57, 36

a   Compute a standard deviation using ungrouped-data procedures.
b   Compute a standard deviation using grouped-data procedures. (Begin your bottom interval at 26 with an interval width of three score points.)
c   Compute a quartile deviation.

2   Would you typically expect a wider range of scores between one standard deviation below the mean and one standard deviation above the mean, or between Q_1 and Q_3? Why?

3   The data below represent intelligence quotients for two sixth-grade classes. Scores in each class were quite evenly distributed.

	$\bar{x}$	σ
Class I	101	12
Class II	105	6

a   In which class would you find the most bright children (IQ of 115 or more)? Why?
b   In which class would you find the most dull children (IQ of 85 or less)? Why?

6

The Normal Curve and Its Applications

When large masses of data are collected from physical or psychological measurements, their frequency polygon often resembles a vertical cross section of a bell; hence we have the familiar term *bell-shaped curve*. An excellent example of such a distribution of data is presented in Fig. 6.1. These data were collected from children on whom the 1937 Stanford revision of the Binet tests was based.* The familiar shape of the bell clearly appears in this figure. These data represent a rather large group of people. Smaller samples of data often do not conform so neatly to the shape of the bell, although its general charac-

* Lewis M. Terman and Maud A. Merrill, "Stanford-Binet Intelligence Scale," Manual for the Third Revision, Form L-M, p. 18, Houghton Mifflin Company, Boston, 1960.

teristics do appear; that is, most of the cases pile up near the center of the distribution, and fewer cases are found at either extreme.

We usually cannot measure an entire population; instead we work with portions of a population so selected as to represent the population as a whole.

Figure 6.1 Distribution of composite IQs of 1937 Stanford-Binet standardization group. (Louis M. Terman and Maud A. Merrill, "Stanford-Binet Intelligence Scale," Manual for the Third Revision, Form L-M, p. 18, Houghton Mifflin Company, Boston, 1960. Reprinted with permission of Houghton Mifflin Company.)

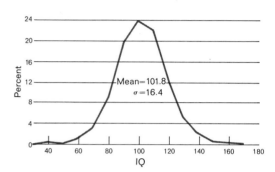

Although measurements taken on such samples may not graph into a perfect bell-shaped curve, we generally believe that the characteristic measured is distributed in the population in the familiar bell shape; therefore, we proceed to treat sample data as though they presented the typical form of the population even though their frequency polygon may deviate slightly from the form of the bell.*

The Normal Curve

The bell-shaped curve is more precisely referred to as the *normal curve*.† This curve has a mathematical formula from which it can be constructed. This formula is

$$Y = \frac{N}{\sigma \sqrt{2\pi}} \, e^{-(x-\bar{x})^2/2\sigma^2}$$

---

* Recent developments in Baysian statistical procedures present alternative hypotheses to normality of populations.

† The normal curve has often been called the *gaussian curve* after K. F. Gauss (1777–1855) who was believed to have developed the formula for it. Later, however, it was discovered that Abraham DeMoivre (1667–1754) had arrived at the formula before Gauss. The application of the normal curve to the study of human behavior received great impetus from the work of Adolphe Quetelet (1796–1874).

where Y = ordinate* for a given value of X

  π = constant equal to 3.1416

  e = second constant equal to 2.7183

We first must determine the values of $\bar{X}$ and σ for a given set of data. Then these figures are put into the formula along with the constants, and values of X are repeatedly substituted in for the computation of successive ordinates in the construction of the normal curve. For example, let us suppose that we have for a population of 1,000 cases a mean IQ of 100 and a standard deviation of 15. We could determine the heights of our ordinates in plotting the normal curve by the formula

$$Y = \frac{1,000}{15 \sqrt{2 \times 3.1416}} \, 2.7183^{-(X-100)^2/2\times15^2}$$

and substituting IQ scores for X along a scale from low to high, we would, by computing the values of successive ordinates, come out with the necessary points for constructing the normal curve. The amount of calculation in this operation is considerable, and fortunately will not have to be done by the typical user of statistics.

The normal curve, however, is not a single curve but a whole family of curves. This idea becomes clear when we study the above formula in more detail. In the example, suppose we retain the mean of 100 and N of 1,000 but change the standard deviation to 5, to 10, to 20. By applying these data to the formula we would produce three normal curves, but the three would not look exactly like each other. They would probably look like Fig. 6.2.

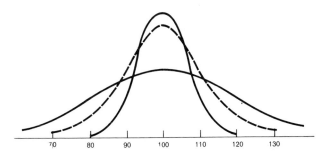

Figure 6.2

   70 80 90 100 110 120 130

Each of these curves fits the requirements of normality, yet their shapes are clearly different. We could similarly vary N and $\bar{X}$ and produce still a greater variety of curves.

Normal curves may vary from rather narrow distributions with relatively

---

* The student may wish to refer to Appendix A, IV, for a review of graphing nomenclature.

long ordinates to rather wide distributions with relatively short ordinates. Curves which deviate from normality tend to vary in two ways: Either they have too few cases in the central area of the curve and are therefore "flattened" in the middle of the distribution, or they have too many cases in the central area and as a result are too "peaked." Therefore we have developed terms to describe these curves that deviate from normality. When samples of data produce comparatively peaked frequency polygons, we say the distributions are *leptokurtic;* when the distribution of cases produces a comparatively flattened distribution, we say this curve is *platykurtic.* *

The fact that we can assume normality in the populations of data that we work with allows us to perform several very useful procedures. These procedures are based on the relations between the mean, the standard deviation, and the various areas under the curve.

In working with the normal curve, we typically use the mean as our starting point and work up or down from there. There are two reasons for this: (1) We often do not know where true zero is for the characteristic with which we are dealing, and so we cannot begin with zero. (2) The curve theoretically does not touch the base line at the extremes because of the possibility, even though rare, of locating in the population a case which scores still higher than our highest score or lower than our lowest score. For these reasons, then, the mean is the most logical "landmark" from which to begin our operations.

In addition we need a unit of measurement to apply to distances above and below our point of departure. This unit is the standard deviation, which gives us a yardstick for siting points along the base line of the curve.

Now we are ready to apply these elements—the mean as a starting point and the standard deviation as a unit of measurement above and below that point on the normal curve. Some very useful facts emerge. We find, as noted in Fig. 6.3, that if we erect an ordinate at one unit (one standard deviation) above the mean, the portion of the area under the curve enclosed by this ordinate, the mean, and the base line is 34.13 per cent of the total area under the curve. The same portion of the area is cut off by one unit below the mean. Similarly, two units above or below the mean cut off an additional 13.59 per cent of the area under the curve, and three units in either direction cut off another 2.28 per cent. *These portions pertain to all curves which fit the criteria of normality*, even though the distribution may be rather widely dispersed (as shown in Fig. 6.3*A*) or comparatively narrowly dispersed (as shown in Fig. 6.3*B*) between these extremes.

---

* These terms are derived from the Greek roots: *leptos*, meaning thin; *platys*, meaning broad or flat; and *kyrtosis*, meaning curvature.

Since portions of the area under the curve represent portions of the total number of individuals we have observed, we can apply the information from Fig. 6.3 to solving many problems. Let us suppose we know that the mean IQ for sixth-grade children in Pinetown is 100 and the standard deviation is 15 IQ points. What portion of the sixth-grade pupils will have IQs below 115? Well, this score is one standard deviation above the mean. Looking at Fig. 6.3, we see that below +1 we have 34.13 per cent, 34.13 per cent, 13.59 per cent, and 2.28 per cent, which add up to 84.13 per cent. We,

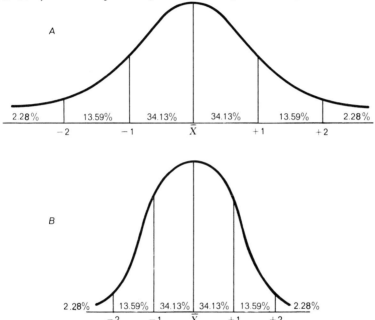

Figure 6.3

therefore, expect that about 84 per cent of the sixth-graders will have IQs less than 115.

How many of Pinetown's sixth-grade children had IQs below 85? As before, we find that 85 is one standard deviation below the mean. Adding up the portions of the curve that fall below that point—13.59 per cent and 2.28 per cent—we find our answer to be 15.87 per cent.

Now let us make a third attack on the problem of bringing additional meaning to score distributions. Suppose Pinetown wanted to provide a special program for slow learners in grade 6. They have defined slow learners as children with IQs from 85 to 70. What portion of their children will come within this range?

Using the procedures illustrated in the previous paragraphs, we find that 85 is one unit below the mean, 70 is two units below, and between these points 13.59 per cent of the cases are expected to appear.

These brief examples show how the normal curve can be applied to solving various problems. The basic procedure tells us to begin at the mean of a distribution, move up or down the scale the necessary number of standard deviations to locate the point in question, and then determine the portion of the curve below that point, or above it, as the problem may indicate.

PROBLEMS

1   A high school counselor has given a general-anxiety questionnaire to all entering freshmen in his high school. The mean for all freshmen was 70; the standard deviation was 10. (a) Herman Ecks has a score of 80. What portion of the class is expected to have lower anxiety scores than Herman's? (b) Janette Zee has a score of 50. What per cent of the class is expected to have anxiety scores higher than Janette's?

2   A manufacturer of schoolroom furniture was interested in making chair desks in as few sizes as possible to fit the varying heights of senior high school students. He decided to build one model for the middle 68 per cent of the high school population. He found that the mean height for the students was 68 inches and the standard deviation was 4 inches. What will be the range of height for the middle 68 per cent of this high school group?

---

z Scores

By now you have noticed that there are essentially two basic steps in solving problems with the normal curve. There is a point in the distribution about which we have a question. We find out how many standard-deviation units that point is from the mean and then determine the portion of individuals (represented by the area under the curve) who come below, or above, that point. Up to now we have dealt with points that are in full standard-deviation units, but very often real problems deal in fractional parts of these units. A more systematic approach is therefore required for these situations. Such a procedure is found in the *z score*.

The *z* score is nothing more than a raw score converted to standard-deviation units. Since standard deviations are measured from the mean, *z* scores begin at that point and range up and down the scale. A score which is one standard deviation above the mean would have a *z*-score equivalent of +1; if a raw score were a half standard deviation below the mean, the *z* score would be −.5, etc.

We convert a raw score to *z* scores in order to determine how many standard-deviation units that raw score is above or below the mean. This allows us then to employ the characteristics of the normal curve in solving problems. The procedure for computing a *z* score is given in Table 6.1.

Table 6.1 Computation of *z* Scores

Formula 6.1	What It Says to Do
$z = \dfrac{X - \bar{X}}{\sigma} = \dfrac{x}{\sigma}$ where X = any given raw score for which we want a *z* equivalent $\bar{X}$ = the mean of the distribution of X scores $x = (X - \bar{X})$ σ = standard deviation of X scores	1. Determine the mean and standard deviation. 2. To find a *z* equivalent for X, first subtract the mean from X to find how many raw-score points X is from the mean. 3. Divide this difference by σ to determine how many standard-deviation units this difference is equal to.

Example For a college freshman class at Hillside University the mean college aptitude-test score is 48, the standard deviation is 8. What is the *z*-score equivalent of a score of 43 at Hillside?

$$z = \frac{X - \bar{X}}{\sigma}$$

$$= \frac{43 - 48}{8}$$

$$= -.625 \quad \text{(That is, a raw score of 43 is .625 of a standard-deviation unit below the mean.)}*$$

* The student who needs a review of negative numbers should consult Appendix A, III. Negative numbers regularly appear in z-score computations.

Since the *z* score is reported in standard-deviation units, it allows us to locate points on the base line of the normal curve. We can then determine portions of cases that come above or below these points by calculating areas under the normal curve. We now know what portions of the group are cut off by whole-unit z scores, but what if we have fractional parts of units? If we are adept at the calculus, we can figure out areas under curved portions of graphs, but fortunately we do not have to do this, since these areas have already been figured out for us and have been put into table form.* Table II in Appendix C is such a table, and it is used in the following manner.

The z-score values are found in column 1; corresponding areas *between* the mean and the z-score points are shown in column 2; and areas *beyond* the z-score points are in column 3. For example, suppose we have found a z score of .25. We find this value in column 1 of the table; and moving across to the next column, we find the figure .0987, a proportion that converts to 9.87 per cent. This is the area between the mean and a z of .25. It should be noted that if we wish to find the entire area below a z of .25, we must add 50 per cent to 9.87 per cent, since half the area of the curve is below the mean.

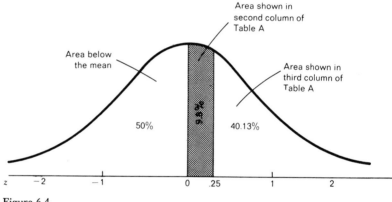

Figure 6.4

Column 3 shows the figure .4013 opposite our z of .25. This is the portion of the area under the curve which lies beyond the z value. Converted to a per cent, .4013 is 40.13 per cent and tells us the area above a z of .25. The whole process is shown in Fig. 6.4.

---

* Suppose we wish to know the area under the normal curve and have no reference to go to. We could slice the area under the curve into many very narrow rectangles, so narrow that their width approaches zero as a limit. (Note figure at right.) Then we could find the area of each of these rectangles and add together as many of these areas as we need to find the magnitude of the portion of the curve we are interested in. This is essentially the procedure used in the calculus.

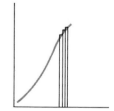

You may by now have noticed that all *z* values in Table II in Appendix C are positive. These data then apply only to the upper half of the curve, the area above the mean. Since the normal curve is a symmetrical one, the solutions applied to *z* values above the mean also apply to *z* values below the mean. Suppose our example in the paragraphs above had dealt with a *z* score of −.25, instead of .25. The solution then would look like Fig. 6.5.

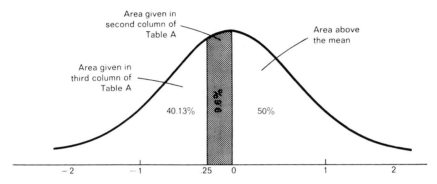

Figure 6.5

If one keeps clearly in mind that *z* scores begin at the mean and move up and down from that point, the application of the data in Table II should cause no problem.

Now some applications of *z* scores and the corresponding areas of the normal curve may help stabilize what we know about the topic. Suppose a high school counselor is faced with a senior boy who is considering enrollment at Midstate University. The boy has an academic aptitude-test score of 650. Is this a high score? We cannot tell from the score alone; we need to know how this score ranks in relation to the average performance of college applicants, that is, the mean. In order to show this relationship we need a yardstick to determine how far 650 is above or below the mean. This yardstick is the standard deviation, and the distance 650 is from $\bar{X}$ in standard-deviation units is our *z* score for 650.

We find that the mean of the academic aptitude-score distribution is 500, and the standard deviation is 100. Applying the *z*-score formula we find that 650 is 1.5 standard deviations above the mean. What portion of the students is expected to fall below this point? Table II in Appendix C tells us that .4332, or 43.32 per cent of the group, lies between the mean and 650, our *z* of 1.5. Since 50 per cent of the students are below the mean, a score of 650 lies above 93.32 per cent of the scores of all test takers. Is a score of

650 a high score?   Certainly it is.   Only 6.68 per cent of the group who took the test scored higher.

Sometimes we have records of an individual's performance on two or more different kinds of measurements and we would like to compare his status on one condition with his status on another.   Unless the scales of two measuring tools are the same, we cannot make a direct comparison.   For example, Johnny has spelled 28 out of 50 words on his spelling test and has solved 11 out of 18 problems in arithmetic.   Direct comparison of his status in arithmetic and spelling cannot be made from these data because they are clearly not in the same scale of measurement.   However, if we convert the two scores to z scores, we put them on a common scale since a z-score unit in one normally distributed set of data represents the same thing as a z-score unit in any other normally distributed variable.

So let us find out if Johnny did better in spelling or in arithmetic.   The spelling-test scores had a mean of 30 and a standard deviation of 5; the arithmetic mean was 10 with a standard deviation of 3.   Johnny's comparison looks like this:

Spelling

$$z = \frac{28 - 30}{5}$$
$$= -.40$$

Arithmetic

$$z = \frac{11 - 10}{3}$$
$$= .33$$

Johnny appears to have done comparatively better in arithmetic than in spelling.

PROBLEMS

1   In a learning experiment students were asked to learn as much as possible of a list of 30 nonsense words in 5 minutes.   They were tested at the end of the 5-minute period to see how many words they had learned.   The mean number of words learned was computed to be 12, and the standard deviation was 4.

   a   Student A had 15 correct words on his test.   What is A's z score?

   b   Sketch a normal curve, locate A's z score on its base line, and erect an ordinate at that point.   What per cent of the group is expected to be below A?   Above A?

2   In the experiment described in Prob. 1, student B had nine correct words on his test.

   a   What is his z score?

b Sketch a normal curve and locate B on the base line. Erect an ordinate at that point. What per cent of the group would be above B? Below B?

c What per cent of the group would fall between A and B?

3 The subjects in the experiment of Prob. 1 also learned a finger-dexterity task, scored on the number of seconds it took to learn the task. The mean number of seconds was 321, with a standard deviation of 60 seconds. Student B of Prob. 2 took 371 seconds to learn the task. Did he do better on nonsense words or on dexterity? (Note: The longer it takes to learn the dexterity task, the lower is the score.)

T Scores

The use of the z score has illustrated the frequent need for changing raw-measurement data to some type of standard scale. Since the z-score scale is often used for this purpose, z scores are sometimes referred to as standard scores. The z score, however, is not the only standard-scoring method. In fact a wide variety of standard-scoring methods could be devised. Any time we express a score in terms of its variation from the mean, with the standard deviation, or multiples of it, as the measure of variation, we have a *standard score*. Another commonly used standard-score method is the T score. Some people find it inconvenient working with a scale that has zero in the middle and half the scores minus values. The T-score scale has solved this problem by placing the mean raw score equal to a T score of 50 and equating the raw-score standard deviation to 10 T-score points. Thus a score one standard deviation above the mean (z score of 1) would have a T score of 60, that is, 50 plus 10. A score one standard deviation below the mean (a z score of -1) would have a T score of 40. Comparable standard-score points for z and T scales are shown in Fig. 6.6.

The computation of a T score is essentially a matter of manipulating the comparable z score. You have seen that the mean of the z scale is zero, while the mean of the T scale is 50. The first step in converting z to T then would be to begin at a scale value of 50 and move up or down from there.

But the T scale has a standard deviation of 10 points, and the z scale has a standard deviation of one. Since z scores are already in standard-deviation units, we can simply multiply the z value by 10 and have a result which tells us how far the score in question is from the mean in terms of a 10-unit standard deviation. This $10z$ value we add algebraically onto our T-score

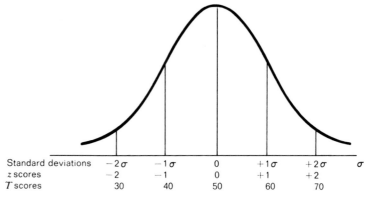

Standard deviations	-2σ	-1σ	0	$+1\sigma$	$+2\sigma$	σ
z scores	−2	−1	0	+1	+2	
T scores	30	40	50	60	70	

Figure 6.6

mean of 50.　The result will be a *T*-score value for the raw score under consideration.　The procedure is formulated as follows.

Table 6.2

Formula 6.2	What it Says to Do
$T = 50 + 10z$ $= 50 + 10\dfrac{(X - \bar{X})}{\sigma}$ $z = \dfrac{X - \bar{X}}{\sigma}$ where X = a given raw score $\bar{X}$ = mean of the distribution of X scores σ = standard deviation of X scores	To convert a raw score to the *T*-score scale: 1. Compute the z score for that raw score. 2. Multiply the z value by 10 and add 50. **Example**　Given a mean of 42 and a standard deviation of 6, what is the *T*-score equivalent of a raw score of 30? 1.　$z = \dfrac{30 - 42}{6} = -2$ 2.　$T = 50 + (-2 \times 10) = 30$

PROBLEMS

1　Vanguard High School has developed its own scholastic aptitude test.　The raw-score mean is 110; the standard deviation is 20.

The school's counselor wishes to report scores in a T scale. In the table below convert the raw scores first to z, then to T, and find the portion of the group that will score below each point.

Raw Score	$X - \bar{X}$	z	T	% Below
132				
126				
112				
90				
86				
70				

2 Suppose you are a counselor explaining to a client the results of his aptitude-test score. Would you prefer to use raw scores, z scores, or T scores? Why?

Standard Scores, Samples, and Populations

We have seen how standard scores can be applied to locating one's position in the group. A similar operation can be applied to samples from a population to see how a given sample ranks in reference to other samples from the same population.

Let us suppose we have 480 boys who report to the city playfield in June to participate in organized baseball. We randomly assign 12 boys to each of 40 teams, and the boys play all summer. At the end of the summer we compute separately for each of the 40 teams the mean number of hits per game. Now every team will not have the same mean number of hits, but if we plotted these 40 means on a graph, we probably would see something like a normal distribution appearing around a point which would be the population (480 boys) mean (Fig. 6.7). A standard deviation could also be com-

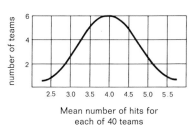

Figure 6.7

Mean number of hits for each of 40 teams

puted for this distribution of means.   In Chap. 5 we called this standard deviation the standard error of the mean to distinguish it from a raw-score standard deviation.   But the use of the standard error is just like the standard deviation—it is a unit of measurement which tells us how distant a given point is from the mean.

Now we can apply something like a *z* score to solving some problems. Team 7 had an average of 3.5 hits per game for the season.   What per cent of the teams ranked higher than team 7?   We could solve this problem if we actually computed the grand mean and the standard error.

Now suppose I am going to be a coach.   What are my chances of being assigned a team which will have an average of 5.4 hits per game for the season?   Suppose I hear about a team with only 2.3 hits per game.   Is it likely this team comes from our population of boys?   Scanning the distribution of Fig. 6.7, we would have to conclude that such a team could only rarely come from random selection from our population of boys.   This application of the basic idea of the standard-score principle, as well as its relation to portions of the normal curve, actually fits into the topic of statistical inference, a topic which will be dealt with at greater length in a later chapter.   However, we solve these problems that deal with many means of samples the same way we solved problems that dealt with raw scores, except here we use the standard error as our yardstick.

Summary

The magnitude of a given measurement or similar observation is not readily apparent when only a raw score is available.   However, when a raw score can be shown in terms of its deviation from the mean, its magnitude begins to be evident.   But we need a yardstick to evaluate the extent of the deviation.   This yardstick is found in the standard deviation.   A score expressed as a deviation from the mean in terms of multiples of the standard deviation is known as a standard score.   Two types of standard scores are commonly used: *z* scores and the *T* scores.   With *z* we equate raw scores to a scale with a mean of zero and a standard deviation of one.   The *T* scale has a mean of 50 and a standard deviation of 10.

One of the most useful applications of standard scores, especially used with *z*, is based on the assumption of normality in the population out of which the measured sample has come.   Since areas under the normal curve, in relation to the standard deviation and fractional parts of it, are known, once we obtain a person's position in the group, as shown by his standard score, we can determine the portion of individuals likely to perform better or worse than that person.

Standard scores are also useful for comparing two measures with each other when the two scales are not in the same units.   If we wish to compare intelligence test results with achievement scores, we can hardly do so until the results of both tests are translated into a common scale.   Such a scale is found in z, T, or similar standard scores.

The idea of portions of the normal curve falling above or below various standard-score points can be applied not only to data on individuals but also to a collection of means of samples from a population.   Thus we can determine the likelihood of getting a sample whose mean is above, or below, various magnitudes and consequently decide whether a given sample is indeed a random selection of cases from a given population.

PROBLEMS

1   Eks University gave college admissions examination A and found their raw-score mean to be 97, the standard deviation to be 12. Compute a z score and a T score for each of the following raw scores:

X	z	T
91		
119		
110		
86		
97		

2   On an admissions test B, Eks University officials found a mean raw score of 78, a standard deviation of 15.   For the following students state whether their performance, relative to all the students at the university, is better on test A of Prob. 1 or on test B.

Student	Raw Score A	Raw Score B
Joe Zibble	95	74
Mary Willdo	110	95
Bill Stronback	88	73

3 For each student in Prob. 2, convert his test A score to a standard score with a mean of 500, a standard deviation of 100.

4 For each of the following z scores state the area under the normal curve between the mean and the z score, the area in the larger portion of curve, and the area in the smaller portion of the curve.

z	$\bar{X}$ to z	Area in Larger	Area in Smaller
1.20			
−.65			
.75			
−.10			

5 Given a distribution with a mean of 50, a standard deviation of 15:
  a What per cent of the group is expected to have scores greater than 68?
  b What per cent will lie between scores of 47 and 60?
  c What per cent will lie between scores of 40 and 47?

7

Correlation and Regression

The admissions officer at Midstate University is looking over the records of last fall's entering freshmen. He notices that students who had high grade point averages in high school tend to do better in college than those who had mediocre high school averages. Across town a young mother who just last year had a course in child psychology decides to keep a monthly growth record of her child. After 6 months she sees a fairly clear picture of increases in height accompanied with increases in weight. And cloistered in his laboratory, an experimental psychologist notices that the more lists of nonsense syllables a student learns, the fewer trials it takes to learn successive lists.

Each of these situations illustrates an example in which change in one condition shows

91

a relation to change in a second condition; that is, two conditions are seen to change together.   Now in none of the above situations would we expect one condition to change a definite, prescribed amount with each unit change in the other condition.   The behaviors described are just not that stable or that closely related.   Nevertheless, clear trends of mutual change do appear in pairs of variables.

In the behavioral sciences we occasionally see two variables which change together almost unit for unit.   In other conditions we observe only a tendency for one to change as the other changes a given amount.   And in still other cases we see no relationship between two variables at all.   Because relationships between pairs of variables may range from very close ones to no relationships at all, we need a technique to indicate the extent to which changes in X are indeed reflected by changes in Y.   This technique is found in what are known as correlational methods.

Correlation in nonstatistical use means that there is a correspondence between two conditions.   In statistical usage correlation refers to techniques which indicate in numerical terms the extent of the relationship between two variables.   It is, then, a measure of relationship with specified limits. These limits are stated in coefficients ranging from zero to ± 1.00.

Suppose I ask you to guess the income of 30 adult males from their shoe sizes.   Chances are that shoe size alone will tell us nothing about income; that is, there is no relationship between these two variables.   Such a condition is indicated by a correlation coefficient of zero.   But suppose I give you 30 pairs of shoes and ask you to guess the size of each left shoe from the size of the corresponding right one.   Now you will very likely guess correctly the size of every left shoe, because as the sizes of right shoes change in pairs, the sizes of the left shoes change an equal amount.   In this case, the correlation coefficient would be $+1.00$, indicating that the relationship is perfect (as one condition changes one unit, the other also changes a specific amount); moreover, the *direction* of change is the *same* for both conditions, indicating a *positive* (or plus) relation.

But sometimes we find that as one condition increases, the other condition decreases.   The higher their high school grade point averages are, the fewer failures we expect to find among college freshmen.   The more years mothers and fathers went to school, the fewer are the high school dropouts in the family.   If one condition increases as the other decreases, there still is a definite relationship between these two conditions.   But since one variable is diminishing as the other expands, we say that the relationship is *negative* (or minus).   If for every unit increase in X we have a prescribed decrease in Y, we would have a perfect negative correlation, or -1.00.

Briefly then, if two variables change together in magnitude in the same direction, the relationship is positive, and the coefficient of correlation between them will be a positive number between zero and +1.00; if two variables change together in magnitude in opposite directions (one increases while the other decreases), the relationship is negative, and the coefficient of correlation between these variables will be a negative number between zero and −1.00; and if a change in magnitude of one variable tells us nothing about the likely condition of the other variable, there is no relationship and the coefficient of correlation will be zero.

But most pairs of conditions observed in the behavioral sciences do not change perfectly together, nor do many even approach a perfect relationship. As a result we see many more correlation coefficients between .50 and .60 than we see between .90 and 1.00. The same is true for correlation coefficients on the negative side. Outside the physical sciences we simply do not expect perfect negative or perfect positive relationships between pairs of variables.

The Scatter Diagram

The relationship between two variables can be illustrated by plotting them on a bivariate graph as we did in Chap. 2. For example, suppose we have the following data, where an X value and its corresponding Y value represent two measurements on the same person.

X: 1, 2,   3, 4
Y: 5, 5.5, 6, 6.5

Graphed on a bivariate format, these data would look like Fig. 7.1. The

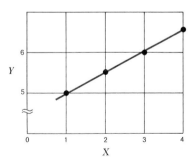

Figure 7.1

graph shows that as X increases a unit of one, Y also increases a specific increment. In other words, as X increases a given amount, Y increases in a proportionate amount, although the increments are of different size. The relationship is therefore a perfect positive one, and the plotted points lie in a straight line.

But all pairs of variables do not progress together unit for unit. Their relationship is less than perfect, although there may be a clear increasing trend in Y for each unit increase in X. Here is an example of this type of relationship, where again corresponding X and Y values are two measurements of the same person.

X: 1,   2,   3,   4
Y: 5.0, 5.6, 6.0, 6.6

Graphed, the data would look like Fig. 7.2. Here the trend of an increase in Y for each unit increase in X is clear, but the data do not progress unit for

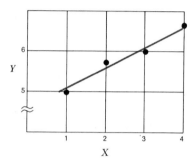

Figure 7.2

unit. Thus, the plotted points fall near, but not directly on, the straight line. Although it is positive, the relationship is not perfect, and the correlation coefficient would be less than 1.00.

Similar examples may be used to illustrate the different relationships. Figure 7.3*A* shows a perfect negative relationship: as X increases a unit, Y decreases a specific increment; Fig. 7.3*B*, a negative relationship which is less

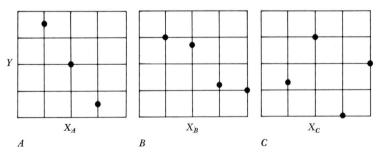

Figure 7.3

than perfect: as X increases a unit, Y has a decreasing trend, but it is not an increment-for-increment change; and Fig. 7.3*C*, a zero relationship: change in X tells us nothing at all about change in Y. We call bivariate graphs such as these *scatter diagrams* or *scattergrams*.

PROBLEMS

1 For each of the pairs of conditions below, tell whether you think the correlation will be positive (high, moderate, or low), zero, or negative (high, moderate, or low).
  a The number of automobiles on the highway and the number of accidents
  b The height and age of elementary school children
  c Mental age and shoe size for adolescents
  d The birthrate and socio-economic level
  e IQ and the number of failures in college
  f The length of the base of a square and the length of its diagonal

---

On our bivariate graphs the relationship between X and Y is revealed by the linearity of the coordinate points. The more nearly the coordinate points fit along a specified line, the more exactly we can anticipate Y once we know what X is. The location of the coordinate points, then, is an important feature of correlation methods. Even when we do not plot them, our computations will proceed as though we had plotted them.

For a given pair of scores we could locate the coordinate point as we did in the figures above by first locating the X value on the base line (the abscissa) and then moving up the Y scale (the ordinate) to find the appropriate Y value, placing our point at this abscissa-ordinate intersection. If we should actually draw in these intersecting lines, we would make a discovery, and so let us take some figures and see what we can find. These data,

X: 1, 2, 3, 4
Y: 2, 3, 4, 5

are graphed in Fig. 7.4. Now let us consider only the second pair of X and Y values, 2 and 3. If we multiply 2 × 3, the product is 6. Now count the number of blocks marked off by the dotted lines. There are six of them. In other words, two X units taken three times (once for each Y unit) produce a rectangle, the diagonal of which (beginning at the intersection of the X and Y axes) would end at the coordinate point.

Possibly, the above comments suggest to the reader that the coordinate points of X and Y can be, in effect, located mathematically.   There are some problems, however, that complicate this process.   For example, X is usually on a different scale than Y; that is, the units are likely to be different, and the mean and standard deviations are different from Y.   But these problems vanish when we convert our X and Y values both to z scores.   Then both X and Y are on the same scale, and when X is zero, Y also will be zero.   In effect then we have set the means of X and of Y at the origin (axes intersection), which is zero.   Now once again multiplying X values by their corresponding Y values (in z-score form), we produce a set of data we can use

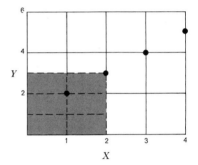

Figure 7.4

mathematically to the same end as we would use a set of plotted coordinate points on a scattergram, that is, to reveal the relationship of X to Y.

The above discussion is presented to provide some insight into the basic formula for computing a correlation coefficient (r_{xy}) *.   That formula is

$$r_{xy} = \frac{\Sigma z_x z_y}{N}$$

Since the sum of anything divided by the number of items summed is the mean of those items, we can now see that the correlation coefficient is a mean —the mean of the cross multiplications of corresponding z scores for X and Y values.

Possibly we can now see too why the maximum correlation is 1.00.   The highest $\Sigma z_x z_y$ value we could get is when each z_x equals its corresponding z_y.   In this case, $\Sigma z_x z_y$ would be equal to Σz_x^2, and since z scores are devia-

---

* This procedure is known as the Pearson product-moment correlation method after Karl Pearson who is credited with its development.   However, Sir Francis Galton had made the preliminary observations that led to the development of the mathematical procedures.

tion scores, $\Sigma z_x^2/N$ would equal σ_z^2, the variance for the z scale, which is always 1. If z_x values are not equal to their corresponding z_y scores, $\Sigma z_x z_y$ must be less than Σz_x^2, hence less than 1.00, and correlation coefficients never exceed a plus or minus 1.00.

The basic method of computing a correlation coefficient is shown in Table 7.1. The procedure of Table 7.1 has a disadvantage, however, in that our data are usually in raw-score form rather than in z-score form. There-

Table 7.1 Computing a Correlation Coefficient

Formula 7.1	What It Says to Do*
$r_{xy} = \dfrac{\Sigma z_x z_y}{N}$ where $z_x = \dfrac{X - \bar{X}}{\sigma_x}$ $z_y = \dfrac{Y - \bar{Y}}{\sigma_y}$ N = number of pairs of X, Y scores	1. Compute a z value for each X and each Y value 2. Multiply z_{x_1} by z_{y_1}, z_{x_2} by z_{y_2}, z_{x_3} by z_{y_3}, . . . , z_{x_n} by z_{y_n}. 3. Add $z_{x_1}z_{y_1} + z_{x_2}z_{y_2} + z_{x_3}z_{y_3} + \cdots + z_{x_n}z_{y_n}$. 4. Divide this sum by the number of pairs of X, Y values.

Example Given the following pairs of z scores representing seven children's positions on the IQ scale and on a reading test, what is the correlation between IQ and reading comprehension R?

Child	z_{IQ}	z_R	$z_{IQ}z_R$
A	1.4	1.0	1.40
B	1.0	1.4	1.40
C	.7	.7	.49
D	.0	.0	
E	− .6	−1.2	.72
F	−1.3	− .6	.78
G	−1.2	−1.3	1.56
		$\Sigma z_{IQ}z_R =$	6.35

$$r_{IQ, R} = \frac{6.35}{7} = .91$$

*The student who needs a review of the use of subscripts should turn to Appendix A, 7b before proceeding.

fore, we need a raw-score procedure in order to circumvent the intermediate step of computing z scores. We get the desired process by simply substituting the z-score formula in Eq. (7.1), thusly:

$$r = \frac{\Sigma \left[\dfrac{(X - \bar{X})}{s} \dfrac{(Y - \bar{Y})}{s} \right]}{N} \qquad \qquad 7.2$$

If we multiply the $(X - \bar{X})$ and $(Y - \bar{Y})$ values together and then substitute $\Sigma X/N$ for $\bar{X}$ and $\Sigma Y/N$ for $\bar{Y}$, it can be shown that the numerator in formula

Table 7.2 Computing a Correlation Coefficient from Raw Scores

Formula 7.4	What It Says to Do
$$r_{xy} = \frac{N\Sigma XY - \Sigma X \Sigma Y}{\sqrt{N\Sigma X^2 - (\Sigma X)^2} \sqrt{N\Sigma Y^2 - (\Sigma Y)^2}}$$	1a. Sum the X scores; sum the Y scores. b. Square each X score and summate the X^2 values; square Y scores and summate Y^2 values. c. Multiply each X score by its corresponding Y score; summate these products. 2. Square the values ΣX and ΣY. 3. Proceed as formulated.

Example Given the following scores on an arithmetic test and corresponding scores on a reading comprehension test, correlate the two sets of scores.

Child	Arithmetic (X)	Reading (Y)	X^2	Y^2	XY
A	3	6	9	36	18
B	2	4	4	16	8
C	4	4	16	16	16
D	6	7	36	49	42
E	5	5	25	25	25
F	1	3	1	9	3
	$\Sigma X = 21$	$\Sigma Y = 29$	$\Sigma X^2 = 91$	$\Sigma Y^2 = 151$	$\Sigma XY = 112$

$$r_{xy} = \frac{6(112) - (21)(29)}{\sqrt{6(91) - (21)^2} \sqrt{6(151) - (29)^2}}$$

$$= \frac{63}{(10.25)(8.06)}$$

$$= .76$$

(7.2) comes out to be the numerator of (7.3). We can similarly deal with the denominator of (7.2). The result is a handy raw-score formula for computing r:*

$$r_{xy} = \frac{\Sigma XY - \dfrac{\Sigma X \Sigma Y}{N}}{\sqrt{\Sigma X^2 - \dfrac{(\Sigma X)^2}{N}} \; \sqrt{\Sigma Y^2 - \dfrac{(\Sigma Y)^2}{N}}} \qquad \textbf{7.3}$$

If a desk calculator is to be used in calculating r, the formula may be rewritten to speed up computation:

$$r_{xy} = \frac{N\Sigma XY - \Sigma X \Sigma Y}{\sqrt{N\Sigma X^2 - (\Sigma X)^2} \; \sqrt{N\Sigma Y^2 - (\Sigma Y)^2}} \qquad \textbf{7.4}$$

PROBLEM

1   I gave a spelling test of 10 words arranged in increasing order of difficulty. I read the words, and my class wrote them on a prepared sheet of paper. A second test was also given; this time students were to check those words in a printed list of 20 words which were spelled correctly. I wish to correlate the written spelling test scores with the recognition test scores. The data I have for my class are as follows:

Student	Written Test	Recognition Test
A	2	5
B	5	8
C	9	15
D	6	12
E	7	11
F	3	9

a   Compute the correlation between the two spelling methods by formula (7.3).

---

* The curious student will want to follow this development in Appendix B.

b   The mean for writing is 5.33, and the standard deviation 2.36, the mean for recognition is 10.00, and the standard deviation 3.16. Compute the correlation coefficient by formula (7.1). How does your result compare with your result in (a)? Which method is the simpler?

Interpretation of *r*

Now that we have computed a correlation coefficient, what does it tell us? There are a number of ways in which *r* may be interpreted; therefore only the most frequently used methods will be pointed out here.

First, r_{xy} can be used to illustrate the portion of variance in *Y* which is associated with *X*. We observe that *X* and *Y* generally increase together. How much of that variance in *Y* is associated with variance in *X*? We find this out by squaring r_{xy}. This gives us the portion of variance σ^2 in one condition which is associated with variance in the other. If r_{xy} is .80, then .64, or 64 per cent, of variance in *Y* is associated with variance in *X*.

The word "associated" is important. Correlation does not show that *X* *causes* a given change in *Y*; it merely shows that the two variables are showing simultaneous alterations. For example, the amount of juvenile delinquency between 1955 and 1965 is correlated with the number of jet aircraft used by commercial airlines. Can we say that the increase in jet aircraft has caused adolescents to resort to antisocial behavior? Or even more absurd, can we say that the increase in the number of delinquents has caused airlines to turn from piston to jet aircraft? Probably both conditions are at least in part due to increasing industrialization, but they have no logical causative relationship. So when we look at r_{xy}^2, we see the portion of *X* variance associated with *Y* variance, but this tells us nothing about causative relationships. Certainly some variables do have a direct influence on others, but correlation techniques do not identify this condition.

A second way we can interpret a correlation coefficient is in terms of the lack of relationship between the two variables. To do this, we compute $\sqrt{1 - r^2}$, and this produces an index of lack of relationship, called the *coefficient of alienation*. The term under the radical tells us the portion of *Y* variance which is not associated with *X*. In other words, the coefficient of alienation is essentially the opposite side of the coin of the coefficient of correlation.

A third way to interpret a correlation coefficient is in terms of how accurately we can predict a *Y* value from a given *X* value. If *Y* changes in a given way as X changes, we should be able to say something about the value of a given Y score once we know X. What is the range of error for such a prediction? This is shown by a kind of standard deviation of errors called the *standard error of estimate*. We shall discuss this more later.

Somewhat related to accuracy of prediction is the improvement over chance that we can make in prediction of Y by knowing the correlation between X and Y. This brings us to the fourth way to interpret r. The *index of forecasting efficiency* is found by subtracting $\sqrt{1 - r^2}$ from 1.00 and multiplying by 100, that is, $(1 - \sqrt{1 - r^2})100$, and it tells us the reduction in errors of prediction over what they would have been if X and Y were unrelated and we were merely guessing at Y scores. Thus, if r_{xy} is .60, $\sqrt{1 - r_{xy}^2}$ is .80, and the index of forecasting efficiency is 20 per cent. This means we can reduce our errors of prediction of Y scores 20 per cent over predictions based on chance alone. We shall dwell more on this topic later.

PROBLEMS

1a Compute r^2 for each of the following values of r: .20, .40, .50, .60, .70, .80, .90, 1.00.

 b Plot the data from (a) on a graph like the one below. Is the variance in X associated with Y a straight-line function, or is it curvilinear? What does this tell us about units of common variance between X and Y as r_{xy} gets larger? What does this say about adding (or subtracting) correlation coefficients?

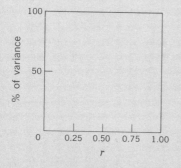

2a For the correlation coefficients on page 102 compute r^2, the coefficient of alienation, and the index of forecasting efficiency, and in your own words tell what each of these figures tell us about Y once we know X.

r	r^2	$\sqrt{1-r^2}$	$(1-\sqrt{1-r^2})100$
.20			
.60			
.80			
1.00			

b As *r* increases, what is the direction of change for r^2? Is it a rectilinear relationship?

c As *r* increases, what is the direction of change for $\sqrt{1-r^2}$? Is it rectilinear?

d As *r* increases, what is the direction of change for the index of forecasting efficiency? Is it rectilinear?

Assumptions in Computing *r*

The nature of the scatter diagram is a very important condition in the formulation of correlation procedures.   The scatter diagrams shown in Figs. 7.1 to 7.3 are very simple because so few cases are shown.   In typical studies we would expect to have many more cases than this, and the data are more likely to distribute themselves somewhat as in Fig. 7.5 for a correlation of

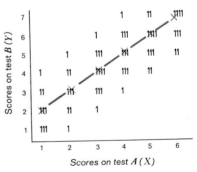

Figure 7.5

about .70.   Here we can see that as *X* increases, *Y* tends to increase, too, but the relationship is certainly not perfect.

Now each of the rows and each of the columns in Fig. 7.5 is called an *array*.   Let us now compute the means for each of the column arrays and see what these points look like.   The small cross in an array locates its approximate mean.   As we look at these points, we notice that they lie in quite a straight line.   The means of the array do not always look this way. Sometimes we have curvilinear relationships such as those shown in Fig. 7.6.

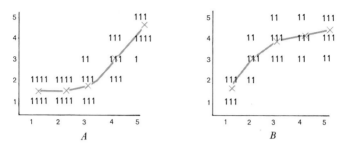

Figure 7.6

A   *B*

And here is the first assumption underlying the product-moment procedure for computing a correlation coefficient.   The relationship between *X* and *Y* is assumed to be a rectilinear one; that is, the means of the arrays are expected to lie in a straight line.   Slight departure from this arrangement can be tolerated, but if a curvilinear relationship exists, techniques other than the product-moment method should be used.*

Now let us look again at Fig. 7.5.   The distribution of points in any array is about like that in any other array.   We actually could compute a standard deviation for each of the arrays; we would then have an indication of dispersion for each of these arrays.

The second assumption of the product-moment procedure is tied to these array dispersions.   We assume that they are all equal.   If they are, we say that they have homoscedasticity,† a necessary condition for the correlation method described above.

Typically, we do not apply exact tests to find out if our data meet these two basic assumptions.   A careful visual study of the scatter diagram usually is satisfactory.   More precise tests of the assumptions are available, however, but are beyond the scope of this chapter.

PROBLEM

1   For each pair of given conditions, indicate whether you believe the assumptions for the product-moment correlation are met, and if not, which assumption is not met.

* The interested student will find the appropriate procedure for handling curvilinear relationships listed in other sources under the topic of correlation ratio.

† The roots are *homo*, meaning the same, and *scedastic*, meaning scatter.

a   Socio-economic status and income
b   Age and IQ
c   Age of females from 10 to 40 years and number of dates per week
d   IQ and grade point average for high school freshmen
e   Automobile speed and rate of gasoline consumption

Regression—The Prediction of Y from X

If any portion of variance in Y changes in some systematic way with a change in X, we should be able to predict Y from X with better than chance accuracy. The way that these predictions are made, and how their accuracy is determined, is the topic of the paragraphs ahead.

If the means of the arrays in a scatter diagram can be seen to fall along a straight line, the slope of this line will tell us how much Y increases for every unit X increases.   This is shown in Fig. 7.7.   We see that Y increases a half

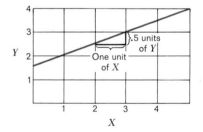

Figure 7.7

unit for every whole unit X increases.   So the first thing we will want to do is to devise a formula for the line that passes through the array means (we call this the *regression line*), and in order to do this, we need to know two things: (1) the slope of the line, that is, the amount of increase in Y with a unit increase in X, and (2) where the line intersects the Y axis, i.e., what the Y value is when X is zero.   Thus the formula for this line is

$$Y = a + bX \qquad\qquad \textbf{7.5}$$

where a is the point where the line intersects the Y axis and b is the slope.

The coefficient b, the indicator of rate of change in Y for a unit change in X, is also called the *regression coefficient*.   The procedure for computing it is presented in Table 7.3.

We now have in hand one of the two bits of information we need to predict Y from X, that is, the regression coefficient.   The second bit, a, is next to be found.   It is computed simply by subtracting from the mean of the Y scale

Table 7.3 Computation of the Regression Coefficient

Formula 7.6	What It Says to Do
$$b_{yx} = \dfrac{\Sigma XY - \dfrac{\Sigma X \Sigma Y}{N}}{\Sigma X^2 - \dfrac{(\Sigma X)^2}{N}}$$ where b_{yx} = rate of change in Y for a unit change in X X = raw scores from which we are predicting Y = raw-score scale to which predictions will be made N = number of pairs of scores observed	1. Multiply each X score by its corresponding Y value, and add these products: $X_1Y_1 + X_2Y_2 + X_3Y_3 + \cdots + X_nY_n$. 2. Add all X scores, add all Y scores, and multiply the two sums: $(X_1 + X_2 + X_3 + \cdots + X_n)(Y_1 + Y_2 + Y_3 + \cdots + Y_n)$. 3. Divide the result of step 2 by N, and subtract from the result of step 1. 4. Square each X score, and summate the squares: $X_1^2 + X_2^2 + X_3^2 + \cdots + X_n^2$. 5. Square the sum of the X scores, $(X_1 + X_2 + X_3 + \cdots + X_n)^2$, and divide by N. 6. Subtract the result of step 5 from that of step 4. 7. Divide the result of step 3 by the result of step 6.

Example Given the following pairs of test scores, find the regression coefficient.

X: 1, 2, 3, 4, 5 $\Sigma X = 15$ $\Sigma X^2 = 55$
Y: 3, 3, 5, 7, 6 $\Sigma Y = 24$ $\Sigma Y^2 = 128$
XY: 3, 6, 15, 28, 30 $\Sigma XY = 82$

$$b_{yx} = \frac{82 - \dfrac{(15)(24)}{5}}{55 - \dfrac{(15)^2}{5}} = 1.00$$

the product of b and the mean of the X scale, thusly:

$$a = \bar{Y} - b_{yx}\bar{X} \qquad\qquad 7.7$$

Now that we are ready to predict a Y value from an X value, let us symbolize predicted scores, as contrasted with actual ones, by means of a prime (Y'). In the example in Table 7.3, b is 1.00, $\bar{X}$ is 3, and $\bar{Y}$ is 4.8. If I have an X score of 2.5, what is my predicted Y score (Y')? The computations would look like this:

$$\begin{aligned} Y' &= a + bX \\ &= (4.8 - 1.00 \times 3) + (1.00 \times 2.5) \\ &= 4.3 \end{aligned}$$

The above procedure applies when we begin our computations with raw data on which we had not computed means and standard deviations. However, if these descriptive statistics are available, the procedure is somewhat simplified. A Y' then can be found by the formula: *

$$Y' = r_{xy} \frac{s_y}{s_x} (X - \bar{X}) + \bar{Y}$$

From the example in Table 7.3 we find that r_{xy} is .88, s_x is 1.58, and s_y is 1.79. Applying these data to the above formula, we predict a Y score from an X score of 2.5 as follows:

$$Y' = .88 \frac{1.79}{1.58} (2.5 - 3) + 4.8$$
$$= 1.0(-.5) + 4.8$$
$$= -.5 + 4.8$$
$$= 4.3$$

This answer is the same as the one found above when the raw-score procedure was applied.

It may also be noted that the b value computed from raw data is equal to the $r_{xy}(s_y/s_x)$ value. In fact, $r_{xy}(s_y/s_x)$ is another way to compute b, and if we substitute it into the formulas for a and substitute the result into $Y' = a + bX$, we come out with the formula which we just used to find the predicted value of 4.3.

PROBLEMS

1 As a high school counselor I would like to devise a procedure for predicting grade point average, GPA, from IQ. I have the following data upon which to base my procedure (too few cases, admittedly).

Student	IQ	GPA
A	90	1.8
B	95	2.1
C	100	2.7
D	105	2.6
E	110	3.0
F	115	3.2

---

* Derivation of this procedure is in Appendix B.

a Compute the predicted GPA for an IQ of 98 using the raw-score procedure.

b Compute r, s_{IQ}, s_{GPA}, and apply these data to the prediction of GPA for an IQ of 98.

2 If $b_{yx} = r_{xy}(s_y/s_x)$, rewrite the formula for r_{xy} in terms of b_{yx}, s_y, and s_x. Now substitute

$$\dfrac{\Sigma XY - \dfrac{\Sigma X \Sigma Y}{N}}{\Sigma X^2 - \dfrac{(\Sigma X)^2}{N}}$$

for b_{yx}, and

$$\sqrt{\dfrac{\Sigma X^2 - \dfrac{(\Sigma X)^2}{N}}{N-1}}$$

for s_x, and

$$\sqrt{\dfrac{\Sigma Y^2 - \dfrac{(\Sigma Y)^2}{N}}{N-1}}$$

for s_y, and see if you can come out with the basic formula

$$r_{xy} = \dfrac{\Sigma XY - \dfrac{\Sigma X \Sigma Y}{N}}{\sqrt{\Sigma X^2 - \dfrac{(\Sigma X)^2}{N}}\sqrt{\Sigma Y^2 - \dfrac{(\Sigma Y)^2}{N}}}$$

The Standard Error of Estimate

In Chap. 5 we saw that a first step in finding the standard deviation was to subtract the mean from each score, square this difference, and add together all these values, dividing by N and taking the square root of the result, that is, $\sqrt{\Sigma(X - \bar{X})^2/N}$. With this thought in mind let us now turn to the scatter diagram in Fig. 7.8. And let us for the moment look only at a single vertical array, say the second one. It looks like a simple frequency distribution, and we have already found that if our data meet the assumptions of the product-moment method, the mean of the array will be the point through which the regression line passes. The mean of the array will also be Y', our predicted value for the X score at the base of this array, 2.

We can now compute a standard deviation for this array by finding how far actual Y scores in the array deviate from the predicted Y', thusly: $\sqrt{\Sigma(Y - Y')^2/N}$. But we do not wish to have to do this for each array, and so we compute a figure, by adding the $\Sigma(Y - Y_1')^2$ values from the first array to the $\Sigma(Y - Y_2')^2$ values for the second array, etc., until all arrays are

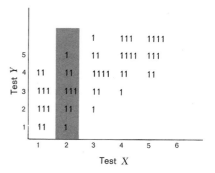

Figure 7.8

represented in the term $\Sigma(Y - Y_i')^2$. We then divide this sum by the total number of cases in the scatter diagram and take the square root of that figure. This produces a standard deviation generalized across all arrays. We call it a *standard error of estimate* and use it just like any standard deviation. Let us take an example.

Suppose that in predicting grade point average from IQ, I find a standard error of estimate to be .50 of a grade point. This figure, applied to a normal curve, will tell me how many actual GPAs are expected to deviate given amounts from the predicted GPA. Figure 7.9 illustrates this point with a

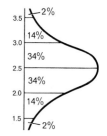

Figure 7.9

predicted GPA of 2.5, when our standard error of estimate is .50. For all persons who are predicted to have a 2.5 GPA, 68 per cent actually will attain GPAs within the range from 2.0 to 3.0; 96 per cent, between 1.5 and 3.5.

The standard error of estimate therefore is really not a new idea at all. It merely applies previously learned procedures—the standard deviation and the normal curve—to data which are arranged only slightly differently from a typical frequency distribution.

The computation of the standard error of estimate by the above method is cumbersome, and fortunately we do not have to use this method. A simpler, but mathematically equivalent, procedure is found to be as follows: *

$$s_{est} = s_y \sqrt{1 - r_{xy}^2} \qquad\qquad 7.8$$

where s_{est} = standard error of estimate

s_y = standard deviation of the Y scores

r_{xy} = correlation between X and Y

Formula (7.8) allows us to get a little more meaning out of r_{xy}. If we square both sides of the equation, we have $s_{est}^2 = s_y^2(1 - r_{xy}^2)$, and this can be rewritten as $r_{xy}^2 = 1 - s_{est}^2/s_y^2$. Now r^2 is the portion of variance in Y which is associated with X. The total variance of Y is 1.00, and if we take away from this the portion of Y variance which is not predicted by X, (s_{est}^2/s_y^2), we have left then the portion of Y variance which is associated with X, or r_{xy}^2. So the ratio of the error variance to the variance of the Y distribution tells us the portion of Y variance not associated with X variance. The larger r_{xy} is, the smaller will be the s_{est}^2/s_y^2 ratio.

The standard error also provides us an additional way in which we can interpret a correlation coefficient, and that is in terms of the accuracy with which Y can be predicted from X. The larger the value of r_{xy}, the smaller is the standard error.

PROBLEMS

1 I have found a correlation between IQ and GPA for college freshmen to be .60; GPA has a standard deviation of .50, and IQ has a standard deviation of 15.

a I predict a GPA of 3.0 for Mary Willslip. What portion of people with Y' like Mary's will actually achieve a GPA of 3.5 or higher?

b I predict for John Plugger a GPA of 2.0. He must have a 1.8 to stay off the probation list. What portion of people predicted to be at 2.0 will actually fall below 1.8? What portion will actually make 3.0 or higher?

2 As an employer of machinists, I have conducted a study to find the correlation between success on the job and mechanical aptitude test. The r_{xy} is .70; test standard deviation is 10; and my job proficiency

* Derivation of this procedure is in Appendix B.

measure has a standard deviation of 5.   I have decided that minimum proficiency is represented by a job success score of 30, but I am willing to accept for employment all persons one standard error of estimate below that point.   What is my minimum acceptable job success score?

Regression Effect

With the data given in a typical scatter diagram we can compute three standard deviations for Y scores: (1) one for the deviation of Y scores from the $\bar{Y}$, (2) one for the deviation of Y scores from the array means, Y', and (3) one for the deviation of array means, Y', from $\bar{Y}$. These three standard deviations and their distributions are schematically shown in Fig. 7.10.

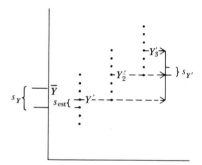

Figure 7.10

We can speculate from this figure that $s_y{}^2 = s_{\text{est}}^2 + s_{Y'}{}^2$, and this can be shown to be true.   We can also see that the spread of Y' values, predicted scores, is less than the Y values, actual scores.   In fact, we see $s_{Y'}$ equal to s_Y only when the correlation between X and Y is ± 1.0.   In other words, we never predict scores as high, nor as low, as actually will be attained.   This tendency for predicted scores to fall toward the mean is called the *regression effect*.   Its result is to present a distribution of predicted scores which is more constricted in dispersion than will be true of actually obtained scores.   The lower the value of r_{xy}, the narrower will be the distribution of predicted scores compared with actual scores.

Correlation of Ranked Data

Sometimes the data that are to be correlated cannot reasonably be supposed to form a scale made up of successive, equal units.   For example, suppose we ask a teacher to rank the students in her class from the most capable to the least capable. Now the extent to which child A exceeds child B in ability is not expected to be equal to the extent to which child B exceeds child C, etc. Thus, the ranks are not believed to represent equal amounts of ability.

Occasionally we have rating-scale data that probably cannot be considered as equal-unit scales. Questionnaire data may also be of this type. In any case, we find occasions when the product-moment method is inappropriate because the data are not from a measuring device which has a common unit at all points along the scale. We therefore need an auxiliary correlation procedure to handle these situations, and this procedure is found in the Spearman rank-order method.

Charles Spearman, the English statistician, devised the statistic called *rho*. Rho represents the correlation of data where the individuals involved have first been ranked in order of magnitude of the trait in question. The correlation then represents the relationship of the ranks for individuals on two characteristics. For example, we may have teachers rank students on ability and correlate this with IQ scores to see if teachers estimate ability about the same way as intelligence tests do. The teachers' reports would already be in ranks, but we would have to rank IQ data, giving a rank of 1 to the highest IQ, 2 to the next highest, etc. In this manner we would have two ranks for each child—the teacher's ranking of the child and the rank of the child's IQ among his peers—and these parallel sets of ranks could be correlated to show the relationship of teachers' estimates of relative ability and test results.

The basic procedure for Spearman's rho is found in the product-moment method. In calculating r_{xy}, we needed ΣX, ΣY, etc. Comparable values can be determined from ranks. For example, the sum of a set of ranks is $n(n + 1)/2$. To devise the correlation procedure for ranked data, we merely substitute into the product-moment formula comparable forms for ranked data [for example, $n(n + 1)/2$ for ΣX, $n(n + 1)(2n + 1)/6$ for ΣX^2, etc.], and the result is the procedure shown in Table 7.4.

Occasionally two or more persons will have the same score, and this complicates the ranking of these individuals. Suppose in the example in Table 7.4 children B and C were both given a scale value of 15 by observer 1. Which child will get a rank of 2, and which 3? We resolve this question by averaging ranks and assigning each child the average of the ranks in question. Therefore, we would add ranks 2 and 3, divide by 2, and give each child a rank of 2.5. The same procedure is also used if we have more than two ranks. If B, C, and D all were given scale values of 15 by observer 1, then we would determine their ranks by $(2 + 3 + 4)/3$, and each would have a rank of 3.

Tied ranks present a problem in the use of rho. Actually rho is a good

Table 7.4   Procedure for Correlating Ranked Data

Formula 7.9	What It Says to Do
$$rho = 1 - \frac{6 \times \Sigma d^2}{n(n^2 - 1)}$$ where rho = correlation between ranked data d = difference between the two ranks for a given individual n = number of individuals ranked	1. Where X is a set of data to be correlated with Y, rank all individuals on the X scale beginning with rank of 1 for the highest X value, 2 for the next highest, etc. Similarly rank Y data. 2. Subtract Y ranks from X ranks to get d. (The sum of all d values should be zero.) 3. Square each d value, and summate squared values. 4. Multiply Σd^2 by 6, divide by $n(n^2 - 1)$, where n is the number of individuals involved in ranking. 5. Subtract the result of step 4 from 1; the result is the correlation between X ranks and Y ranks.

Example   The following data represent sociability ratings submitted by two graduate psychology students after observing a group of 10 nursery school children for 1 hour.   Correlate the ratings of the two observers.

Child	Observer 1	Observer 2	Rank 1	Rank 2	d	d²
A	18	15	1	2	−1	1
B	14	16	4	1	3	9
C	15	14	3	3	0	0
D	17	13	2	4	−2	4
E	12	9	6	7	−1	1
F	13	10	5	6	−1	1
G	10	8	7	8	−1	1
H	9	7	8	9	−1	1
I	7	11	9	5	4	16
J	6	6	10	10	0	0
					0	34

$$rho = 1 - \frac{6(34)}{10(100 - 1)}$$
$$= 1 - .21$$
$$= .79$$

estimate of the product-moment procedure to the extent that we have relatively few tied ranks.   As the number of tied ranks increases, the more rho is expected to depart from the product-moment correlation coefficient.   An example may illustrate the deviation of rho from r_{xy} when tied ranks are evident.

Suppose we have 10 more nursery school children rated by two observers using a sociability scale. We have the following results:

Child	Observer I	Observer II	Rank I	Rank II	d	d²
A	19	16	1	2	−1	1.00
B	16	17	2.5	1	1.5	2.25
C	16	14	2.5	3	− .5	.25
D	12	13	4	4	0	0
E	11	12	5.5	5.5	0	0
F	11	12	5.5	5.5	0	0
G	10	9	7	7.5	− .5	.25
H	9	9	8	7.5	.5	.25
I	8	6	9	10	−1	1.00
J	7	7	10	9	1	1.00
					0	6.00

$$rho = 1 - \frac{6(6)}{10(100 - 1)}$$
$$= .96$$

And if we apply the product-moment procedure to the actual raw data, assuming they each represent an equal-unit scale, we get the following result:

$$r_{xy} = \frac{1,489 - \frac{(119)(115)}{10}}{\sqrt{1,553 - \frac{(119)^2}{10}} \sqrt{1,445 - \frac{(115)^2}{10}}}$$
$$= .93$$

The difference between rho and r in this case is not dramatic, but it does illustrate the fact that the two indicators of relationship will not be identical if ranks are tied. The product-moment correlation for the data in Table 7.4 will, however, produce an r of .79, just like the rank-order method. (The interested student may wish to prove this statement by computing r for the data in Table 7.4.)

Summary

Correlation is a procedure for indicating in quantitative terms the relationship between two variables. The relationship is stated in terms of a coefficient of correlation which runs between ± 1.00 and zero. If as X increases one unit, Y also changes by a constant number of units, the coefficient will be 1.00; if as X changes one unit, we can say nothing at all about Y, the correlation is zero; and if as X increases one unit, Y decreases a constant number of units, the coefficient will be -1.00. Most correlations in the behavioral sciences are somewhat less than ± 1.00, indicating a less than perfect relationship between variables being observed.

There are several ways to interpret a correlation coefficient. It can be used to show the portion of variance in X which is associated with Y; it can be used to show the lack of relationship between X and Y; it can be used to show the accuracy of prediction of Y from X; and it can point up the increase in accuracy of a prediction over a random guess.

The standard procedure for computing a correlation coefficient is the product-moment method. It assumes that the relationship between X and Y is rectilinear and that the distribution within a given array has a dispersion equal to that of all other arrays. We call this characteristic homoscedasticity.

Sometimes data are taken from a scale which does not have a common unit at all points on that scale. They essentially indicate rank order of the individuals. In this case the product-moment method is not appropriate, and Spearman's rank-order method (rho) is used to indicate relationships between pairs of ranked data.

The prediction of Y from X is often less than perfect. The standard error of estimate is a kind of standard deviation which tells us how far our predictions are likely to be in error and for what portion of the individuals. This is done by applying the standard error to the normal curve with the predicted score as the mean and by figuring areas under the curve for given numbers of standard errors.

Correlation procedures indicate relationship but do not reveal causality. If X is related to Y, we cannot state that X is causing Y, or vice versa.

PROBLEMS

1 Age is proposed as a condition which is related to length of time a group of surgical patients stayed in the hospital. The following data were collected to illustrate this proposition. Correlate age of the patients with length of stay in the hospital.

Age	Days in Hospital
42	12
36	10
32	11
29	6
26	14
24	6
22	9
18	3
15	8

2 I wished to find out if fraternal twins are alike in their hand-eye coordination, and so I gave a group of 10 pairs of twins a test of maze tracing. Their scores follow.

Score for First Twin	Score for Second Twin
5	4
2	3
7	5
3	4
4	4
3	2
5	6
8	7
1	3
6	7

a Correlate the performances of the pairs of twins.
b A given subject has a score of 6. What score is his twin expected to make?
c What will be the expected range of scores for the middle 68 per cent of subjects whose twins made a score of 6?

3 A psychiatrist ranked 10 children on their adjustment to school. These same children were also given a personality inventory. The

psychiatrist's rank and the inventory score are given for each child. Correlate these data.

Psychiatrist's Rank	Inventory Score
10	62
9	75
8	58
7	42
6	48
5	32
4	34
3	39
2	41
1	38

4 For each correlation coefficient below find the portion of variance in X associated with Y and the coefficient of alienation.

a .20

b .80

c −.40

5 As correlation increases, what changes appear in the variance in X associated with Y? What change occurs in the coefficient of alienation?

8

Probability and Statistical Inference

The topic of probability holds great significance in the study of human behavior, because so many events do not occur each time there is an occasion for them to do so. Therefore, we want to know the likelihood of occurrence of a possible event so that we may make reasonable predictions based on the portion of occasions in which the event is known actually to occur.

For example, a schoolboy is taking a test for which he is not fully prepared. Four of the true-false items are unknown to him. If he makes completely random guesses at the answers to these, how many trues and how many falses should we expect him to make? You are right to say two of each; however, completely random responses could end up with other combinations. He could mark

117

three true and one false, three false and one true, all false, or all true.   These combinations are less likely to occur in random marking than a two-true–two-false arrangement, but they could happen.   In other words, the two-true–two-false arrangement is the most likely one, but the most likely events do not occur every time they are expected to, and so we wish to know in what portion of the total number of occasions will the most likely events, as well as events with lesser likelihood, occur.

A second situation may help to elaborate this idea.   Suppose we have four pennies (analogous to four true-false examination questions) and of course we can turn up a head or a tail on each coin (analogous to true or false, as some students who hav'   ·ken this kind of examination will attest).   We toss the four pennies into the air, and when they settle, we count the number of heads and tails.   On the first toss we get all tails.   Believing something to be wrong with the toss to produce such one-sided results, we try again.   This time we get one tail and three heads.   We now decide to toss 20 times (analogous to 20 students randomly responding to our four true-false items) to see what the cumulative results would be.   The number of occurrences of various combinations is given in Fig. 8.1.   This figure is the actual result of

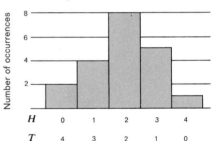

Figure 8.1

tossing four pennies 20 times; however, other distributions are certainly possible.   Nevertheless, the figure tells us something about the probability of getting various combinations of heads and tails from tossing four pennies. Our tossing four coins 20 times is analogous to repeating an experiment 20 times with four subjects, each time determining the nature of a single random sample from a population.   If we were risking something of considerable value on our ability to guess the number of heads in a four-coin toss, we certainly would not guess zero or four.   Our best bet would be to guess that on a purely chance basis two heads would turn up, because in our 20 repetitions of our experiment more samples produced two heads than any other number. Although this is the most likely arrangement of random events, it is far from being the only one.

In a similar manner we predict that a sample of children from a given population will do such and such; they may or may not do so, but the study of behavior concentrates on the likelihood of their doing so. We predict that the events with the highest likelihood will occur. We are sometimes wrong, but with the knowledge of the frequency of possible outcomes, we can know how often we are apt to be wrong.

A definition of probability is now in order. *The probability of an event is the proportion of times that the event would occur if the chances for occurrence were infinite.* Suppose I flip a group of four pennies repeatedly 10,000 times. The most common outcome is two heads, two tails. No heads, or all heads, are comparatively uncommon outcomes. On 3,694 occasions I have two heads among the four coins, and dividing this by 10,000, I have a probability of .3694, or very nearly .37, the value that an infinite number of tosses would bring, as we shall see later. In other words, the probability of getting two heads from a toss of four coins is .37. Similarly, if I had four extremely difficult true-false items and an infinite number of high school seniors responded to them on a pure guess basis, we would expect the probability for two trues to be .37 also. We will abbreviate the probability of an occurrence of an event as p, and the nonoccurrence as $(1 - p)$, or q. Thus, for the probability of getting two heads from a toss of four coins, $p = .37$ and $q = .63$. The sum of all probabilities for various events will always add up to 1.00.

After you toss your pennies the 10,000th time, I place into your tired hand four more pennies. Surreptitiously I have altered each of these by embedding a small piece of lead in the shoulder of Mr. Lincoln, making the head sides heavier and more likely to fall downward. Now you toss these pennies into the air and find that they all come up tails. You likely will conclude that it is very unlikely (although not impossible) that my treated coins are from the population of coins for which you found no heads to be a rather uncommon result.

Now if we think of each coin toss as an experiment with four cases and keep in mind that we have repeated the original experiment 10,000 times, the basic idea of probability illustrated by the coin tosses can be generalized to studies in human behavior (although here we typically conduct experiments using more than four individuals). With the repeated coin experiments we decided what the probability was of getting a given outcome (two heads) from many replications of the experiment within a given population. Then we conducted another experiment with treated coins and speculated that the treated coins were very likely not from the population of previous coins in terms of the characteristics of "flipability."

Similarly we determine the nature of a given group of people, take a sample of cases, and subject them to a treatment (e.g., learning, frustration, psychotherapy). We then compare the nature of the treated sample with what we have decided is characteristic of untreated samples to see if the treatment has altered the characteristic being observed. We make this comparison in terms of the probability of getting from the untreated population a sample that looks like our treated sample. If the likelihood of getting such a sample is remote, as it was with our treated coin, we conclude that the sample probably is from a population different from the one with which we began.

Let us apply this idea to a true-to-clinic event. We are studying the effect of nondirective counseling on psychological maladjustment. We shall continue our study for a month, after which time we shall classify our cases as improved or unimproved (like heads and tails?); the probability for improvement will be the ratio of improved cases to total cases (like tossing a group of, say, 10 coins and recording the proportion of heads). From a group of outpatients awaiting psychiatric treatment we determine that successive samples of untreated maladjusted persons will show a probability of improvement of .51; that is, the most common proportion of improved cases in the samples of untreated patients we have observed is .51. Our sample of counseled patients, however, shows a proportion of improvement of .73. In looking at our study of uncounseled patients, we decide that it is extremely rare that a sample of uncounseled persons would produce a proportion of improvement of .73, and we may wish to conclude that the counseled group is now a sample from a different population in terms of personal adjustment.

To this point we have used probability information but have not looked at the nature of the data (the distribution obtained by tabulating successive probabilities found in repeated samples) with which we have been working. In observing probabilities for a given event occurring in a number of samples, we first note that the probability of the event's occurrence is not always the same from one sample to the next, but the probabilities for our samples do appear to cluster around a given value. As with any variable data, we can make up a frequency distribution of these probabilities from repeated samples and can compute a mean and a standard deviation.

A theoretical distribution of expected outcomes of alternative events (like heads or tails) in the population can be computed by expanding the binomial*

$$(p + q)^n$$

where p = probability of one event
q = probability of the alternative to the event
n = number of times the event can occur

The sum of the coefficients of the terms in the expanded binomial gives us the

---

* Students not familiar with the binomial expansion can get some help from Appendix A, VI.

number of times that given combinations of the events, such as heads and tails, will be expected to occur out of the total number of occasions equal to the sum of the coefficients of all the terms in the expanded binomial. For example, $(p + q)^4$ would expand to $1p^4 + 4p^3q + 6p^2q^2 + 4pq^3 + 1q^4$. The sum of all coefficients is 16. The probability of getting four p's and no q's is $\frac{1}{16}$, or .06; the probability of getting three p's and one q is $\frac{4}{16}$, or .25; and so on.

Now suppose I have 5,000 names of boys and 5,000 names of girls, all mixed together in a barrel. I stir vigorously and draw out four names, replacing the name before each successive draw. What is the probability of getting the names of four boys and no girls? Of three boys and one girl? The answers here are also found in the expanded binomial above. We have a probability of .06 of getting all boys—not a very likely event; we have a probability of .25 of getting three boys and one girl, etc. The basic idea of probability can now be seen to generalize from coins to the area of human events.

But expanding the binomial is not the only way to determine the probability of obtaining various combinations of events. The French mathematician Blaise Pascal, who lived in the seventeenth century, devised a method for determining the frequency of various combinations when $p = .50$. This procedure is illustrated in Table 8.1. In the left-hand column n refers to the

Table 8.1 Pascal's Triangle

n				Frequencies of Combinations						Sum
1					1	1				2
2					1	2	1			4
3				1	3	3	1			8
4			1	4	6	4	1			16
5		1	5	10	10	5	1			32
6	1	6	15	20	15	6	1			64
7	1	7	21	35	35	21	7	1		128
8	1	8	28	56	70	56	28	8	1	256

number of events combining to yield various outcomes. When we find the row containing the n equal to the number of occasions for an occurrence, we move across this row where the numbers indicate relative frequencies of various combinations. For example, suppose we have four true-false items ($n = 4$). How many times will we expect to find all four items marked true by chance alone? How many papers will have three items true and one false, two true and two false, one true and three false, and all false? Reading across the row that goes with an n of 4, we find answers to these questions. We shall get by sheer chance *one* paper with all true, *four* papers with three true and one false, *six* with two true and two false, *four* with one true and three false, and one with all false, out of a total of 16 papers.

Now we have defined probability in terms of proportion of occurrences, that is, the fraction of the total number of occurrences that is accounted for by the desired outcome. Well, the total number of events (sum) in the row associated with our experiment ($n = 4$) is 16, and to find what portion of 16 is accounted for by each combination of events, we simply divide each of the frequencies given across the row by 16. Thus, we find that the probability of getting a paper marked four trues by chance is $\frac{1}{16}$, or .06. The probabilities for the other combinations in order would be .25, .37, .25, and .06. These are the same probabilities we found by expanding the binomial $(p + q)^4$. The sum of these probabilities should be 1.00, and it would be 1.00 except for rounding errors.

The distribution can now be applied to interpreting the results obtained from actually administering the above true-false test. If our obtained distribution of response combinations approaches the theoretical probabilities based on the binomial expansion, we may wish to conclude that our class was responding to our four items on a clearly random basis. But if our obtained distribution deviated markedly from the expected proportions, we may wish to conclude that something other than chance was influencing the mode of response seen in our class.

PROBLEMS

1 Suppose I toss a group of three coins an infinite number of times. What proportion of the tosses will produce three heads and no tails? What proportion will produce two heads and one tail? One head and two tails? Three tails?

2 Assuming that there are as many boys as girls in a given school system, I decide to randomly select a sample of eight cases. What is the probability of getting eight boys and no girls? What is the probability of getting seven boys and one girl? Of getting four boys and four girls?

We now see the binomial distribution as a kind of frequency distribution where successive sample proportions are tabulated. Therefore, we can compute basic descriptive data on this distribution just as we do with any distribution. The mean of a binomial distribution is found by the formula

$$\bar{X} = np \qquad \textbf{8.1}$$

where n is the number of events (X) that may occur on a given occasion and p is the probability of an occurrence for a single event. Thus in tossing four coins repeatedly for an infinite number of times, the mean number of heads (X) that will appear will be $4 \times .50$, or 2.

We can check this against Pascal's triangle. The sum of the row where n is 4 is 16. The row indicates that one time we shall get four heads; four times we shall get three heads (3×4 is 12 heads); six times we shall get two heads (2×6 is 12 heads); four more times we shall get one head (1×4 is 4); and one time we shall get no heads. The total number of heads is $4 + 12 + 12 + 4 + 0$, or 32, heads out of 16 repetitions of the four-penny toss. The sum of the heads divided by the number of tosses ($\frac{32}{16}$) gives us an average of 2 heads per toss. This is exactly what we got when we multiplied np.

In a 10-item true-false test marked on a random basis how many trues should we expect to find on the average? Applying our formula to this problem, we have $10 \times .50$, or 5 items marked true on a random basis.

Just as we can compute a mean for the binomial distribution, we can compute a standard deviation. The formula is

$$\sigma = \sqrt{npq} \qquad \textbf{8.2}$$

where n = number of occurrences possible for a given event
p = probability of getting X on any occurrence
$q = 1 - p$
Applying our formula to the four-penny toss, we get

$$\sigma = \sqrt{4 \times .50 \times .50}$$
$$= \sqrt{1.0}$$
$$= 1$$

Thus, with a mean of two heads per toss of four coins, plus and minus one standard deviation will run from one head to three heads.

It should be noted that the mean and standard deviation of the binomial distribution are *parameters*, not sample estimates of the population. If each four-penny toss is to be a separate experiment—a sample of the population of similar experiments—then the mean found by combining an infinite number of samples will be the population mean. Thus, if we took an infinite number of samples of four pennies each, found the number of heads that turned up for each sample, summed these numbers of heads, and divided this sum by the number of samples observed, we would have a mean number of heads for a population of four-penny tosses.   This is essentially what np gives us.   Likewise, the number of heads in the various samples would distribute themselves around the mean number, and a standard deviation could be found ($\sqrt{npq}$) which would indicate dispersion of sample values around the population mean.   In the behavioral sciences students are usually dealing with samples from a population, not whole populations.   However, we often wish to know if sample "a" is in fact from population "A."   We can compute the sample characteristics, but we need the population data in order to see if our sample is indeed like the intended population.   The above formulas provide these needed data.

The binomial distributions we have dealt with to this point have been based on a number of repetitions of a four-case sample—four coins tossed simultaneously.   We noticed that many of the samples produced two heads and two tails; fewer samples produced all heads and no tails or no heads and all tails.   In other words, the sample data accumulate near the population mean (np) with noticeably fewer samples appearing with probabilities markedly different from that mean.

This generalization seems warranted from our work with a four-case sample, but suppose we had 24 pennies instead of 4.   Now instead of 5 possible outcomes we have 25.   What would the frequency distribution of sample probabilities look like in this situation?   We would see that it begins to approach a bell shape, although it does not yet fit the formula for a normal curve.   The area in the tails of our distribution is greater than in a typical normal curve, and the central area is leptokurtic.

If we should extend our cases beyond 30, the table of the normal curve can be used as a basis for reading probabilities for various combinations of outcomes.   Thus for a 30-case sample of coins (30 coins tossed at once) the population mean would be

$$\bar{X}_p = np$$
$$= 30 \times .5$$
$$= 15 \text{ heads}$$

and the standard deviation would be

$$\sigma_p = \sqrt{npq}$$
$$= \sqrt{30 \times .5 \times .5}$$
$$= 2.7$$

Thus we can determine probabilities of getting various outcomes by determining the area under a normal curve, with a mean of 15 and a standard deviation of 2.7, by using what we already know about z scores and their relation to various curve areas.

How many samples (30 coin tosses) are expected to have four or fewer heads? First we must remember that to represent four heads in a discrete series which parallels a continuous one, the 4 is the midpoint of the unit between 3.5 and 4.5. We may now apply the usual z procedure:

$$z = \frac{X - \bar{X}}{\sigma}$$
$$= \frac{4.5 - 15}{2.7}$$
$$= -3.89$$

And looking on our table of areas under the normal curve (Table II in Appendix C), we find that when 30 coins are tossed at once, less than 1 per cent of the samples will produce four or fewer heads—a rare occasion indeed. It should be noted here that if our sample value were above the mean, we would use the lower limits of its interval. For example, if our sample produced 20 heads, our z value would be $(19.5 - 15)/2.7$, since all values above 19.5 would be part of the interval labeled 20. If the sample value is less than the population mean, we use the upper limits of the interval.

PROBLEMS

1   From the enrollment of an elementary school I wish to choose randomly a sample of 50 children. In the total enrollment there is one boy for every girl ($p = .5$).
a   What per cent of random samples would produce more than 35 boys?
b   What per cent of random samples would produce less than 12 girls?

2   In the last election in a given county there were six registered Democrats for every five Republicans. What per cent of random samples of 40 registered voters in the county would have more than 25 Democrats in them?

To this point we have dealt with very simple data in which the cases can take only one of two values, such as heads and tails, true and false. We have done this because it is the most direct illustration of the idea of probability.

Each successive sample of observations is not expected to produce the same proportion of a given alternative as every other sample, but we see that with many repeated samples a distribution of proportions appears, and with that distribution we can determine the likelihood of getting a sample with a given proportion of the desired alternative.

But in problems in the social sciences individuals often may take any one of a range of values rather than just one of two. However, the basic procedures used in the exercises with coins also apply to problems which deal with data with wider ranges of outcomes; that is, we can set up a distribution of outcomes based on many samples randomly drawn from a given population and then determine the likelihood of getting a particular sample outcome from this population. The basic difference is this: With coins and similar individuals which have only two alternatives, we used sample *proportions* as our basic data and made up a frequency distribution from these proportions; with data taken from individuals who may take any one of a range of values, we shall use sample *means* as our basic data, and our distribution will be made up of these sample means.

An example will illustrate the analogy. Early in this chapter we took four coins and tossed them as a group repeatedly 10,000 times. We then could count the number of heads each time, make a proportion out of the number of heads by dividing it by 4, and plot these 10,000 proportions on a frequency distribution. This distribution then allowed us to establish the frequency of occurrence for various randomly determined outcomes in tossing four coins. We found that all four coins being heads, or all four being tails, is a rather infrequent event compared with the outcome of two heads and two tails.

Now suppose from the population of ten-year-old children I draw a random sample of four children, determine their IQs, and compute a mean IQ for the sample. I repeat this process 10,000 times, just as I did with the coins. The means will be different from sample to sample, but we can make a frequency distribution of these sample means and decide from this the likelihood of getting a randomly drawn sample that has a given mean. In fact we shall see that our distribution of sample means will look something like the familiar bell-shaped curve, that we can compute a standard deviation for it, and that we can determine the number of samples that will appear between different points under the curve. What we have just observed follows from what statisticians call the *central-limits theorem*. This theorem states that if a large number of equal-sized, randomly selected samples are drawn from a given infinite population, if for each sample the mean is computed for a given trait, and if these means are put together into a frequency distribution, this distribution will fit the characteristics of the normal curve. (An assumption is made that sample sizes are large; that is, there are at least 30 cases in a sample.)

Whenever we deal with data which represent characteristics of samples rather than characteristics of individuals, we call the resulting frequency distribution a *sampling distribution*. Since we treat these distributions much the way that we treat any normal distribution, let us begin by computing the standard deviation for our sampling distribution of means. It is found by the formula

$$\sigma_{\bar{x}} = \frac{\sigma_x}{\sqrt{N}} \qquad\qquad 8.3$$

where $\sigma_{\bar{x}}$ is the standard deviation of the sampling distribution of means, σ_x is the standard deviation for the population of X scores, and N is the number of cases in the samples that we selected to make up our sampling distribution. In order to distinguish this standard deviation from the one based on data from individual cases, we give it a different name. We call it the *standard error of the mean*, but it is simply the standard deviation of a distribution of a very large number of means of samples which were randomly drawn from a given population.

But what is the mean of our sampling distribution of means? If a sampling distribution is indeed based on an infinite number of equal-sized samples from the population, the mean of the sampling distribution will be the mean of the population.

Now let us apply what we have just observed. Suppose again we are dealing with the population of ten-year-old children. The population mean IQ for these people is 100, and the standard deviation is 15. And suppose I am going to study a group of 36 ten-year-olds randomly selected from the population. What would a sampling distribution of 36 case samples look like? Well, the mean would be 100, and the standard deviation would be

$$\sigma_{\bar{x}} = \frac{15}{\sqrt{36}}$$
$$= 2.5$$

From our knowledge of the normal curve we immediately know that 68 per cent of randomly drawn samples of 36 ten-year-olds will have mean IQs between 97.5 and 102.5. (This is one standard error above, and one below, the mean of the sampling distribution.) Also we would expect only 2 per cent of random samples of 36 cases each to have mean IQs beyond 105, or two standard errors above the mean of the sampling distribution. It should be clearly noted here that to this point we have not actually selected a single sample from our population. We need to know only the population mean, the population standard deviation, and the number of cases we expect to select in a sample that we may wish to study.

Now knowing all this about our population of ten-year-old children, I decide to teach reading using a special secret method which I have not yet exposed to the world. I want to use a sample of ten-year-olds as my subjects, and I want them to be "typical." I therefore randomly select 36 ten-year-olds and measure their intelligence. Their mean IQ is 107. Is it likely that I could randomly get such a sample from the population of children ten years of age?

We apply two bits of knowledge to the solution of this problem. First we wish to know where in a sampling distribution 107 comes, and secondly we want to know what portion of sample means would fall beyond this point in the distribution. The first item we find by applying the z-score procedure; the second comes from reference to the table of areas under the normal curve (Table II in Appendix C).

So let us now solve our problem. The mean of 107 has a z score in this case as follows:

$$z = \frac{\bar{X} - \bar{X}_t}{\sigma_{\bar{x}}}$$

where $\bar{X}$ is the mean of our sample, $\bar{X}_t$ is the mean for the total population, and $\sigma_{\bar{x}}$ is the standard error of the mean—the standard deviation for this sampling distribution of means.

So we find the necessary information in this manner:

$$z = \frac{107 - 100}{2.5}$$
$$= 2.8$$

Our sample mean is 2.8 standard errors away from the mean of our sampling distribution; and looking at Table II in Appendix C, we find that much fewer than 1 per cent of randomly drawn samples are expected to have means as large as 107. Shall we say that we have a "typical" sample of ten-year-old children? Our sample in fact is pretty unusual among randomly selected samples from our population.

Sometimes we select a sample from a population, give the sample some kind of special treatment, and then ask if it is still a sample from the original population. The assumption is that our treatment has altered the characteristics being observed in such a way that the sample now may be no longer representative of its original population. We therefore test the sample mean, after treatment, against the population mean to see if our sample is now a rather rare one for a population like ours.

Suppose now that in your dark and musty cellar you have formulated a drug which, when injected into white mice, appeared to make them much more alert mentally. You believe it is at last ready to be tried out on a group of human subjects. A random sample of 100 cases is drawn from our population of ten-year-olds, and they are given a capsule of the drug, followed 10 minutes later by an intelligence test. We find that the average IQ for the sample is 104. For a population of IQs we previously found the mean to be 100, the standard deviation to be 15. Is our sample a likely one from this population?

We solve the problem this way: The standard error for a sampling distribution of means of 100 case samples would be

$$\sigma_{\bar{x}} = \frac{15}{\sqrt{100}}$$
$$= 1.5$$

and to find the number of standard errors our sample is from the mean of the distribution, we compute a z value:

$$z = \frac{104 - 100}{1.5}$$
$$= 2.66$$

Consulting Table II in Appendix C, we find that less than 1 per cent of the samples randomly drawn from our population have means as great as 104. Has our drug really changed the mental ability of our sample? Chances of randomly selecting this kind of a group are indeed remote, and so certainly we would want to take a more detailed look at our drug.

In the above examples we looked at sample values in terms of their similarity to the population values. How divergent, in terms of z scores, can a sample value be before we say it is too unlikely to be considered a sample from the basic population? Statisticians in the behavioral sciences have two points, beyond either of which we say the sample is so unlikely that we do not believe it is from the population under consideration. These points are the z values of 1.96 and 2.58. If we consult Table II in Appendix C, we see why these points have been selected. First, ± 1.96 leaves 2.5 per cent of the sample means in each tail of the curve (a total of 5 per cent), while ± 2.58 leaves $\frac{1}{2}$ per cent in each tail (a total of 1 per cent). These values are known as the 5 per cent level of confidence and the 1 per cent level, respectively, because these are the portions of randomly drawn samples whose means are at least this remote.

In determining whether a sample is to be rejected as randomly drawn from the defined population, we are free to use either criterion point. We begin by hypothesizing that our sample mean is *not* different from the population mean at, say, the 5 per cent level. *Such a statement of no difference is called a null hypothesis.* Then we test the difference to see if indeed the z value is greater than, in this case, 1.96. If it is, we believe the sample mean is sufficiently different from the population value to say that our sample is not a randomly selected group from the defined population; that is, we *reject* the null hypothesis.

In the example where we applied a drug to our sample of ten-year-olds, our null hypothesis would be that there is no difference at the 1 per cent level between our sample mean and the mean of the population. Since the difference produced a z value of 2.66, we reject the null hypothesis. In other words we believe that it is rather remote that such a sample would be randomly selected from our population.

Type I, type II errors But here we have a dilemma. One per cent of the samples randomly drawn from our population will produce z values beyond 2.58. If we reject all such samples, we run the risk of making a mistaken conclusion in 1 out of every 100 replications of our study, since by sheer chance 1 out of 100 samples will indeed be this remote. We call this a type I error. On the other hand some randomly drawn samples from *other* populations will look like samples from the population we are studying, and although these samples should be rejected, they are in truth accepted as being from our population. This is a type II error. For example, suppose I am dealing with the population of children who are ten years old and I am studying mental age. An occasional random sample will give me a mean mental age of, say, twelve years, and my standard error indicates that I should reject at the 1 per cent level this sample as being from my ten-year-old population. But random selection will once in awhile produce samples of ten-year-olds who indeed have mean mental ages of twelve, and they should be included in my ten-year-old population. Now suppose I happen to get a sample of eleven-year-olds by accident and find that this sample has a mean mental age of ten years. I would likely say that this sample is from my ten-year-old population, and again I would be in error. In other words, my 5 and 1 per cent criteria lead me sometimes to reject samples that are truly from my population and sometimes to accept samples that are not from my population.

The criterion for rejecting the null hypothesis is important here. If we set the 5 per cent level as the point for rejecting sample values, we increase the likelihood of rejecting samples that are in truth random samples from our population; that is, 5 per cent of all samples will fall by the wayside. On the other hand, the 5 per cent level decreases the likelihood of accepting a sample as being from our population when in truth it is not. (Why is this so?)

The 1 per cent criterion reverses what we said in the last paragraph. Since only 1 out of 100 samples from our population will be erroneously rejected, this reduces the likelihood of rejecting samples which should in truth be accepted. However, this 1 per cent point increases the likelihood of accepting samples which are from other populations and should be rejected. Figure 8.2 is a graphic description of this problem. Thus the selection of the

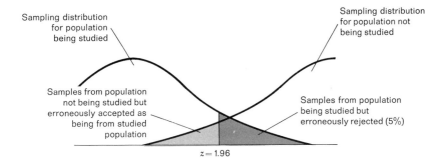

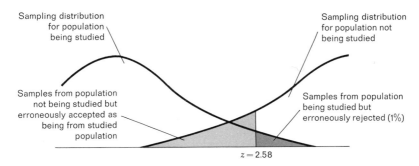

Figure 8.2

5 per cent or the 1 per cent limit depends upon the kind of errors we can best tolerate. Can we afford to reject 5 per cent of the samples from our own population in an effort to reject more samples from other populations? If so, the 5 per cent level is appropriate. But if we wish to reject as few samples as possible from our population and can afford to accept, erroneously, a more than occasional sample from other populations, then the 1 per cent level is to be chosen.

To this point we have dealt only with data in which we knew the population standard deviation.   Suppose we do not have this information.   How will we compute the standard error?

If we do not know the population standard deviation, we must estimate this parameter from sample data.   The sample standard deviation s_x is our best estimate of the population value, and so the estimated standard error becomes

$$\text{est } \sigma_{\bar{x}} = \frac{s_x}{\sqrt{N}} \qquad\qquad 8.4$$

and our z value is computed as

$$z = \frac{\bar{X} - \bar{X}_{\text{tot}}}{\text{est } \sigma_{\bar{x}}}$$

and the resulting figure is evaluated according to Table II in Appendix C. It must be noted, however, that in order to use this formula, s must be computed as an estimate of the population standard deviation as described in Chap. 5.

PROBLEMS

1   I have found that for all high school seniors in Forestville the average height is 68 inches, the standard deviation is 4 inches.   I have a group of 49 students that I wish to study in reference to the relation of nutrition and height.   My sample has a mean of 66 inches.   Can I consider (at the 5 per cent level) that this is a random sample from the senior class in reference to height?

2   Suppose I have a group of 36 children who have a mean height of 54 inches, a standard deviation in height of 3 inches.   Is it likely this is a random sample from a population whose mean is 52.1 inches?   (Test at the 5 per cent level.)

3   In the following situations state whether it is better to risk a type I or a type II error and why.

   a   It is extremely costly to get together a group of people who have been randomly selected from a given population, and so I wish to reject as few as possible of the samples which may be part of my population.

   b   I have a drug which I believe may cure a previously incurable disease.   However, it has undesirable side effects, and so I do not wish to apply it to anyone who I am not quite sure is from my population.

c I wish to make a conclusion about teaching arithmetic to children of low intelligence. I believe that the conclusion may not be tenable for brighter children, and so I wish to select children who are truly from the lower intelligence group.

t Distribution

To this point we have been talking about a sampling distribution of means based on an infinite number of randomly selected samples of at least 30 cases each. We have seen that the means of such samples produce a normal distribution. Suppose that our samples were composed of less than 30 cases, say 20 or even 15 cases each. How would this affect the shape of the sampling distribution?

When samples are less than 30 cases in size, a noticeable change in the shape of the sampling distribution does begin to appear. The nature of the change produces a curve which, with decreasing sample N's, becomes increasingly leptokurtic, with increasingly larger areas in the tails of the curve. In other words, as sample sizes decrease, the sampling distribution of their means becomes more pointed in the middle and has relatively more area in its tails. Such a distribution is known as the *t distribution*, or *"Student's" distribution*.* Figure 8.3 compares the normal curve (*A*) with two *t*

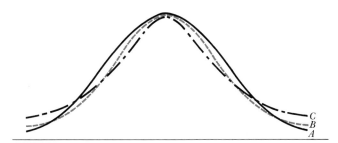

Figure 8.3

distributions (*B* and *C*). Curve *A* is obtained by plotting means of large samples; *B*, by plotting means of smaller samples; *C*, by plotting means of even smaller samples than *B*.

It should be emphasized that the *t* distribution is not a single curve but a

---

* For many years some companies in England maintained the custom under which employees published materials only under the company name. Company personnel therefore often used pen names for their private publications. Thus, W. S. Gosset used the name of "Student" when he published his first work with *t* in 1908.

whole family of curves, the shape of each being a function of sample size.   The smaller the sample, the greater are the portions of the area under the curve that appear at the extremes of the distribution and the more the middle of the curve becomes peaked, whereas the larger the sample size, up to about 30 case samples, the more nearly the *t* distribution approaches the shape of the normal curve (beyond 30 case samples the two distributions become very much alike).

Since we know the nature of Student's distribution, we can apply it to the solution of problems in the same way as we applied the normal curve; i.e., we locate a point on the base line in standard-error units and then find the per cent of the area under the curve that lies beyond that point.   Since the distribution is made up of means of many samples, the area beyond our point will represent a certain portion of sample means that are greater, or smaller, than the one we are considering.

Table III in Appendix C provides us with areas under the curve for *t* distributions based on various sizes of samples.   However, since we usually apply *t* to problems involving the null hypothesis and accept or reject the hypothesis that is at the established 5, or 1, per cent level, Table III provides only the *t* values for those points.

Since the shape of the sampling distribution changes with different sample sizes, Table III reports different values for sample *N*'s.   If relatively more of the area under the curve is in the curve *X* tails than in the curve *Y* tails, then beginning at the mean we must move further along the base line to locate the point in *X* beyond which 5 per cent of the sample means will fall than we would in curve *Y*.   Figure 8.4 illustrates this fact.   Therefore, if the samples

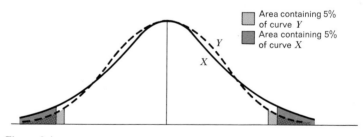

Figure 8.4

represented in our sampling distribution are made up of 10 cases, it will take 2.262 standard errors to reach the point on the curve beyond which 5 per cent of the sample means will fall, whereas if we have samples of 30 cases, it takes only 2.045 standard errors to reach the point beyond which 5 per cent of the samples will appear.

The student who has consulted Table III in Appendix C has found that the t values reported above actually correspond with the rows labeled 9 and 29, not 10 and 30, case samples. The explanation of this lies in *degrees of freedom*.

The degrees of freedom associated with a given sample are determined by the number of observations that are free to vary. Suppose boys in a physical education class are shooting baskets with a basketball. Student A made 10 baskets. Can we tell from this how many baskets he has missed? Or how many he has attempted? No. But suppose we know that each student was allowed 15 tries. Now we can determine the number of misses since the number of successes and the total number of attempts determine the number of misses. Only two of our three conditions, then, are free to vary independently of the third condition. If we know the number of misses and successes, the total number of shots can only be one value; if we know the number of successes and the total number of attempts, the number of misses can only be one value. Thus, only two of the conditions are free to vary independently of the third. The third condition is always determined once we know the other two. We therefore have one restriction on our data and two degrees of freedom.

Now when we deal with a sampling distribution of means, we have a similar situation. For simplicity let us suppose that we have only two samples in our sampling distribution of means. Now the mean of a sampling distribution is the population mean, and the sum of deviations around the mean of any distribution is zero; that is, for our sampling distribution, $(\bar{X}_1 - \bar{X}_{\text{tot}}) + (\bar{X}_2 - \bar{X}_{\text{tot}}) = 0$, or $\Sigma(\bar{X}_i - \bar{X}_{\text{tot}}) = 0$. If we know $\bar{X}_1$ and $\bar{X}_{\text{tot}}$, $\bar{X}_2$ can only be one value. Or if we know $\bar{X}_2$ and $\bar{X}_{\text{tot}}$, $\bar{X}_1$ can only be one value. Thus, since the distribution mean must be a given value, we have one restriction on the freedom of observations to vary, and our degrees of freedom are $N - 1$.

Returning now to our problem with t, we look up t values in Table III under degrees of freedom, which in the above problems is $N - 1$. (We shall see later that degrees of freedom may be other than $N - 1$, however.) Thus for our sample of 30 cases we have $N - 1$, or 29, degrees of freedom; for 10 cases, 9 degrees of freedom, and these determine the row of Table III which we consulted to get the 5 per cent value of t.

Previously we had decided if our sample mean was a likely member of a sampling distribution based on a population with a given mean value by use of the formula

$$z = \frac{\bar{X} - \bar{X}_{\text{tot}}}{\text{est } \sigma_{\bar{x}}}$$

and evaluated the result by referring to Table II in Appendix C. But with samples sizes of less than 30 cases, we shall solve these problems with the formula

$$t = \frac{\bar{X} - \bar{X}_{tot}}{\text{est } \sigma_{\bar{x}}}$$

and refer to Table III in Appendix C for an evaluation of the result.

Thus, suppose we have randomly drawn a sample of 25 six-year-olds, found their IQs, and found the mean to be 105, the standard deviation to be 15. Is it likely that this is a random sample from the population whose mean is 100? We solve the problem with t as follows:

$$\text{est } \sigma_{\bar{x}} = \frac{s_x}{\sqrt{N}}$$
$$= \frac{15}{5} = 3$$
$$= \frac{105 - 100}{3}$$
$$= 1.66$$

and consulting Table III, with 24 degrees of freedom, we find the t value necessary for the 5 per cent level to be 2.06. Since our value is less than this amount, we accept the hypothesis that our sample could well be from the population with a mean of 100. The pertinent sampling distribution is shown in Fig. 8.5.

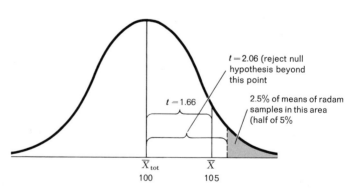

$t = 2.06$ (reject null hypothesis beyond this point

$t = 1.66$

2.5% of means of radam samples in this area (half of 5%

$\bar{X}_{tot}$ $\bar{X}$
100   105

Figure 8.5

Estimating population mean from sample   In the above problems we have been trying to determine whether a sample is from a population with a given mean. The procedure may also be reversed, in which case we have a sample mean and want to know the mean of the population from which the sample came. Unfortunately we cannot determine the exact mean for the population, but we can state the limits within which the population value is most likely to occur. In other words, we state an interval of values within which we believe the population mean will fall and the probability of finding the population value within that interval. We call this process the *interval estimate*, and it is done as follows.

Chances are (at the .05 level) that the mean of a large sample from a population is not going to lie more than $1.96\sigma_{\bar{x}}$ from the population mean. Thus, we believe that the population value will be within $1.96\sigma_{\bar{x}}$ of the sample mean. However, we do not know whether our sample mean is greater or smaller than the population value, and so we must mark off $1.96\sigma_{\bar{x}}$ above, as well as below, our sample mean. This then yields the range within which the population mean is most likely to lie (at the .05 level).

Let us take an example to illustrate this procedure. Suppose I have a sample of children randomly drawn from the population of lower-class families. I tabulate the number of childhood diseases these children have had, and I wish to say something about the mean number of diseases for the population of lower-class children. For my sample I find the mean to be 5, the standard deviation to be 2.1, and I have 36 cases in the sample. The first step is to find the standard error of the mean:

$$\text{est } \sigma_{\bar{x}} = \frac{2.1}{\sqrt{36}} = \frac{2.1}{6} = .35$$

Thus the population mean should lie between 4.3 and 5.69, that is, the sample mean, 5, plus and minus 1.96 est $\sigma_{\bar{x}}$. This range is sometimes referred to as the *fiducial limits*.

PROBLEMS

1   I have a sample of 50 children whose mean height is 61 inches, with a standard deviation of 4.5 inches. What is the range (at the .05 level) within which we shall expect to find the mean height of the population from which my sample came?

2   A sample of 36 college freshmen have a mean number of errors on a finger-maze problem of 17.6, with a standard deviation of 3.2.

What is the range within which we shall expect to find (at the .01 level) the mean errors for the population from which my sample came?

Summary

Probability deals with the likelihood of a given event's occurrence. In random selection, we cannot predict the outcome of every event, but we can make probability statements which tell us the proportion of events which will have a given outcome.

When there are only two possible outcomes for each event, such as heads and tails, true and false, etc., the probabilities for various combinations of events may be found by expanding the binomial $(p + q)^n$, where p is the probability for one outcome, q is $(1 - p)$, and n is the number of events being observed. Pascal's triangle, Table 8.1, may also be used to establish probabilities if p is .50.

Since some outcomes of events are more likely than others, an infinite number of repetitions of events produces a frequency distribution in which frequencies pile up around a central, most probable outcome. Using a z-score approach, we can compute a mean and standard deviation for such a distribution and from it determine the probability for various combinations of events.

The basic idea of probability which arises out of simple events like coin tossing can be applied to studies of human behavior. Instead of recording proportions of outcomes in our frequency distributions, we often tabulate means of an infinite number of samples. This frequency distribution is called a sampling distribution of means and can be used to determine the probability of randomly choosing a sample with a mean of a given magnitude. Again, a z-score technique is applied for this purpose. The standard deviation of a sampling distribution of means is called a standard error of the mean.

When samples are small (less than 30 cases), we still may construct a sampling distribution and use it to determine the probability of randomly selecting various-sized sample means. However, the shape of the sampling distribution deviates from normality increasingly as sample sizes get smaller. We call these distributions t, or Student's distributions, but we use them very much like normal curves, except we note that their characteristics change with the number of degrees of freedom.

The sampling distribution of the mean may be used to determine the likelihood that a sample is from a given population. It also allows us to state the interval within which a population mean will come once we know the mean of a sample from that population.

PROBLEMS

1 I am going to toss a group of five pennies. Construct a probability distribution for all possible outcomes. What is the probability of getting:
   a Five tails?
   b Three heads, two tails?
   c One head, four tails?
2 I have given a 34-item true-false test. If all students mark their papers randomly, what is the expected mean number of trues marked? What is the expected standard deviation of the distribution of trues? What proportion of papers are expected to have 27 or more trues marked?
3 In a given population of children the mean height is 43 inches, the standard deviation is 6 inches. I have a sample of children with a mean of 45.1 inches. Is it likely (5 per cent level) that this is a random sample from the described population? (N = 36)
4 I have a sample of 46 children. Their mean IQ is 112, the standard deviation is 11. Could this be a random sample (1 per cent level) from a population with a mean IQ of 115? What is the range within which the population mean will fall (5 per cent level)?
5 A sample of 10 college co-eds had a mean of seven dates per month, with a standard deviation of two dates. Is it likely (at 5 per cent level) that the population of co-eds from which these girls came has a mean of nine dates per month? What is the interval within which the mean falls for the population from which these girls are a sample (1 per cent level)?

9

Testing Differences between Means

In a learning experiment two groups of 35 cases each have been randomly selected from all students enrolled in introductory psychology. Group I has studied nonsense syllables 10 minutes every hour for 3 hours whereas group II has studied 5 minutes every half hour for 3 hours. At the end of the 3 hours each group is given a test of recall to see which practice procedure has led to the best retention. We now ask: Is the mean performance for one group superior to that of the other?

No doubt we would also test the above groups on their ability to recall new material before the study exercise and again afterward to see if practice on these tasks has improved ability to retain new material in general. Again, we compare mean performances—this

140

time the mean of the test scores following practice with the mean preceding practice.

These are only a few of the many possible circumstances in which we wish to compare performance of one group with another, or compare performance of a group before some kind of experience with their performance after that experience. An appropriate technique for this comparison is the *t-test*.

In Chap. 8 we saw that if we successively drew random samples from a given population, computed their means, and put these means into a frequency distribution, the result was a normal curve. We called this a sampling distribution of means, and with it we could state the chances of getting a sample whose mean was above, or below, a given value.

Now, instead of selecting only one sample at a time, let us select *pairs* of samples, compute the mean for each sample in the pair, subtract the first sample mean from the second, and record this *difference*. We repeat this process many, many times, recording only the differences between the two sample means.

This procedure would produce a list of numbers (differences) which could then be arranged into a frequency distribution. We would see that our distribution looks like a normal one, and we could calculate the dispersion of scores around its central point. We would then have a sampling distribution of differences between means, and just as we can state how many scores are expected to fall beyond given points in a raw-score distribution, we can state how many differences between means will fall beyond given points.

Now let us actually do what we have just described. From a population of college freshmen we take nine pairs of random samples of five cases each. (This is neither enough pairs nor enough cases in a sample to build adequately a sampling distribution of mean differences, but it is sufficient for our example.) We collect IQs on the samples we select, compute the mean IQ for each sample in a pair, find the difference between means for the paired samples, and record this difference in a distribution, thusly:

	Pair I		Pair II		Pair III	
	113	116	126	120	121	118
	115	113	103	117	118	124
	112	115	117	126	117	119
	117	126	121	108	119	108
	113	110	118	119	120	116
$\bar{X}_i$	114	116	117	118	119	117
$(\bar{X}_1 - \bar{X}_2)$	−2		−1		2	

	Pair IV		Pair V		Pair VI	
	125	109	117	120	119	125
	120	119	119	115	125	104
	118	121	116	119	109	118
	114	121	111	116	117	120
	113	114	117	110	120	118
$\bar{X}_i$	118	117	116	116	118	117
$(\bar{X}_1 - \bar{X}_2)$	1		0		1	

	Pair VII		Pair VIII		Pair IX	
	109	117	117	121	112	117
	117	120	122	115	115	122
	119	115	119	126	120	113
	113	110	104	109	112	110
	122	118	122	119	121	118
$\bar{X}_i$	116	116	117	118	116	116
$(\bar{X}_1 - \bar{X}_2)$	0		−1		0	

Now if we put the differences between means $(\bar{X}_1 - \bar{X}_2)$ into a frequency distribution, we get Table 9.1. (Actually only nine pairs of randomly selected samples probably could not be expected to produce a sampling distribution of differences between means which is quite as symmetrical as Table 9.1, but for illustration purposes our sampling was especially fortuitous.)

We can now see that our distribution of differences between means does indeed appear as if it might turn out to be a normal curve if more differences

Table 9.1   Distribution of Differences between Means

$(\bar{X}_1 - \bar{X}_2)$	f
+2	1
+1	2
0	3
−1	2
−2	1

were added to the data. Indeed if an infinite number of pairs of sufficiently large samples are selected and their mean differences recorded, the distribution will be normal, and if the samples are truly randomly drawn from a common population, the mean of this sampling distribution will be zero.

Now suppose from our population of college freshmen I select two samples of five cases each and find that the difference between their mean IQs is 3. Is it likely that each of these samples is a random selection from our freshmen students? The distribution in Table 9.1 suggests that such a pair of samples

Table 9.2 Computation of the Standard Error of the Difference

Formula 9.1	What It Says to Do
$s_{\text{diff}} = \sqrt{\dfrac{s_1^2}{N_1} + \dfrac{s_2^2}{N_2}}$ where s_1^2 and s_2^2 = variances of samples 1 and 2, respectively N_1 = number of cases in sample 1 N_2 = number of cases in sample 2	1. Compute the variance for each sample (see Chap. 5 for review). 2. Divide the variance of sample 1 by N_1 and the variance of sample 2 by N_2. 3. Add the results of step 2. 4. Take the square root of the figure obtained in step 3.

Example We have two samples of 40 girls each randomly selected from all those who have just enrolled as college freshmen. The mean age for sample 1 is 220 months, and the standard deviation is 6 months; for sample 2 the mean age is 223 months, and the standard deviation is 7 months. What is the standard error of the difference between mean ages?

$$s_{\text{diff}} = \sqrt{\frac{6^2}{40} + \frac{7^2}{40}}$$
$$= \sqrt{2.12}$$
$$= 1.46$$

That is, remembering that the distribution of differences between means is a normal one, we find that 68 per cent of the pairs of random samples $(N = 40)$ drawn from our population would be expected to have *differences* between their means not to exceed ± 1.46 months.

is unlikely, and so we conclude that they are not samples from the same population. Apparently at least one of the samples comes from some other population of students.

From the distribution of differences in Table 9.1, we could compute a mean and a standard deviation and decide just what per cent of pairs of samples would have a difference between ± 1, between ± 2, etc., just as we do with any normal distribution. However, to do this with assurance that our data are reliable, we would first have to collect many pairs of samples, and we would wish to have samples larger in size. This is an arduous—if not prohibitive—job, and luckily we do not have to do it. Instead we can compute the standard deviation for a sampling distribution of differences between means by using the descriptive data from each of the two samples in a given pair. We call this standard deviation the *standard error of the difference*, and it is found, as shown in Table 9.2, for a pair of samples that (1) are large (30 or more cases each) and (2) do not have correlated means—that is, the selection of a case for one sample in no way influences the selection of any case in the other sample.

In formula (9.1) it would be desirable to use population, rather than sample, variances. However, we seldom have population data available, and the sample variance, when appropriately calculated,* is our best estimate of the population value.† Therefore, we substitute the sample data in the formula and proceed with the calculations.

PROBLEMS

1 Given the following means from pairs of samples, compute their differences and arrange the differences into a distribution.

   a Does it appear likely that from this population we would get a pair of samples with a difference between their means equal to three points?

   b Does it appear likely that we would randomly select from this population a pair of samples whose means differ as much as six points?

* See page 69.

† We have to this point assumed that our samples come from a common population or from two populations with equal variances, and so our sample variances are therefore not unequal. Formula (9.1), however, may be applied when variances are in fact unequal *provided* that samples are large (30 or more cases in a sample).

$\bar{X}_1$	$\bar{X}_2$	diff	$\bar{X}_1$	$\bar{X}_2$	diff
27	26		29	25	
29	24		27	24	
24	27		26	25	
26	26		25	23	
26	24		26	26	
23	28		24	27	
26	27		23	24	
27	24		25	25	
26	27		24	28	
25	27		27	27	

2   In a learning experiment a psychologist selected two samples of 30 sixth-grade boys each. He first wanted to know if they were samples from a common population of learners, and so he compared them on IQs. The first sample had a mean IQ of 102 and a standard deviation of 10 IQ points, and the second sample had a mean of 100 with a standard deviation of 11 points.

a   Compute the standard error of the difference.

b   In your own words, what does this figure tell us?

Now if our two samples are either from a *common* population or from two populations with equal variances (an assumption we *must* make if our sample sizes are small, that is, less than 30 cases), we estimate the population variance best by *pooling* the data from the two samples. We do this by first finding the sum of the squared deviations of scores around the mean of sample 1, $\Sigma(X_i - \bar{X}_1)^2$, and then adding this amount to the sum of the squared deviations of scores around the mean for the second sample, $\Sigma(X_j - \bar{X}_2)^2$. This gives us a pooled sum of squared deviations, which divided by the degrees of freedom, now $(N_1 - 1) + (N_2 - 1)$ or $N_1 + N_2 - 2$, provides an estimate of the variance of the population from which the samples came. As before, the variance is divided by the number of individuals, and the square root is taken to get the standard error. But this time we have two samples, and so we divide the variance by $N_1 + N_2$. Table 9.3 illustrates the procedure for estimating the population variance and computing a standard error of the difference by the *pooled-variance* method.

Table 9.3 Pooling Variances to Compute a Standard Error of the Difference

Formula 9.2	What It Says to Do
$$s_{\text{diff}} = \sqrt{\frac{\Sigma(X_1 - \bar{X}_1)^2 + \Sigma(X_2 - \bar{X}_2)^2}{N_1 + N_2 - 2}\left(\frac{1}{N_1} + \frac{1}{N_2}\right)}$$ $$= \sqrt{\frac{\Sigma X_1^2 - \dfrac{(\Sigma X_1)^2}{N_1} + \Sigma X_2^2 - \dfrac{(\Sigma X_2)^2}{N_2}}{N_1 + N_2 - 2}\left(\frac{1}{N_1} + \frac{1}{N_2}\right)}$$ where s_{diff} = standard error of the difference X_1 = scores in the first sample, with mean $\bar{X}_1$ X_2 = scores in the second sample, with mean $\bar{X}_2$ N_1 = number of cases in the first sample N_2 = number of cases in the second sample	1. Compute the sum of the squared deviations around the mean for the first sample: $\Sigma(X_1 - \bar{X}_1)^2$, or $[\Sigma X_1^2 - (\Sigma X_1)^2/N_1]$. 2. Compute the sum of the squared deviations around the mean of the second sample: $\Sigma(X_2 - \bar{X}_2)^2$, or $[\Sigma X_2^2 - (\Sigma X_2)^2/N_2]$. 3. Add the result of step 1 to the result of step 2. 4. Divide the result of step 3 by the degrees of freedom $(N_1 + N_2 - 2)$. 5. Multiply the result of step 4 by the combined reciprocals of N_1 and N_2, that is, $1/N_1 + 1/N_2$. 6. Take the square root of the result of step 5.

Example Given the following data, compute the s_{diff}.

Sample I
$\Sigma X_1 = 150$
$\Sigma X^2 = 2{,}644$
$N = 31$

Sample II
$\Sigma X_2 = 86$
$\Sigma X^2 = 924$
$N = 31$

$$s_{\text{diff}} = \sqrt{\frac{2{,}644 - \dfrac{(150)^2}{31} + 924 - \dfrac{(86)^2}{31}}{31 + 31 - 2}\left(\frac{1}{31} + \frac{1}{31}\right)}$$

$$= 1.67$$

PROBLEM

1 Given the following two sets of data representing the number of simple additions made by 10 subjects in each of two samples in a 4-minute period:

Sample 1	Sample 2
10	7
8	8
8	6
7	7
7	8
7	9
6	11
5	5
4	4
3	3

a   Compute the standard error of the difference using the pooled-variance method and figuring the sum of the squared deviations for each sample by the formula $\Sigma(X_1 - \bar{X}_1)^2 + \Sigma(X_2 - \bar{X}_2)^2$.

b   Compute the standard error of the difference using the formula $\Sigma X_1^2 - (\Sigma X_1)^2/N_1 + \Sigma X_2^2 - (\Sigma X_2)^2/N_2$.

c   Which of the procedures (a or b) did you find the most economical in time?

Sample size and the sampling distribution of differences   To this point we have dealt primarily with pairs of samples of at least 30 cases in each sample. When samples are this large, the sampling distribution of differences between means is essentially normal, and standard errors [computed by either formula (9.1) or formula (9.2)] can be used to establish areas under the normal curve, just like any standard deviation, and a table of z can be used for the resulting interpretation. However, very often we deal with pairs of samples of less than 30 cases. The sampling distribution of differences in this situation takes on the characteristics of t, not z. With small samples we also assume that the variances are equal, and pooling is the prescribed procedure [formula (9.2)] for calculating the standard error.*

Tests of significance   We now return to the original question posed at the beginning of this chapter. Is the performance of one group statistically different from the performance of another? The answer to this question lies in the *t-test*.

---

* See page 151 for a possible exception.

We have just seen that a sampling distribution of differences between pairs of sample means follows Student's distribution if the sample sizes are less than 30 cases; beyond that sample size, the distribution is essentially normal. Knowing the shape of the distribution of differences between pairs of sample means and the standard deviation of such a distribution (the standard error of the difference), we can determine what portion of the pairs of randomly drawn samples will have mean differences beyond given limits. For example, if with samples of 30 cases we have a standard error of the difference equal to 1.85, then 32 per cent of the pairs of random samples will have $\bar{X}_1 - \bar{X}_2$ differences greater than ± 1.85. Figure 9.1 illustrates this

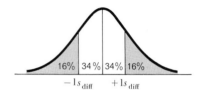

Figure 9.1

fact. (We must keep in mind, however, that portions of the curve in relation to the standard error change with degrees of freedom when we use Student's distribution.)

If we can tell what portion of differences between pairs of sample means will fall beyond given points, our next step is to establish again our 5 per cent and 1 per cent limits and determine the number of standard errors it takes to get to those points. If the difference between the means of the two samples we are observing is less than the number of standard errors it takes to get to the 5 per cent point, our difference is not significant for that criterion. Likewise, if our difference is less than the 1 per cent point, it is not significant at that criterion. However if the difference exceeds either or both of these criterion points, we say that it is significant at the 1 or 5 per cent level, whichever point the difference exceeds.

The procedure just described is the *t*-test. Its step-by-step accomplishment is shown in Table 9.4.

To this point we have not decided whether a given *t* value is significant at the 1 (or 5) per cent criterion. Let us now decide that question.

In the use of the *t*-test we consult Student's distribution to determine the significance of the difference between our means. But when we use Student's distribution, we remember that the shape of the curve varies with the size of the samples involved. Therefore, before entering the table of *t* values we must first determine the number of degrees of freedom involved in our data.

If our samples are large and we have computed the standard error of the

Table 9.4 The Computation of the *t*-test

Formula 9.3	What It Says to Do
$t = \dfrac{\bar{X}_1 - \bar{X}_2}{s_{\text{diff}}}$ where $\bar{X}_1$ = mean of the first sample $\bar{X}_2$ = mean of the second sample s_{diff} = standard error of the difference	1. Compute the mean for sample 1 and the mean for sample 2. 2. Determine their difference. 3. Compute the standard error by the appropriate method [formula (9.1) or (9.2)]. 4. Divide the difference between means by the standard error.

Example Two samples of 19 students now have practiced a letter-cancellation task. One sample practiced for three 10-minute sessions; the other practiced six 5-minute sessions. Their final scores were as follows. Compute the *t* value for the difference between the means of the two samples.

Sample 2

10, 14, 13, 11, 9
11, 15, 12, 13, 12
$\Sigma X_2 = 120$
$\Sigma X_2{}^2 = 1,470$

Sample 1

20, 12, 17, 16, 18
14, 16, 19, 15
$\Sigma X_1 = 147$
$\Sigma X_1{}^2 = 2,451$

$$s_{\text{diff}} = \sqrt{\dfrac{1,470 - \dfrac{(120)^2}{10} + 2,451 - \dfrac{(147)^2}{9}}{10 + 9 - 2}\left(\dfrac{1}{10} + \dfrac{1}{9}\right)}$$

$= .994$

$$t = \dfrac{16.3 - 12.0}{.994}$$

$= 4.33$ With $10 + 9 - 2$ degrees of freedom, significant at the 1 per cent level, the null hypothesis is rejected.

difference with formula (9.1), our *t* distribution approximates a normal curve, and the difference between the means is significant for two-tailed tests at the 1 per cent level if the *t* value is 2.58 and at the 5 per cent level if 1.96. However, if we have small samples and have pooled our variances to maximize the accuracy of our estimate of the population variance, then the *t*-test result is evaluated by entering the table of *t* with $N_1 + N_2 - 2$ degrees of freedom, the denominator of the variance as computed in formula (9.2).

Since we pooled variances in computing the *t* value in Table 9.4, to evaluate our results, we will enter the table of *t* values with $N_1 + N_2 - 2$ degrees of freedom. We therefore look in Table III of Appendix C in the row that corresponds with $10 + 10 - 2$, or 18, degrees of freedom. Here we find that a *t* of 2.101 is needed for significance at the 5 per cent level and 2.878 at the 1 per cent level. Since our *t* value in Table 9.4 was 4.68, it is unlikely that we would draw two samples at random with means as different as the means in Table 9.4. In other words, the difference between our means is more than 2.101 standard errors from the mean of a sampling distribution of differences. Therefore, it is unlikely that so great a difference would appear by chance among pairs of randomly selected samples.

Testing variances for differences before pooling We have seen above that in small-sample problems, as well as in large-sample problems where pooled variance is used, we assume that both samples come from populations with a common variance. To be sure we meet this assumption, we should first test our sample variances for the significance of their difference before pooling the variances. This is called a *test of homogeneity*. We make this test with the formula

$$F = \frac{s_i^2}{s_j^2} \qquad\qquad 9.4$$

where s_i^2 is the larger of the two variances and s_j^2 is the smaller, and determine its significance by entering Table IV of Appendix C with $N_i - 1$ degrees of freedom for the numerator and $N_j - 1$ degrees of freedom for the denominator, where *i* is the sample with the larger variance and *j* is the sample with the smaller variance. *F* values that are larger than the table values show a significant difference in the sizes of the two variances in the ratio. We should note, however, that the *F* table involves only *one* tail of the curve, so values listed in the table as the .05 level are, for our present test, actually the .10 level, and those listed as .01 values are the .02 level.

We test the hypothesis that both samples in Table 9.4 came from populations with the common variance, thus:

$$F = \frac{56.0}{33.0} = 1.68$$

We then enter Table IV with $N_i - 1$, or 8, degrees of freedom for the numerator and $N_j - 1$, or 9, degrees of freedom for the denominator. Moving down the N_1 (df = 8) column in the table to the N_2 (df = 9) row, we find that an *F* value of 3.23 is needed to be significant at the 10 per cent level;

therefore, we accept the hypothesis that our samples come from populations with common variances and rest assured that we were correct in pooling our variances. (F was a one-tailed test, so probabilities were doubled.)

PROBLEM

1 Two randomly selected groups of 20 subjects each were chosen from beginning classes in educational psychology.   One group was given training in estimating the area of rectangles; the other group was a control group with no training.   At the end of the training period both groups were given a test of estimating areas of circles.   The number of correct estimations by each subject in each group is given below:

Training Group		Control Group	
18	15	17	16
14	13	13	12
17	9	18	11
15	14	14	13
12	16	12	16
8	13	16	12
16	21	9	15
14	9	8	11
10	15	14	15
13	14	10	14

a Test the variances for homogeneity.
b Test the hypothesis that there is no difference between the sample means.   (Note sample size before selecting method for computing the standard error of the difference.)

An approximate test when variances are unequal and samples are small
Suppose that when we complete our F test, we find that the variances are indeed significantly different and our sample sizes are too small to apply

formula (9.1) as it now stands.   Must we abandon a test of the significance of the difference between means?

Luckily we may test the hypothesis that the means of the populations from which the samples came are different, irrespective of hypotheses concerning the population variances.   In this case we take s_1^2, the first sample variance, as the best estimate of σ_1^2 and s_2^2, the second sample variance, as the best estimate of σ_2^2 and compute a t value as follows:

$$t = \frac{\bar{X}_1 - \bar{X}_2}{\sqrt{\dfrac{s_1^2}{N_1} + \dfrac{s_2^2}{N_2}}} \qquad\qquad \textbf{9.5}$$

However, the value of t found by formula (9.5) *cannot* be evaluated by consulting Table III in Appendix C.   Instead we compute an approximation of the t value for the 5 per cent level as follows: *

$$t_{.05} = \frac{t_1 \dfrac{s_1^2}{N_1} + t_2 \dfrac{s_2^2}{N_2}}{\dfrac{s_1^2}{N_1} + \dfrac{s_2^2}{N_2}} \qquad\qquad \textbf{9.6}$$

where t_1 is the table value of t at the 5 per cent level with $N_1 - 1$ degrees of freedom and t_2 is the 5 per cent level for $N_2 - 1$ degrees of freedom.   This computed t value is then used in place of the table value.   Our null hypothesis in this case is that the samples have been chosen from two populations, the means of which are equal.   If our obtained value from formula (9.5) is *larger* than that found by (9.6), the difference between the means is significant at the 5 per cent level, and the null hypothesis is rejected; that is, the samples are not believed to have come from populations which have equal means.

Testing the difference between means when observations are correlated between samples   Suppose I want to conduct a study in which teaching method A is compared with method B.   Now I quickly see that if one group of subjects is more intelligent than the other, my results will be distorted. I therefore match on intelligence each subject in the A group with a subject in the B group.   This control eliminates the possibility of getting a mean difference on achievement which is due merely to intelligence; however, since the selection of a child for one group influences the selection of a child in the other group, the observations in group A will be correlated with group B to the extent that intelligence is a factor in getting scores on the achievement test given at the close of the study.

---

* See Allen Edward, "Statistical Analysis," rev. ed., p. 139, Holt, Rinehart and Winston, Inc., 1958.

Other possibilities for correlating observations also exist. For example, we may wish to compare husbands with wives on an attitude scale, fathers with sons on an intelligence test. Or we may wish to give a test of some type to a group of subjects, administer an experimental treatment, then readminister the test to the same people. The pretest and posttest will no doubt be correlated because the same individuals are responding to the items both before and after the treatment, and certainly not all personal traits reflected by the test are presumed to be altered by the treatment.

When the data in one sample are correlated with the data in the other, we must alter our procedure for the *t*-test to acknowledge the fact that changes in one set of data will be reflected in the other. Typically in studies of this type a subject in one sample is matched in some way with a subject in the other sample. The extent to which the samples are different then depends upon the way that the subjects in one sample differ from their matched partner in the other sample. That is, the difference between sample means will be equal to the mean of the matched-pair differences. The data in Table 9.5 illustrate this fact. We have five matched pairs of subjects. The mean of their score differences is equal to the difference of the group means, that is, $\bar{X}_1 - \bar{X}_2 = \bar{D}$. Therefore, in paired data, we may substitute $\bar{D}$, the mean of differences between pairs of subjects, for $\bar{X}_1 - \bar{X}_2$ in doing a *t*-test.

Table 9.5 Illustration of $\bar{X}_1 - \bar{X}_2 = \bar{D}$

	IQs for Subjects		
	Sample A	Sample B	$IQ_A - IQ_B$
	115	110	5
	112	113	-1
	110	110	0
	108	105	3
	100	97	3
ΣX	545	535	$10/5 = 2$
$\bar{X}$	109	minus 107	equals 2 $\bar{D}$ equals 2

It now appears that the differences between the scores of paired subjects in matched groups may be put into a distribution themselves. If so, we might compute a standard deviation of those differences just as we compute any

Table 9.6   *t*-test for Paired Data

Formula 9.8	What It Says to Do

$t = \dfrac{\bar{D}}{s_{\text{diff}}}$
 where $\bar{D}$ is the mean of the differences in scores between pairs of matched subjects
 	
 $s_{\text{diff}} = \dfrac{s_D}{\sqrt{N}}$
 where s_D is the standard deviation of difference scores and N is the number of differences (or number of matched pairs)
	The procedure applies to situations where each subject in sample A is paired with a subject in sample B.
	 1. Compute the score differences for all pairs of subjects $(X_{1A} - X_{1B}, X_{2A} - X_{2B}, \text{etc.})$.
	 2. For these differences (D) compute a mean ($\Sigma D/N$).
	 3. Compute a standard deviation of differences as follows:
	    a Square all D values and find their sum $(D_1{}^2 + D_2{}^2 + \cdots + D_n{}^2)$.
	    b Sum all D values $(D_1 + D_2 + D_3 + \cdots + D_n)$.
	    c Apply (a) and (b) in formula (9.7) to get the standard deviation of D values (s_D).
	 4. Divide s_D by $\sqrt{N}$, where N is the number of pairs in the two samples, to get s_{diff}.
	 5. Divide $\bar{D}$ by s_{diff} to get the t value and enter Table III (Appendix C) with $N - 1$ degrees of freedom, where N is the number of pairs, or number of differences.

Example   Two samples of 10 high school seniors each have been matched on IQ before beginning an experiment in learning words in a fictitious language. They were then allowed 20 minutes to study the meanings of words, after which they were tested for the number of words learned. Group A studied in pairs, one student reading the words to the other; the students in group B studied alone. Did the different procedures result in different achievement? Our null hypothesis is that there is no difference between the groups in number of words learned.

Number of Words Learned

Group A	Group B	D	D^2	
10	11	-1	1	$\bar{D} = \frac{5}{10} = .5$
9	7	2	4	
9	8	1	1	$s_D = \sqrt{\dfrac{15 - \dfrac{(5)^2}{10}}{9}} = 1.18$
8	9	-1	1	
8	6	2	4	$s_{\text{diff}} = \dfrac{1.18}{\sqrt{10}} = .37$
7	6	1	1	
7	8	-1	1	$t = \dfrac{.5}{.37} = 1.35$
5	4	1	1	
4	3	1	1	With 9 degrees of freedom
4	4	0	0	insignificant, the null
		$\Sigma D = 5$	$\Sigma D^2 = 15$	hypothesis is accepted.

standard deviation, but we must substitute difference scores for the raw scores we used in describing data in Chap. 5. The formula would be

$$s_D = \sqrt{\frac{\Sigma D^2 - \frac{(\Sigma D)^2}{N}}{N - 1}}$$

$$9.7$$

and we saw in Chap. 8 that the standard error is found by dividing a standard deviation by the square root of N. Therefore, if we divide s_D by $\sqrt{N}$, the number of *differences* (or the number of matched *pairs* in our samples), we have a standard error—of what? Since the basic data are differences, it must be a standard error of the difference, but this procedure takes into account the correlation in observations of the two samples. Previous standard errors of the difference have assumed that the correlation between groups is zero.

The entire procedure for computing a t-test of correlated samples (paired cases) is given in Table 9.6.

PROBLEMS

1 An undergraduate student in a psychology laboratory wished to test the hypothesis that adolescent boys are brighter than their fathers. He collected IQs on 10 fifteen-year-old boys and also on their fathers. The data are below. Test the null hypothesis for these data.

Sons	Fathers
115	120
114	117
114	112
110	118
108	102
107	95
105	107
100	106
97	93
95	99

2   An opinion scale was developed to assess attitudes about the desirability of attendance at a given private college for women.   The scale was scored so that a low value reflected a negative attitude toward attendance, a high value a positive attitude.   It was then administered to 15 mothers and their 15 teen-age daughters.   The results are below.   Test the null hypothesis for these data.

Mothers	Daughters
53	48
59	57
32	46
43	59
37	42
46	40
39	45
48	36
42	56
45	42
49	39
47	55
46	39
55	58
50	45

One- or two-tailed test   In Chap. 8 we saw that it is sometimes reasonable to believe that the population mean is only above, or only below, the sample mean.   In such cases we are dealing with only one tail of the distribution.   In our table of t the column listed as the 5 per cent level provides values which leave 2.5 per cent in each of the two tails of the curve.   If we are doing a one-tailed test we would use the column in Table III of Appendix C listed as the .10 level.   The data in this column represent points beyond which lies 5 per cent of the area under the curve in each tail of the distribution.

Similarly when we test the difference between two means, it is sometimes logical to believe that differences can only go in one direction, that is, that a given mean can change only in one direction.   In this case, when using the 5 per cent level as our criterion for rejecting the null hypothesis, we look for the desired value of t under the column headed .10 level of confidence, since half of that .10 (or 5 per cent) will be in the tail in the one direction in which we expect the change. Likewise, if we are using the .01 level as our criterion, we would consult the column headed .02 for a one-tailed test. Figure 9.2 illustrates this idea for the 5 per cent level.

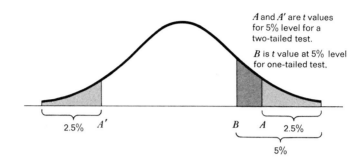

A and *A'* are *t* values
for 5% level for a
two-tailed test.

B is *t* value at 5% level
for one-tailed test.

2.5%   *A'*   *B*   *A*   2.5%

Figure 9.2   5%

Summary

Just as the means of an infinite number of randomly drawn samples from a population produce a normal curve when plotted in a frequency distribution, so do the differences between means of randomly drawn samples. We call this distribution of differences between means a sampling distribution of differences.

Like the data from any normally distributed characteristic, the sampling distribution of differences has a standard deviation which can be used as a yardstick for determining the number of differences between means of randomly drawn samples that are expected to fall beyond given points. We can then establish the likelihood of getting by chance two means with a given difference.

If we are observing two samples of individuals, we compare the ratio of this difference between their means and the standard error of the difference with points in Student's distribution beyond which either 5 or 1 per cent of the sample differences are expected to fall. If our two sample means differ more than the number of standard errors reported as the 5 or 1 per cent criterion points, we judge the samples to be different significantly at the criterion point exceeded. This procedure is known as the *t*-test.

In doing a *t*-test the selection of the correct procedure for computing the standard error of the difference is especially important.

1 When N is large, we may pool variances if the two samples come from populations with a common variance. But if samples come from populations with unequal variances, unpooled procedures can be applied.

2 When sample N's are small, we must assume the samples have come from populations with common variances. If this assumption is reasonable, the pooled-variance technique is the appropriate one for computing the standard error of the difference.

3 If samples are small and cannot be presumed to come from populations with a common variance, unpooled procedures can be applied. However, table values of t must be revised before we can test the significance of the difference between the means being observed. Revision of the table values can be made by means of formula (9.6).

4 When the data in the two samples are intercorrelated, revisions in the t procedure must be made to accommodate for the fact that values in one sample partially determine values in the other. Special techniques must be employed for these situations.

PROBLEMS ON THIS CHAPTER

1 A curriculum supervisor is studying two methods of teaching reading. Fifty first-graders are assigned randomly to method A, fifty to method B. After six weeks of instruction the following statistics were computed from an achievement test in reading:

	$\bar{X}$	s
A	47	9
B	51	10

Test the hypothesis that there is no difference between the means of the two samples.

2 In Prob. 1 there were 26 girls in method A and 24 girls in method B. The basic data for the girls were as follows:

	$\bar{X}$	s
A	51	9
B	54	11

Test the hypothesis that there was no difference between achievement of girls in one sample compared with the other. (Should the curriculum supervisor test for homogeneity of variance here?)

3   A psychologist is studying the effect of drugs on accuracy of hand-eye coordination. He uses a star-tracing problem as his measure of accuracy. He has 30 subjects in the drug X group and 34 subjects in the placebo group. The number of errors made were as follows:

	$\bar{X}$	s
Drug X	34.3	9
Placebo	37.6	7

Test the null hypothesis for these two groups of subjects.

4   On a repeat of the study in Prob. 3 the psychologist had a group of 10 subjects who took drug X and a group of 12 who took the placebo. The results were as follows:

	$\bar{X}$	s
Drug X	32.1	11
Placebo	35.0	6

Test the null hypothesis for these two samples. (Apply F for homogeneity of variance at the 5 per cent level.)

5   The psychologist in Probs. 3 and 4 repeated his study on a third group of 12 subjects. Half the group got drug X, half a placebo, and they were tested. Two days later the half who got the placebo took drug X, and those who had first taken the drug got the placebo. Again the test was given; thus, two scores were available on each subject. The scores were as follows:

Subject	Drug X	Placebo
A	28	26
B	24	31
C	29	31
D	36	35
E	34	35
F	37	39
G	31	32
H	39	41
I	29	31
J	28	29
K	35	36
L	33	33

Test the null hypothesis for these two sets of data.

10

Introduction to Analysis of Variance

The t-test, as we have just seen, is a satisfactory procedure for determining whether the means of samples A and B are sufficiently different to say that such a difference is unlikely as a result of chance selection of random samples. But the t-test is limited primarily to situations in which we are dealing with only two samples at a time. Suppose we have three samples, all of which are being observed simultaneously. For example, we are studying the effect of alcohol on hand-eye coordination. Group A takes 2 ounces of alcohol 5 minutes before tracking a stylus along a wire; group B has 1 ounce; and group C has none at all. Are these three groups from the same population of stylus trackers?

At first we might think that a reasonable

solution would be to apply the t-test to each of the possible pairs of group means, that is, A and B, A and C, B and C.   In the present case, where we have only three tests to make, the labor is not extensive.   But suppose we had five groups.   Ten tests would have to be made.   And suppose we had eight groups, 12 groups, 15.   Clearly the t-test is an inefficient procedure here. Also, with increasing numbers of sample pairs the probability increases of getting two samples the means of which are by chance significantly different, even though all pairs of samples are from the same population.

However, another, and probably more serious, problem arises from multiple t-tests done on the same body of data.   The various differences between means are not independent of each other.   For example, suppose we have three samples of children and have means for nonsense-syllable learning on these samples.   The difference between means A and B is 3, between A and C is 4.   Now what is the difference between B and C?   Did you say 1?   How did you decide that?   The difference between B and C is clearly tied to the differences between A and B, and A and C.   In other words, one difference in the three is not independent of the other differences, and with this non-independence of differences the t-test—which is tied to a distribution of differences between pairs of means of independent, random samples—does not appear to be entirely satisfactory.

What we now need is a procedure for simultaneously testing the differences between several groups.   This procedure is found in the *analysis of variance*.

The analysis of variance deals with, as its name implies, variances. Variance is simply the arithmetic average of the squared deviations of scores from their mean; that is, a variance is the square of the standard deviation. In the procedures ahead we shall therefore be repeatedly dealing with $\Sigma(X - \bar{X})^2$, which in Chap. 5 we saw was equal to $\Sigma X^2 - (\Sigma X)^2/N$.   These values are the sum of squared deviations of scores from their mean and are often called simply the *sum of squares*.

Up to this point we have dealt with standard deviations (and variances) based on two kinds of data: (1) the standard deviation of raw scores from the mean of the group and (2) the standard deviation of group means from the population mean (which we called a standard error of the mean).   In the analysis of variance we shall simply borrow these two ideas to make up a single procedure.

Partitioning of variance   Suppose we have collected IQs on five randomly selected samples of ten-year-old children, 20 in each sample.   My best estimate of the population mean (we shall call it the *grand mean* or *total mean* to distinguish it from sample means) would be the sum of the entire 100 cases divided by N.   Now let us look only at Susan who is a member of sample 3.

How far does her IQ deviate from the grand mean? We could find that out in one of two ways. We could subtract the grand mean ($\bar{X}_t$) from Susan's IQ score ($X_s - \bar{X}_t$). Or we could find how far the mean of sample 3 (Susan's sample) deviates from the grand mean ($\bar{X}_3 - \bar{X}_t$) and then algebraically add to this the amount that Susan's score deviates from her group mean ($X_s - \bar{X}_3$). The sum of these two deviations would tell us how far Susan's score deviates from the grand mean; that is,

$$(X_s - \bar{X}_t) = (\bar{X}_3 - \bar{X}_t) + (X_s - \bar{X}_3)$$

In other words, the deviation of a given score from the grand mean can be partitioned into two clearly distinct segments—the deviation of the score from the mean of its group and the deviation of that group mean from the grand mean.

What we have done to this point is analogous to figuring out how far a workman must travel to work in the morning. We could measure the miles from the workman's residence to the factory directly (analogous to $X_s - \bar{X}_t$), or we could measure the miles from the bus stop in his neighborhood to the factory (analogous to $\bar{X}_3 - \bar{X}_t$) and then add algebraically the distance from his residence to the bus stop (analogous to $X_s - \bar{X}_3$). We now ask: Are the various bus stops (means of samples) on the whole more widely dispersed around the factory than the workmen are dispersed around the bus stops?

The variance, we noted earlier, is found by summing the squared deviations of scores from their mean and dividing by the degrees of freedom. If deviations of scores from the grand mean can be divided into two parts— deviations of sample means from the grand mean and deviation of scores from sample means—then variances may also be divided into two similar parts. We call the variance based on deviation of sample means from the grand mean the *among-groups variance** and the one based on deviations of scores from sample means the *within-groups variance*. The rationale of analysis of variance lies in the fact that *both the within-groups variance and the among-groups variance are estimates of the population variance.*

Having found these two variances, we pose this question: *Do the sample means vary around the grand mean more than the individual scores vary around the sample means?* If the sample means *do* vary around the grand mean *more than* the individual scores vary around their sample means, the samples are comparatively widely dispersed from each other; but if the sample means vary around the grand means *less than* individual scores vary around their sample means,

---

* Some texts refer to this as *between-groups variance*, which grammatically leaves something to be desired.

the samples are very much like each other in score values.   Figure 10.1 illustrates this point.

Figure 10.1*A* and *B* each show three samples of individuals.   The individuals in the samples in *A* are dispersed around the sample means to exactly the same extent as the individuals in the *B* samples; that is, the within-groups variance in *A* is equal to the within-groups variance in *B*.   However, the sample means in *A* are much more widely dispersed around the grand mean

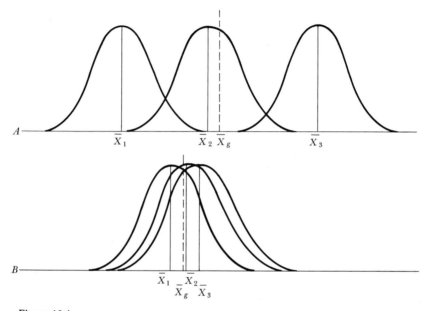

Figure 10.1

than those in *B*.   In other words, the among-groups variance in *A* is much greater than the among-groups variance in *B*.   Considering these two items of information, we may wish to conclude that the samples in *A* are not just random samples from the same population.

The conclusion, then, as to whether the samples came from different populations or from the same population is based on the size of the within-groups variance as compared with the among-groups variance.   We can state this comparison in a ratio, known as the *F* ratio, thusly:

$$F = \frac{s_{ag}^2}{s_{wg}^2}$$ **10.1**

where s_{ag}^2 is the among-groups variance and s_{wg}^2 is the within-groups variance. If s_{ag}^2 and s_{wg}^2 are really estimates of the variance of the same population, the F ratio will approach 1.0; however, if in a given problem they are each estimates of variances of different populations, the F ratio will clearly deviate from 1.0.

How do we compute these variances? If we remember how pooled variances were found for the t-test, we have the basic technique for computing the s_{wg}^2, so let us deal with it first. The procedure for dealing with a three-sample problem is

$$s_{wg}^2 = \frac{\Sigma(X_1 - \bar{X}_1)^2 + \Sigma(X_2 - \bar{X}_2)^2 + \Sigma(X_3 - \bar{X}_3)^2}{(N_1 - 1) + (N_2 - 1) + (N_3 - 1)} \qquad \textbf{10.2}$$

Now if we square each of the numerators, as we did in computing the variance in Chap. 5,* we can come up with the formula

$$s_{wg}^2 = \frac{\Sigma X_1^2 + \Sigma X_2^2 + \Sigma X_3^2 - \left[\dfrac{(\Sigma X_1)^2}{N_1} + \dfrac{(\Sigma X_2)^2}{N_2} + \dfrac{(\Sigma X_3)^2}{N_3}\right]}{N_t - 3} \qquad \textbf{10.3}$$

where X_1, X_2, X_3 = scores from samples 1, 2, 3
$\qquad N_1, N_2, N_3$ = number of cases in samples 1, 2, 3
$\qquad\qquad N_t$ = total number of cases, or $N_1 + N_2 + N_3$

The generalized procedure for dealing with n number of samples is given in Table 10.1.

Now let us turn to the numerator of the F ratio, the among-groups variance s_{ag}^2. Since this figure indicates the extent to which the sample means vary around the grand mean, a first impression may suggest that it is found by applying the formula $\Sigma(X_i - \bar{X}_t)^2/(k - 1)$. However, we found that for *each* $(X - \bar{X}_t)$ deviation there were two components, $(X - \bar{X}_i)$ and $(\bar{X}_i - X_t)$. Therefore, we have an $(\bar{X}_i - \bar{X}_t)$ component for the deviation of each X score from the grand mean, so in computing the sum of squares for among-groups variance, we must repeat the $(\bar{X}_i - \bar{X}_t)$ for all cases within a sample and then for all samples. The procedure for this operation would be

$$s_{ag}^2 = \frac{\Sigma N_i(\bar{X}_i - \bar{X}_t)^2}{k - 1} \qquad \textbf{10.4}$$

For our three-sample example this would be done as follows:

$$s_{ag}^2 = \frac{N_1(\bar{X}_1 - \bar{X}_t)^2 + N_2(\bar{X}_2 - \bar{X}_t)^2 + N_3(\bar{X}_3 - \bar{X}_t)^2}{3 - 1}$$

---

* If this procedure is not familiar to the student, he should turn to pages 66–67 and review the procedure.

Table 10.1   Computational Procedures for the $s_{wg}{}^2$

Formula 10.3

$$s_{wg}{}^2 = \frac{\Sigma X_1{}^2 + \Sigma X_2{}^2 + \cdots + \Sigma X_n{}^2 - \left[\dfrac{(\Sigma X_1)^2}{N_1} + \dfrac{(\Sigma X_2)^2}{N_2} + \cdots + \dfrac{(\Sigma X_n)^2}{N_n} \right]}{N_t - k}$$

where $s_{wg}{}^2$ = within-groups variance
$X_1, X_2, \ldots, X_n$ = individual scores in samples 1, 2, . . . , n
$N_1, N_2, \ldots, N_n$ = number of cases in samples 1, 2, . . . , n
N_t = total number of cases in all samples
k = number of samples

What It Says to Do

1. For each sample, square each score and sum these squared scores to get $\Sigma X_1{}^2$, $\Sigma X_2{}^2, \ldots, \Sigma X_n{}^2$.
2. For each sample, sum all scores and then square these sums to get $(\Sigma X_1)^2, (\Sigma X_2)^2, \ldots,$ $(\Sigma X_n)^2$.
3. For each sample, divide the $(\Sigma X)^2$ value by N for that sample.
4. a   Sum all $\Sigma X_i{}^2$ values.
   b   Sum all $(\Sigma X_i)^2/N_i$ values.
   c   Subtract the value of step b from the value of step a.
5. Divide the result of step 4 by $N_t - k$.

which when each of the enclosed values is squared becomes equal to the formula

$$s_{ag}{}^2 = \frac{\dfrac{(\Sigma X_1)^2}{N_1} + \dfrac{(\Sigma X_2)^2}{N_2} + \dfrac{(\Sigma X_3)^2}{N_3} - \dfrac{(\Sigma X_t)^2}{N_t}}{k - 1}$$

The generalized procedure for the among-groups variance is given in Table 10.2.

We began this chapter by pointing out that the deviation of a given case from the grand mean can be divided into two parts: (1) the deviation of the individual from his sample mean and (2) the deviation of this sample mean from the grand mean. The deviations around the grand mean for a group of scores for combined samples, then, can be partitioned into the within groups deviations and the among groups deviations. In other words, the total

Table 10.2   Computation of the Among-Groups Variance

Formula 10.5

$$s_{ag}^2 = \frac{\dfrac{(\Sigma X_1)^2}{N_1} + \dfrac{(\Sigma X_2)^2}{N_2} + \cdots + \dfrac{(\Sigma X_n)^2}{N_n} - \dfrac{(\Sigma X_t)^2}{N_t}}{k - 1}$$

where $\qquad s_{ag}^2$ = among-groups variance

$\Sigma X_1, \Sigma X_2, \ldots, \Sigma X_n$ = sums of individual scores in samples 1, 2, . . . n

ΣX_t = sum of individual scores in all samples combined

$(\Sigma X_1 + \Sigma X_2 + \cdots + \Sigma X_n)$

$N_1, N_2, \ldots, N_n$ = number of cases in samples 1, 2, . . . , n

k = number of samples observed

What the Formula Says to Do

1. For each sample, sum all scores to get $\Sigma X_1, \Sigma X_2, \ldots, \Sigma X_n$; square these values and divide each by the number of cases that went into that sum; summate all resulting values.
2. Sum the sample sums $(\Sigma X_1 + \Sigma X_2 + \cdots + \Sigma X_n)$ to get the sum of all cases (ΣX_t); square this value and divide it by the total number of cases in all samples combined.
3. Subtract the result of step 2 from the result of step 1.
4. Divide the result of step 3 by 1 less than the number of samples in the analysis $(k - 1)$.

sum of squares of the combined groups should be equal to the sum of the two partitioned sums of squares, that is

$$ss_t = ss_{ag} + ss_{wg}$$

We can compute the total variance by the procedure

$$ss_t = \Sigma(X - \bar{X}_t)^2$$

or by the equivalent procedure

$$ss_t = \frac{\Sigma X_t^2 - \dfrac{(\Sigma X_t)^2}{N_t}}{N_t - 1}$$

We can then use this figure to short-cut other computations; for example, $ss_{wg} = ss_t - ss_{ag}$. We can also check the computations since the sum of ss_{ag} and ss_{wg} should equal an independent calculation of ss_t.

The F test   Now that we have the components in hand, we are ready to complete the F test.   As noted earlier, the F test is based on the ratio between the among-groups variance and the within-groups variance.   We pose the null hypothesis that there is no difference between these two variances.   We determine the significance of F values quite the way we determine the significance of t values; that is, we refer to a frequency curve, albeit the shape of the F curve is typically quite skewed.   Nevertheless from such a frequency distribution we can determine the likelihood of getting F values of a given magnitude for various combinations of degrees of freedom—which brings up our next point.

In a t-test we have only one value for degrees of freedom, but in an F test

Table 10.3   Completion of an F Test on Three Randomly Selected Samples of College Freshmen

(The data represent numbers of algebra problems solved in a 3-minute time period by high school seniors.)

Sample 1		Sample 2	Sample 3	
	5	5	6	
	3	3	4	
	1	3	4	
	4	1	2	
	2	4	3	
ΣX_i	15	16	19	$\Sigma X_t = 50$
$\Sigma X_i{}^2$	55	60	81	$\Sigma X_t{}^2 = 196$

$$s_{wg}{}^2 = \frac{55 + 60 + 81 - \left[\dfrac{(15)^2}{5} + \dfrac{(16)^2}{5} + \dfrac{(19)^2}{5}\right]}{15 - 3} = 2.30$$

$$s_{ag}{}^2 = \frac{\dfrac{(15)^2}{5} + \dfrac{(16)^2}{5} + \dfrac{(19)^2}{5} - \dfrac{(50)^2}{15}}{3 - 1} = .86$$

$$F = \frac{.86}{2.30} = .37$$

With $N - k$, or 12, degrees of freedom in the denominator and $k - 1$, or 2, degrees of freedom in the numerator, we consult Table IV in Appendix C and find that we must accept the null hypothesis.

we have degrees of freedom for the s_{ag}^2 and for the s_{wg}^2. In Table IVa in Appendix C we find the 5 per cent level by first locating in the left marginal column the degrees of freedom associated with s_{wg}^2, the denominator $(N_t - k)$, and then moving across that row to the column at the top of which is the number of degrees of freedom associated with s_{ag}^2, the numerator $(k - 1)$. This column-row cell will contain the F value at the 5 per cent level. Table IVb contains F values for the 1 per cent level. If our F ratio is less than the 5 per cent value, the null hypothesis is accepted; if it exceeds one or both of these criterion values, we reject the hypothesis at the level of the point surpassed. In so doing we have completed the F test. An example is laid out in Table 10.3.

PROBLEMS

1 Three samples of nine-year-old boys are selected from a grade school for the purpose of testing physical training methods. Sample 1 was a control group and received no special training; sample 2 had 1 hour of work a day in such group sports as volleyball, touch football, and basketball; sample 3 had calisthenics 30 min daily. At the end of 2 weeks a physical fitness test was administered to all groups. Their scores are below. Test the null hypothesis for these samples.

Sample 1	Sample 2	Sample 3
10	10	7
11	9	9
9	5	6
6	6	5
8	8	3
7	7	2

2 Compute the mean for each sample of Prob. 1. Does $(N_1 \bar{X}_1^2 + N_2 \bar{X}_2^2 + N_3 \bar{X}_3^2 - N_t \bar{X}_t^2)/(k - 1)$ equal, except for rounding errors, the value you found for the among-groups variance? If means of samples are already available, is this method faster than formula (10.5)?

Assumptions in analysis of variance   The distribution of F values is known to take on certain characteristics with different combinations of degrees of freedom.   However, these characteristics are known only under certain conditions which we assume to be present.   These conditions are (1) that all populations from which samples have been drawn are normally distributed; (2) that the variances for the populations from which samples have been drawn are equal; and (3) that the individuals being observed have been randomly selected from the populations represented by the samples.

The values in Table IV in Appendix C are precise only when we have met the above assumptions.   However, in actual practice it has been observed that one or more of these assumptions can be "bent" without appreciable loss in the adequacy of the F test.   The researcher strives to meet the assumptions of the F test, but he usually finds that if his data are reasonably close to meeting the assumptions, his conclusions based on the F test are not markedly affected.

Summary

The t-test is an adequate procedure for testing the null hypothesis when we have means of only two samples to consider.   However, we often have more than two samples to consider at one time, and so an alternative procedure is needed for testing the hypothesis that all samples could likely be from the same population.   The analysis-of-variance procedure is appropriate for such a test.

The procedure is based on the fact that the deviation of a given score from the population mean can be divided into two parts: (1) the deviation of the score from its sample mean and (2) the deviation of the sample mean from the population mean.   Therefore, out of the total variance of all individuals around the population mean we can compute two variances: (1) one for scores around their sample means and (2) one for sample means around the grand mean.

We then put these two variances into a ratio which is called the F ratio. If the variance of sample means around the grand mean is conspicuously greater than the variance of scores around the sample means, the samples must be, relatively speaking, widely dispersed around the grand mean, very likely not representing random samples from the same population.   However, if the sample means are very narrowly dispersed around the grand mean, compared with score dispersions around their sample means, the samples are likely all to be random samples from a common population.

PROBLEMS

1 A curriculum supervisor has undertaken a study of the value of grade reports to parents in the promotion of achievement. Three groups of fourth-grade students have been randomly chosen from all fourth-graders in the L. B. Johnson Elementary School. Group 1 gets a conventional report card every 8 weeks; a parent-teacher conference is held every 8 weeks for group 2; and group 3 is given no report at all. At the end of the year tests are given in all subject areas. Raw scores for arithmetic problems are given below. Test, at the .05 level, the hypothesis that the three samples are from a common population.

Sample 1	Sample 2	Sample 3
12	14	8
10	8	11
11	19	13
11	15	9
8	10	7
10	11	5
7	13	6
9	12	8
10	9	7
6	12	10

2 In the study described in Prob. 1, the spelling test scores were as below. Test the null hypothesis for spelling.

Sample 1	Sample 2	Sample 3
8	5	10
2	10	4
10	2	5
4	6	2
7	8	6
5	4	4
6	7	7
5	12	8
6	5	6
4	1	7

3   A medical team wished to study the relationship between cigarette smoking and various diseases. They selected five groups of subjects; four groups consisted of patients in a city hospital, and one was made up of a random selection of visitors to the hospital. The number of cigarettes smoked per day by each subject is given below. Test the null hypothesis (at the 1 per cent level) for these data.

Lung Diseases	Heart Disease	Digestive Diseases	Kidney Disorders	Visitors
32	19	17	12	12
17	26	26	15	15
28	30	30	10	36
24	17	35	20	17
21	34	20	18	20
38	15	15	30	25

11

Chi Square and Other Nonparametric Procedures

In testing hypotheses in previous chapters, we computed characteristics of a sample or samples in order to make some conclusions about characteristics of the population; that is, we dealt with statistics as estimates of parameters. These procedures are characteristically called *parametric tests*.

However, in many situations our data clearly do not fit the assumptions necessary for parametric tests. For these situations methods have been developed which are free of the assumptions characteristic of operations such as t and F. Such procedures are called *nonparametric tests*. They are carried out, however, not without their own assumptions. This chapter will deal with a minimum number of these methods, including chi square, the sign test, and the median test. These three, along with rank-order correlation, can be applied to a majority of situations requiring nonparametric analysis.

Chi square   A number of studies in the social sciences deal with counting of individuals who appear in various categories.   We often wish to compare this count with the number of individuals that an a priori hypothesis says should appear in these categories.   For example, suppose we are studying the political affiliations of women who belong to the Read Along Book Club. We find that there are 23 Republicans, 18 Democrats, and five women who belong to political parties other than the two major ones.   In Table 11.1,

Table 11.1   Fictitious Political Affiliations of Women in a Club

Parties	Observed Frequency	Expected Frequency
Republican	23	18.4
Democrat	18	20.7
Other	5	6.9
Total	46	46.0

these data are our observed frequencies, i.e., our actual count within the categories.   We have noted that in the last election in this book club's county, 45 per cent of the registered voters were Democrats; 40 per cent were Republicans; and 15 per cent were of other parties.   If the ladies in the book club distributed themselves among the political parties in the way that the total registered electorate did, we would have 40 per cent of the 46 members affiliated with the Republicans, 45 per cent with the Democrats, and 15 per cent with other parties.

Now we ask ourselves: Are the political affiliations of these ladies typical of any sample from the county population, except for sampling error, or do their affiliations deviate so widely from the expected affiliations that we must conclude that it is not a chance deviation?

To find out how much the observed frequencies f_o do deviate from the expected f_e, we could subtract the expected frequency of each party from the actual frequency $(f_o - f_e)$ and add together these differences for all parties. However, if deviations from the expected value in one party is a large positive, in another a large negative, as many differences could be positive as negative, and we may well end up with a sum of $(f_o - f_e)$ being zero even though a considerable difference existed between expected and observed frequencies in our data.   In fact, the sum of random fluctuations from the expected values should be zero.   Therefore, our problem is that in adding deviations, a deviation of actual frequencies from the expected value in one cell could be obscured by a similar deviation in the opposite direction in another cell. We get around this problem in chi square by squaring for each cell in the table the difference between the observed and expected frequencies, $(f_o - f_e)^2$. Thus, all values are positive.

A second problem is tied to the magnitude of an observed-minus-expected difference relative to the number of frequencies involved.   For example, the 10-point difference in A of Table 11.2 is small in proportion to the number of

Table 11.2   Illustration of the Importance of Differences Relative to the Size of the Expected Frequencies

Category	A	B
Observed frequency	1,510	12
Expected frequency	1,500	22
Difference	10	10

individuals involved.   However, the same difference in B is proportionately great.   In other words, the importance of a given $f_o - f_e$ is relative to the size of the expected group.   Therefore, we divide the squared difference between the actual and expected frequencies by the expected frequency, $(f_o - f_e)^2/f_e$.   This puts the squared difference in proportion to the number of cases expected in the cell.   We then add up for all cells these squared-differences-divided-by-the-expected-frequency values, and this is our chi square.   The procedure is given in Table 11.3 in a step-by-step outline.

Significance of chi square   Chi square is based on the idea that if the hypothesis upon which the expected frequencies are computed is correct, deviations of actual frequencies from the expected ones will be random fluctuations only.   From our work in previous chapters we know that when there are random fluctuations around any point, it is mathematically possible to compute the proportions of cases that deviate various amounts from that

Procedure for Computing Chi Square

Formula 11.1	What It Says to Do
$$\chi^2 = \Sigma \frac{(f_o - f_e)^2}{f_e}$$ where f_o = actual (observed) frequency for a given cell and f_e = expected frequency for that cell	1. Determine the number of individuals that fall into each category being observed (f_o). 2. By means of an a priori hypothesis determine the number of individuals that are expected to fall into each category (f_e). 3. For each cell, subtract f_e from f_o, square the difference, $(f_o - f_e)^2$, and divide the result by f_e. 4. Sum the results of step 3 for all cells, that is, $\chi^2 = \dfrac{(f_{o_1} - f_{e_1})^2}{f_{e_1}} + \dfrac{(f_{o_2} - f_{e_2})^2}{f_{e_2}} + \cdots + \dfrac{(f_{o_n} - f_{e_n})^2}{f_{e_n}}$, where subscripts 1, 2, . . . , n refer to various classified groups or cells in a table such as Table 11.1.

Example We are studying color preferences of women college freshmen. We have begun with the basic colors of red, blue, yellow and have asked 60 women to select the color they like best from a card containing a 1-inch square of each of the three colors. We get the following distribution of choices:

Red	Blue	Yellow
13	27	20

We test the hypothesis that the observed choices do not differ from a random selection and make the test as follows: The above data are the observed frequencies, and our hypothesis is a random distribution of selections, or a third of the total responses in each category.

f_o	f_e	$\dfrac{(f_o - f_e)^2}{f_e}$
13	20	2.45
27	20	2.45
20	20	.00
	$\chi^2 =$	4.90

point. With these proportions we could build frequency curves which, although they may be unlike the binomial distribution in shape, can be used, in relation to degrees of freedom, to determine the likelihood of getting scores which deviate various amounts by chance alone. Then if our obtained deviations could be achieved only rarely by chance, we may wish to conclude that something other than chance was operating. The chi-square test, being tied to deviations, operates in a manner very much like this.

How do we determine the degrees of freedom in a problem such as the example in Table 11.3? Until now degrees of freedom have been associated with the number of individuals in a sample and the number of restrictions imposed by such a condition as the population mean. In chi square, degrees of freedom are tied to the number of classifications into which we have sorted our individuals, and the number of restrictions imposed are determined by the total observations in the categories. In Table 11.1, we have three categories which must add up to 46 cases. We are free to vary the frequencies in two of the categories; but when the cases in two categories are established, the frequency in the third category is also determined, since it is the total number of cases less the frequencies of the "free" cells. We, therefore, have $k - 1$ degrees of freedom, where k is the number of categories into which we have segmented the classification variable. In the example of girls choosing colors we had three color categories for sorting, and so degrees of freedom is $3 - 1$, or 2.

It must be noted that the procedure shown in Table 11.3 for computing degrees of freedom pertains to problems in which the data have been sorted on a single variable only, e.g., political party. Later we shall classify observations under two variables, such as social class and political party, simultaneously. We shall take a second look at degrees of freedom at that point.

The significance of the chi-square value can be determined by consulting Table V of Appendix C. Here we have listed for various degrees of freedom the chi-square values beyond which various percentages of chi squares will fall by chance alone. As in previous tests, we typically set the 5 or 1 per cent levels as our criterion of significance and accept or reject the null hypothesis in relation to these values of chi square.

For the problem in Table 11.3, we have 2 degrees of freedom. In Table V in Appendix C we see that a chi-square value of 5.99 is necessary for significance at the 5 per cent level. Since our value of 4.90 is less than the table value, we accept the hypothesis that freshman women have a preference for color which does not differ from a random arrangement.

In the example of Table 11.3 we found our expected frequencies by hypothesizing a random distribution of the variable being observed, but any hypothesis that has foundation may be used to establish expected frequencies. For example, we may have reason to believe that one out of three men prefers convertible cars to nonconvertibles, whereas only one out of five women prefers convertibles. This a priori proposal then could be the basis for determining how many men and how many women from a given group should be expected to choose a convertible.

A second example of this approach is found in analyzing items on certain tests. Suppose we have four alternatives on a multiple-choice test. Did our class respond to a given item on a random basis? If so, the responses of the group should be equally distributed among the four choices. Our expected frequency would be .25N for each of the four alternatives to the test item. We could then compare these expected frequencies with actual student responses to see if the class did indeed respond to the item essentially on a random basis.

Other hypotheses may also be appropriate. For example, we may have reason to believe that the second of four alternatives to a test item should get as many choices as all other alternatives combined and that alternatives 1, 3, and 4 are equally attractive; that is, the remaining half of the responses are equally spread over these three choices. In this case, the expected frequency for the second alternative would be $\frac{1}{2}N$, and the expected frequency for all other alternatives would be $\frac{1}{6}N$.

A test of independence with two variables of classification Sometimes we wish to classify our observations under each of two different conditions simultaneously. For example, we may wish to consider urban-rural residence and preference for the three basic colors. Here we would be asking whether one variable of classification is independent of the other. (By independence we mean that knowledge of one characteristic for an individual tells us nothing about the other characteristic for that person.) Double-classification problems such as this require a second procedure for determining the expected frequencies, and so let us look at the following table to see if we can come up with a method for establishing these expected values. In the data below, we are comparing regular college students with part-time students on their feelings about the adequacy of social events at college X. The row and column totals are called *marginal totals*. A table laid out like the one below is called a *contingency table*, because it reflects the extent to which frequencies in one variable (student status) are contingent upon—or dependent upon—frequencies in the other variable (attitude).

	Satisfied	Dissatisfied	Totals
Regular	40	30	70
Part-time	40	10	50
Totals	80	40	120

In the data above, we look first at the totals. Out of the 120 students in all, 70 were regular students; 50 were part-time. Also, 80 were satisfied, and 40 were dissatisfied with social events. Now if the two groups are independent in their attitudes, the proportion of regular students who are satisfied with social events will be the same as the proportion of part-time students who are satisfied, and similarly, the proportion of regular, dissatisfied students will be the same as the proportion of part-time, dissatisfied students. Therefore, of the total of 70 who are regularly enrolled, $\frac{80}{120}$ will be expected to appear in the satisfied category, and $\frac{40}{120}$ will fall into the dissatisfied category, or

f_e for regular, satisfied students $= 70 \times \frac{80}{120} = 46.67$
f_e for regular, dissatisfied students $= 70 \times \frac{40}{120} = 23.33$

In a like manner, we can also determine the expected frequencies for part-time students. There were 50 of these people in all, and if the categories are independent, these 50 people will be divided between the satisfied and dissatisfied categories in proportion to the marginal totals for those two categories. That is,

f_e for part-time, satisfied students $= 50 \times \frac{80}{120} = 33.33$
f_e for part-time, dissatisfied students $= 50 \times \frac{40}{120} = 16.67$

We now generalize this procedure for computing expected frequencies when we are testing the hypothesis that the categories are independent. First we get row and column totals and the grand total. The expected frequency for any given cell in our contingency table is then found by multiplying that cell's row and column totals and dividing this product by the grand total. In the table below the expected frequencies are found as listed.

A	B	C	T_1
D	E	F	T_2
T_3	T_4	T_5	T_g

$$f_{eA} = \frac{T_1 \times T_3}{T_g} \qquad f_{eB} = \frac{T_1 \times T_4}{T_g} \qquad f_{eC} = \frac{T_1 \times T_5}{T_g}$$

$$f_{eD} = \frac{T_2 \times T_3}{T_g} \qquad f_{eE} = \frac{T_2 \times T_4}{T_g} \qquad f_{eF} = \frac{T_2 \times T_5}{T_g}$$

where A, B, C, D, E, and F are classification categories; T_1 and T_2 are the total frequencies in rows 1 and 2; T_3, T_4, and T_5 are column totals; and T_g is the grand total of all frequencies in the table.

Now let us return to the problem above to see if student status at X university is independent of attitude about social events. We can now check the calculations of expected frequencies which we made above. In chi square the sum of the expected frequencies must equal the sum of the actual frequencies. Our actual frequencies totaled to 120, and our expected frequencies, rounded to two decimal places, also total to 120. With this knowledge we can proceed with increased confidence in our computations. The chi square becomes

f_o	f_e	$\dfrac{(f_o - f_e)^2}{f_e}$
40	46.67	.95
30	23.33	1.91
40	33.33	1.33
10	16.67	2.67
	$\chi^2 =$	6.86

The degrees of freedom for a two-variable classification problem follows essentially the same procedure as a one-variable classification situation; however, we have added restrictions because both row and column totals impose limitations. We noted earlier that the degrees of freedom in a single row (or column) arrangement were 1 less than the number of classification cells. However, in a two-way classification, each cell in a row (restricted by the row total) is also a cell in a column (restricted by a column total). The operation of such restrictions can be illustrated best by an example such as Table 11.4.

Table 11.4 Data for Illustrating Degrees of Freedom in Chi Square

	Class 1	Class 2	Class 3	Total
Group I	A	B	C	20
Group II	D	E	F	30
Total	10	26	14	50

Once the frequencies for cells A and B are determined, cell C is not free to vary if the row is to add up to 20.   Also, once cell A is established, cell D is not free to vary if the column is to add up to 10.   Following this procedure, we find that once any two of the cells are set, no other cell frequency in the table is free to vary.   In other words, we have only 2 degrees of freedom (df) in the above situation.   The results of this logical procedure for arriving at degrees of freedom is duplicated in the following formula: df $= (r - 1)(c - 1)$, where r is the number of rows, and c the number of columns in the table.

Now for our problem relating enrollment status to satisfaction with social events, we have $(r - 1)(c - 1)$, or 1, degree of freedom.   We consult Table V in Appendix C and find that a chi square of 6.86 with 1 degree of freedom is significant at the 1 per cent level of confidence.   This tells us that the way frequencies spread themselves for one variable (student status) is dependent upon the way the frequencies are dispersed for the other variable (attitude).   In other words, if a chi-square test rejects the hypothesis of independence, we accept the hypothesis of dependence.   Our knowledge of X does indeed tell us something about Y.

Correction for small frequencies in a 2 × 2 table   When we have a small sample of cases, the usual computation of chi square gives us an overestimate of the true value.   As a result, we reject some hypotheses which in fact should be accepted.   We can avoid this problem in 2 × 2 tables, however, by applying what is known as *Yates's correction.**

The procedure is a simple matter of subtracting .5 from the absolute value of the $f_o - f_e$ values in each of the four cells of the table.   For example, if our table had frequencies like

4	9	13
7	6	13
11	15	26

we could calculate the expected frequencies by our usual method and find them to be

$$f_{e_1} = \frac{11 \times 13}{26} = 5.50 \qquad f_{e_2} = \frac{15 \times 13}{26} = 7.50$$

$$f_{e_3} = \frac{11 \times 13}{26} = 5.50 \qquad f_{e_4} = \frac{15 \times 13}{26} = 7.50$$

* F. Yates, a British statistician, explored the small-frequency problem in a paper prepared for the Royal Statistical Society in 1934.

Then we would compute our chi square in this manner:*

$$\frac{(|4 - 5.5| - .5)^2}{5.5} = .18$$

$$\frac{(|7 - 5.5| - .5)^2}{5.5} = .18$$

$$\frac{(|9 - 7.5| - .5)^2}{7.5} = .13$$

$$\frac{(|6 - 7.5| - .5)^2}{7.5} = .13$$

$$\chi^2 = \overline{.62}$$

Now if the Yates's correction were *not* applied in the calculation, the chi square would have been somewhat larger, that is,

$$\frac{(4 - 5.5)^2}{5.5} = .41$$

$$\frac{(7 - 5.5)^2}{5.5} = .41$$

$$\frac{(9 - 7.5)^2}{7.5} = .30$$

$$\frac{(6 - 7.5)^2}{7.5} = .30$$

$$\chi^2 = \overline{1.42}$$

Yates's correction is applied when the least expected frequency in any cell is less than 5. If expected values are 5 or greater, the uncorrected procedure gives a reasonably accurate estimate. Yates's correction is suitable for tables which have only 1 degree of freedom, but suppose we have more than a single degree of freedom. Then if all except one of the cell expectations are large, we may achieve a reasonably close approximation of chi square with calculations in the usual manner without Yates's procedure.

We can occasionally avoid the problem of small frequencies in cells by combining categories. For example, suppose we have taken an opinion survey to find out how people feel about a proposed tax bill; we compare Republicans with Democrats on five categories of an agreement scale and get the following frequencies:

* The vertical lines used to enclose numbers mean that we are dealing with the absolute value of the difference regardless of sign.

	Strongly Disagree	Disagree	Undecided	Agree	Strongly Agree
Democrats	2	4	25	14	10
Republicans	8	7	12	9	3

By condensing our scale to include agree, undecided, disagree categories, we would have six cells all of which would be large enough for computing chi square directly with reasonable assurance that our chi square was quite accurate. The table then would look like this:

	Disagreeing	Undecided	Agreeing
Democrats	6	25	24
Republicans	15	12	12

When computing chi square, one is often faced with the dilemma of proceeding with a small cell frequency and maintaining categories which have research significance, or combining cells and achieving a more accurate estimate of chi square but losing categories. The choice is one which must be made again for each individual problem.

Assumptions and limitations in chi square Like all statistical analyses, chi square is based on certain assumptions which must be met if the analysis is to produce dependable results. The essential limitations to the use of chi square, arising out of the basic assumptions, are:

1 Individual observations must be independent of each other. The response that subject A gives to a questionnaire should have no influence on the response of subject B. The fact that co-ed X chose red as her favorite color should not influence co-ed Y's choice, etc. Independence of individual observations also means that a given individual can be represented only once in an analysis. Two encounters of the same person in the data cannot, of course, be independent observations.
2 Chi square must be limited to frequency (or counting) kinds of data. Sometimes a category is defined by a measurement, e.g., all students

between IQs 100 and 110, but these people within a category are counted for the data that are to be analysed. Measurements themselves cannot be analysed by chi square. For example, it is not legitimate to establish $f_o - f_e$ by comparing children's IQs with the average for a defined class.

3   The sum of the expected frequencies must equal the sum of the actual frequencies.

4   As noted earlier, with 1 degree of freedom no expected frequency should be less than 5, unless Yates's correction is applied. If we have more than 1 degree of freedom, one small cell may not distort the results markedly. If cell categories can be reasonably combined to eliminate small cell expectancies, this alternative may be considered. However, a posteriori manipulations tend to deteriorate experimental sophistication.

PROBLEMS

1   A school social worker wished to see if absence from class is tied to social class standing. He went to the school attendance records for the semester and made up the following table of persons who had been absent:

	Absence		
	1 day	2–5 days	More than 5 days
Middle class	25	12	5
Lower class	20	10	8

Are the social classes independent in their attendance behavior?

2   A very obscure item was placed in a history test. The correct answer to the question could only be found in a footnote of a reserve book. The instructor decided that if the class had not read the foot-

note, their responses should be equally distributed across the four multiple-choice alternatives. If the class had read the footnote, the distribution of frequencies would not be random. The number of times each alternative was chosen is given below. Decide whether the class may have read the footnote.

Alternative	A	B	C	D
Number of times chosen	7	17	9	11

3   A student group wished to poll the student body to see if students generally preferred lecture or discussion-type classes. They believed that high achievers may look at the problem differently than low achievers, and so they divided the group on the basis of the previous semester's grade point average. The obtained data were these:

Achiever Status	Preferred Lecture	Preferred Discussion
Above 2.5	10	10
Below 2.5	16	4

Is preference for type of class independent of academic achievement?

The Sign Test

An English teacher has divided his class into two groups, matching individuals in group A with those in group B on a pretest of knowledge of parts of speech. Group A then practices diagramming sentences while group B writes stories and evaluates one another's themes. At the end of a 6-week period a posttest of parts of speech is a gain given. Does one group now achieve better than the other?

This problem looks like a correlated *t*-test situation, but if we cannot meet the basic parametric assumptions of *t*, we can apply the sign test. If the groups are equal in achievement, for each member in A that surpassed his matched partner, there should also be a member of B who surpassed his partner. The sign test then merely counts the number of cases in one group who exceed their matched partners and compares this with the number of persons in the second group who exceed their matched partners. A's who surpass B's or B's who surpass A's will be a randomly determined event, like heads or tails on a coin toss.

The basic procedure for the sign test is as follows. Let us use the data in Table 11.5 for illustration. Here we see scores for groups A and B, arranged

Table 11.5 Posttest Results of an English Test for 12 Pairs of Subjects in Grade 12 Who Were Matched on a Pretest

Group A	Group B	Sign (A − B)
21	16	+
10	14	−
14	8	+
21	13	+
28	10	+
19	19	0
14	17	−
12	11	+
11	13	−
18	18	0

so that matched partners are side by side. Then for each pair we subtract B from A (we get the same results if we subtract A from B); and if A is larger than B, we assign that pair of individuals a plus; if B is larger than A, the pair gets a minus. If our groups have changed about equally, the pluses and minuses will be randomly distributed around a median of zero. Our null hypothesis is therefore that the median difference is zero. If there are con- siderably more of one sign than the other, the distribution of differences is clearly not random, and the hypothesis of equal change in the two groups must be rejected.

The null hypothesis is tested, when there are 10 or fewer cases, by use of the binomial expansion* with $p = .5$ and N equal to the number of pairs observed. In Table 11.5 we had 10 matched pairs; 5 of these were assigned pulses; 3, minuses; and 2, zeros. We drop the zero pairs and deal with an N of 8.

By chance alone we would expect 4 pluses and 4 minuses from the 8 pairs with differences beyond zero. The question we now ask is: Do the 5 pluses differ significantly from our chance value of 4? We now find the probability of getting 5 pluses in a binomial expansion, where p is .5. We can do this by expanding the binomial $(p + q)^8$, or we can read the values from Pascal's triangle, Table 8.1, and compute the probability of getting 5 or more pluses. The line in Pascal's triangle where N is 8 reads: 1, 8, 28, 56, 70, 56, 28, 8, 1, which sums to 256 individuals. Since the median (70) is the point where p is .50, that is, 4 pluses out of 8, we move to the right and find that 56 would represent the number of times out of 256 we would expect to get 5 pluses out of 8; 28 times we should get 6 out of 8, 8 times we should get 7 pluses, and 1 time we should get 8 pluses out of 8 chances. Thus, to determine the probability of getting 5 or more pluses out of 8, we would add $56 + 28 + 8 + 1$ and divide this sum by the total of 256. The resulting probability would be .36. If we set our criterion points, as we have in previous tests, at the .05 or .01 point, we see that our value of .36 is far from significant. We thus accept the null hypothesis and in fact say that we very easily could have obtained 5 pluses out of 8 on a chance basis alone. Therefore, we have no basis for concluding that one group progressed further than the other during the training weeks.

We agreed that we would use the binomial expansion to determine significance if the number of pairs being observed is 10 or less. If there are more than 10 pairs, we may use the normal curve as an approximation of the probabilities. The necessary z values are found with a mean of $.5N$ and a standard deviation of $\sqrt{N(.25)}$. The z value for a given number of pluses (X) would then be

$$z = \frac{(X \mp .5) - .5N}{\sqrt{N(.25)}} \qquad \textbf{11.2}$$

If the number of pluses is *more* than $.5N$, we would use $X - .5$; if the pluses are *less* than $.5N$, we would use $X + .5$ in computing z. This procedure corrects for the discontinuity of the data. For example, the lower limit of the interval

---

* The reader may wish to consult Chap. 8 for a review of probability as it is associated with the binomial expansion.

that represents 5 pluses out of 8 is actually 4.5.   Thus $5 - .5$ includes the entire interval represented by 5.

Having computed our z value, we can consult a table of areas under the normal curve to determine the proportion of samples that would have more pluses than our obtained number.   Either a one-tailed test or a two-tailed test may be applied, depending upon the nature of our hypothesis.

PROBLEMS

1   Fourteen students were given a test and 30 minutes later again given the same test to see if practice actually influenced their scores. The results of the pretests and posttests are below.   Using a two-tailed test at the .05 level, apply the sign test of significance to these data.

Pretest	Posttest
109	149
108	107
108	108
103	138
103	101
99	98
94	129
94	130
94	91
91	139
91	91
89	87
88	134
71	119

2   Using the data given in Prob. 1, compute a $\Sigma(X_{pre} - X_{post})/N_{pairs}$ for the plus differences, and again for the minus differences.   Does the relative size of these two means compare favorably with your test of significance?   What does this say about the strength of the sign test in reflecting magnitude of differences?

The Median Test

The median test is a nonparametric procedure which is used to test the hypothesis that two or more groups come from populations which have the same median. Suppose we have two reading groups in Miss Dexter's fourth-grade class. We want to compare reading group A's reading ability with reading group B's ability. We give reading tests to both groups to determine their status. Now if groups A and B are both from populations with a common median, we can combine them to get the best estimate of that median—we shall call it the *grand median*. We can now actually count the number of cases above, and the number below, the grand median in A, and the number of cases above and below the grand median in B. If A and B are indeed from populations with common medians, 50 per cent of each group should fall above the grand median and 50 per cent below. These then are our expected frequencies for each group above and below the grand median. Applying the chi-square method, we can compare the actual frequencies in these segments with their expected values.

An example may illuminate the procedure. Let us return to Miss Dexter's reading groups and look at their records. We find that for the 6-week period the class has made the scores in reading comprehension recorded in Table 11.6. The grand median is found by use of the frequency distribution of Table 11.7 which combines both groups. The grand median, computed in the manner described in Chap. 3, is 18.5.

Table 11.6 Gain Scores for Reading Speed
Achieved by Two Groups of Students

Group A	Group B
15	22
21	21
18	19
14	23
16	19
21	22
15	17
18	19
20	17
17	16

Table 11.7   A Frequency Distribution of Combined
Groups from Table 11.6 to Be Used
for Computing the Grand Median

X	f
23	1
22	2
21	3
20	1
19	3
18	2
17	3
16	2
15	2
14	1

We now count the scores that appear above and below the grand median
for group A and the scores above and below the grand median for group B.
The result of this classification would be a typical contingency table as used
for chi-square analyses and would look like this:

	Group A	Group B
Above	3	7
Below	7	3

Applying chi square to these data, with an expected frequency of half of each
of groups A and B above and half below the grand median, we would have

$$\frac{(3 - 5)^2}{5} = .80$$

$$\frac{(7 - 5)^2}{5} = .80$$

$$\frac{(7 - 5)^2}{5} = .80$$

$$\frac{(3 - 5)^2}{5} = .80$$

$$\chi^2 = \overline{3.20}$$

With 1 degree of freedom, $(r - 1)(c - 1)$, we look this value up in the chi-square table (Table V in Appendix C) and find that it is not significant at the .05 level.

The median test can also be applied to more than two groups.   The same general procedure applies.   First we combine all groups and compute a grand median.   Then for each group we count the number above and below the grand median and compute a chi-square test with 50 per cent of each group expected above, and 50 per cent below, the grand median.   In our example above we had equal-sized groups; however, this is not a requirement for the median test.   We may proceed as usual even though the observed groups differ in number.

PROBLEMS

1   A curriculum supervisor wished to test the advantage of a new procedure of teaching mathematics in grade 6.   There are four rooms of children in the sixth grade; half are randomly assigned to take method A, half method B.   After 6 weeks their scores on an arithmetic test are as follows.   Test the hypothesis that the two groups are from populations with common medians.

A	B
28	29
27	26
27	24
25	22
25	21
25	20
24	20
23	19
20	19
20	19
19	18
18	18
15	17

2   A psychologist is studying a new drug called *Larnin* for its effect on the ability to learn.   He assigned 32 subjects to three groups.

Group A got one grain of Larnin; B got two grains; and C got an inert powder. Each group was then asked to study a list of nonsense words for 10 minutes, after which they were tested for the number of words learned. Their scores are given below. Test the hypothesis that all three groups are from populations with a common median.

A	B	C
10	11	12
9	11	12
8	10	11
8	10	11
7	8	9
6	5	8
6	5	8
6	5	7
5	4	5
3	4	5
	3	5

Summary

We are often faced with the problem of dealing with data which do not fit the assumptions necessary for employing parametric tests such as t and F. Therefore, a variety of nonparametric tests have been devised for the analysis of such data.

Three nonparametric procedures are adequate for dealing with the majority of problems. Chi square handles frequency data in which we have sorted cases into defined categories and wish to see if the observed frequencies depart significantly from frequencies that would be expected from a given hypothesis about the way cases will be sorted. The sign test deals with paired sets of data which were collected under different circumstances. If the differences between the two sets of data are randomly distributed, the median difference between the pairs of scores will be zero. The sign test, then, tests the hypothesis that the obtained pair differences are zero. The third procedure, the median test, says that if several samples of individuals all come from populations with a common median, each sample should have

50 per cent of its cases above and 50 per cent below the grand median of the combined groups. We then can count for each group the number of cases that actually do fall above and below the grand median and test these observed frequencies against the expected 50-50 split of frequencies in each group by the chi-square procedure.

It should be noted that generally speaking parametric tests are more powerful than nonparametric tests in terms of accepting true hypotheses and rejecting false ones. That is, conclusions based on parametric tests are more reliable than those based on nonparametric tests. So when the data meet the assumptions of parametrics, parametric devices should be applied. However, for the many situations which do not fit these assumptions, nonparametric devices are very useful.

PROBLEM

1　In the following situations decide which procedure—chi square, the sign test, or the median test—is the appropriate technique for analysis. (We are assuming in each case that the data do not meet the assumptions of a parametric test.)

a　I have a group of kindergarten children who are to be used to test some reading-readiness materials. I give them a pretest on reading readiness and a posttest. I want to see if they have changed significantly from pretest to posttest.

b　I have randomly assigned three groups of emotionally disturbed children to three treatments. I have a psychiatrist rank the members of the total group on adjustment after 6 weeks of treatment. I wish to see if the effects of the treatments are different.

c　I wish to know if women's opinions about the death-penalty laws are independent of men's opinions. I ask a group of women and a group of men whether they are in favor of, opposed to, or undecided about the death-penalty law.

d　I wish to see if there is a difference between fathers and their sons in the amount of anxiety they show in regard to test taking. I attach a galvanometer to the arm of each subject, then announce that I am going to give him an intelligence test. The galvanometer reading will be my measure of anxiety, and I will show one set of readings for fathers, one set for their sons.

Appendix **A**

Review of
Arithmetic
and Algebraic
Processes*

Since a basic knowledge of algebraic processes is salient to successful progress in statistical methods, a few basic rules for computation, readily available, would appear to be important aids to the student. These rules, with illustrations and problems (answered on pages 239–241), are presented below.

I. Order of Operations

Purpose Suppose we have the following situation to deal with: $6 + 9 \div 2 \times 4 = ?$ Is the answer 28, 24, 42, 6.8? These answers result from completing the required operations in different orders of adding, multiplying, and dividing. The purpose of this section is to prescribe procedures for carrying out basic arithmetic with numbers and fractions so that all computers will arrive at a common and correct answer.

Rules

1a When both multiplication and addition (or subtraction) are called for in a computational procedure, the multiplication should be done

* For a more detailed presentation the student should see Helen Walker, "Mathematics Essential for Elementary Statistics," rev. ed., p. 382, Holt, Rinehart and Winston, Inc., New York, 1951.

first, unless parentheses tell us otherwise. Therefore, $10 + 5 \times 4 = 30$, but $(10 + 5) \times 4 = 60$; $2 \times 10 - 5 = 15$, but $2 \times (10 - 5) = 10$.

1b When both division and addition (or subtraction) are called for, the division is done first, unless parentheses tell us otherwise. Therefore, $10 + 4 \div 2 = 12$ but $(10 + 4) \div 2 = 7$; $15 \div 5 - 3 = 0$, but $15 \div (5 - 3) = 7.5$.

1c When both multiplication and division are called for in one computational process, parentheses must be used to illustrate the order. Therefore, $20 \times 6 \div 2$ is not acceptable, but $20 \times (6 \div 2)$ or $(20 \times 6) \div 2$ is acceptable.

2 In the situation where an expression enclosed in parentheses is either multiplied or divided by a term outside the parentheses, the expression outside is distributed over all terms inside the parentheses according to the process (multiplication or division) indicated. This is called the *distributive law*. (Also note rule 7c.) Therefore

$$4(7 + 3) = (28 + 12) = 40$$
$$\tfrac{1}{2}(8 - 4) = (4 - 2) = 2$$
$$X(Y + Z) = XY + XZ$$
$$\frac{1}{X}(Y + Z) = \frac{(Y + Z)}{X} = \frac{Y}{X} + \frac{Z}{X}$$
$$\left(\frac{\Sigma X}{N}\right)^2 = \frac{(\Sigma X)^2}{N^2}$$

3 Multiplying or dividing both the numerator and the denominator of a fraction by the same number does not change the relationship represented by the fraction; adding a number to, or subtracting it from, both the numerator and denominator does alter the basic relationship represented by the fraction. Therefore

$$\frac{1}{2} = \frac{2}{4} = \frac{3}{6} \quad \text{and} \quad \frac{x}{y} = \frac{ax}{ay} = \frac{azx}{azy}$$

where a and z are constants, but

$$\frac{1}{2} \neq \frac{2+1}{2+2} \quad \text{and} \quad \frac{x}{y} \neq \frac{a+x}{a+y}$$

4 To add or subtract two fractions, both fractions must be in the same denomination; that is, they must have common denominators. Therefore

$$\frac{1}{3} + \frac{1}{2} = \frac{2}{6} + \frac{3}{6} = \frac{5}{6} \quad \text{and} \quad \frac{a}{x} + \frac{b}{y} = \frac{ay}{xy} + \frac{bx}{xy} = \frac{ay + bx}{xy}$$

5 To multiply two fractions, we simply multiply the two numerators and then the two denominators. Therefore

$$\frac{2}{3}\left(\frac{2}{5}\right) = \frac{4}{15} \qquad \left(\frac{a}{x}\right)\left(\frac{b}{y}\right) = \frac{ab}{xy}$$

6 To divide one fraction by another one, invert the divisor and multiply it times the dividend. Therefore

$$\frac{2}{3} \div \frac{2}{5} = \frac{2}{3} \times \frac{5}{2} = \frac{10}{6} = 1\frac{2}{3} \qquad \frac{a}{x} \div \frac{b}{y} = \left(\frac{a}{x}\right)\left(\frac{y}{b}\right) = \frac{ay}{bx}$$

Problems

1 Complete the designated operations:

a $12 \times 7 + 4 \times 6 - 1 =$ b $5 + 12 \div 2 - 3 =$
c $(5 \times 6) \div 3 + 7 =$ d $3(4 + 6) =$

e $a(x + 2y) =$ f $i^2\left[\Sigma fd^2 - \frac{(\Sigma fd)^2}{N}\right] =$

2 Which of the following terms stated as equal are in fact not equal:

a $(8 \times 4) + 3 = 8 \times (4 + 3)$ b $(7 \div 2)4 = 7 \div (2 \times 4)$

c $(ab) + x = a(b + x)$ d $\frac{a}{b} = \frac{na}{nb}$

e $\frac{\Sigma x}{N} = \frac{N\Sigma x}{N^2}$

3 Complete the designated operations:

a $\frac{2}{3} \times \frac{7}{8} =$ b $\frac{a}{b} \cdot \frac{x}{y} =$

c $\frac{1}{N}\left(\frac{\Sigma X^2}{N}\right) =$ d $\frac{2}{3} \div \frac{1}{4} =$

e $\frac{x}{y} \div \frac{a}{b} =$ f $\frac{2}{3} + \frac{3}{4} =$

g $\frac{zx}{y} - \frac{a}{b} =$

II. Symbols

Purpose The purpose of this section is to review some common symbols and the operations which they indicate. The symbols used in algebra and statistics are merely shorthand ways of stating quantitative values, processes, or relationships.

Rules

7a   Alphabetic symbols usually stand for numbers.   Therefore, N usually means the number of observations made, X usually stands for a raw score of some kind, etc.

7b   Since there are only 26 letters in the alphabet (52 if we count capitals and small letters), we occasionally run out of letters to represent numbers.   We save letters by subscripting.   A subscript is a number or symbol which tells us "which one" of the quantities in a given class is being considered.   Therefore, X_1 would indicate the first number in the group of numbers called X; X_2 would be the second one, etc.   For example, let us use IQ as the condition to be labeled X, and let us suppose we have five children's IQs to deal with.   Then X_1 would be the first child's IQ; X_2 would be the second child's IQ; and X_5 would be the fifth child's IQ.   Subscripts are adjectives telling which one.

7c   Signs tell us what is to be done with numbers or indicate a relationship between numbers.   The signs for adding, subtracting, multiplying, and dividing are familiar, but signs showing relationships, other than the equals sign, are not so common.   Some of these are:

1 $<$ means less than; $a < b$ means a is less than b.

2 $>$ means more than; $a > b$ means a is more than b.

3 $\leq$ means equal to or less than; $a \leq b$ means a is equal to or less than b.

4 $\geq$ means equal to or more than; $a \geq b$ means a is equal to or more than b.

5 $\neq$ means not equal; $a \neq b$ means a and b are not equal.

6 Σ means the sum of; ΣX means the sum of all the X values. $\sum_{i=1}^{n} X_i$ means the sum of all X values from X_1 to the nth, or last, X. If this designation is not used, it is assumed that all X values are to be summed.   The above designation could be written $\sum_{i=1}^{7} X_i$, in which case we add only the first 7 X's.   The value of the procedure lies in situations where we are using less than all the cases available, and that will seldom occur in this book.   Therefore, we shall use ΣX to mean the summation of all X values, ΣY to mean the summation of all Y values, etc.

7d   Brackets and parentheses are used to single out operations that may be thought of as a single value, and as a result they indicate the order of many processes. Therefore, $(5 + 4)(6) + 1 = (9)(6) + 1$, or $(30 + 24) + 1$. It is clear that if addition (or subtraction) is the process within the parentheses, it may be done first, or the multiplication (or division) may be done first as long as we follow the distributive law described in rule 2. Thus, $2(4 + 1) = 2(5)$ or $(8 + 2) = 10$, and

$$\frac{(X_1 + X_2 + X_3)}{N} = \frac{X_1}{N} + \frac{X_2}{N} + \frac{X_3}{N} \quad \text{and}$$

$$\frac{a(X_1 + X_2)}{N} = \frac{aX_1 + aX_2}{N} = \frac{aX_1}{N} + \frac{aX_2}{N}$$

Problems

1 We have the following IQs for four boys: Joe 105, John 110, Dick 100, Tom 107.
   a If we let N stand for the number of observations, what does N equal?
   b What is the value of X_3? X_1?
   c What is the value of $\Sigma X/N$?
   d What is the meaning of the following statements?
      (1) $X_2 > X_1$ (2) $X_3 < X_1$
      (3) $(X_1 + X_2) > (X_3 + X_4)$ (4) $X_1 \neq X_2$
      (5) $A = \Sigma X^2$

2 Which of the following statements are correct?

   a $(a + b)(c) = a + bc$ b $\dfrac{(X - Y)}{2} = \dfrac{X}{2} - \dfrac{Y}{2}$
   c $(N - 1)(N) = N^2 - N$
   d $\Sigma[X^2 - 2XM + M^2] = \Sigma X^2 - 2\Sigma XM + \Sigma M^2$

3 State in words what each of the following equations says in symbols. X stands for IQ scores; N is the number of observations; C is a constant equal to 50; $\bar{X}$ is the average.

   a $\bar{X} = \dfrac{\Sigma X}{N}$ b $\dfrac{\Sigma(X - C)}{N} = \bar{X} - C$

   c $\dfrac{\Sigma(XC)}{N} = \bar{X}C$ d $\dfrac{\Sigma(X - \bar{X})}{N} = 0$

   e $\displaystyle\sum_{i=1}^{4} X_i \neq \sum_{i=5}^{8} X_i$

4 Put into algebraic shorthand the following statements:
   a The sum of the ages of 10 boys, divided by the number of boys observed, is the average age for these boys.

b   If we divide each of four numbers by a fifth number, then add these four results, we have a quantity which is equal to the sum of the four numbers divided by the fifth one.

c   The sum of four numbers, each of which was squared before summing, minus the sum of the numbers, the quantity of which is squared and then divided by the number of numbers, is equal to Σx^2.

III.   Positive and Negative Numbers

Purpose   This section reviews computations with positive and negative numbers.

Rules

8a   If numbers are to be added and they have the same sign, add the absolute value of the numbers and sign the answer with the common sign.

8b   If numbers are to be added and they have unlike signs, subtract the smaller from the larger and sign the result with the sign of the larger number.

8c   When we subtract one number from another number, we change the sign of the number to be subtracted and proceed as in (a) or (b) accordingly.   Therefore, $7 - (-4) = 7 + 4$, or 11; $-10 - (-3) = -7$.

8d   If we multiply a positive number by a negative number, the answer is a negative number.   Therefore, $+8 \times (-4) = -32$; $-7 \times 6 = -42$.

8e   When we multiply two numbers with like signs, whether positive or negative, the answer should be signed positively.   Therefore, $-7 \times (-3) = 21$; $7 \times 3 = 21$.

8f   The rules for multiplication apply also to division; unlike signs between divisor and dividend produce a negative quotient, whereas like signs between a divisor and dividend produce a positive quotient.

Problems

Find the answers to the following:

1	$(-8) + (+4) - (-1) =$	**2**	$(+7) - (+3) + (-6) =$
3	$(-6) + (-2) - (+1) =$	**4**	$(-7) - (+4) + (-6) =$
5	$-2(+6) =$	**6**	$-4(-7) =$
7	$(-18) \div (-6) =$	**8**	$(+24) \div (-4) =$

IV. Functions

> **Purpose** This section illustrates methods of dealing with two conditions, one of which changes in a prescribed manner with every given change in the other. When this happens, we say one condition is a function of the other.

Rules

9a A variable is a quantity which may take any one of a set of values, this set being termed the *range of the variable.*

9b One variable is called a *function f* of the other if for every value of the one, there is one or more corresponding values of the other. Therefore, in the equation $y = bx$, y and x are variables, and y is a function of x, that is, $y = f(x)$. The y is called the dependent variable, x the independent variable, and b is a constant; that is, it takes only one value.

9c Functions can be graphed by arbitrarily inserting values for the independent variable (x) and solving the equation for the dependent variable (y). Therefore, if $y = bx$ and $b = 2$,

If X is	0	1	2	3	4
Then Y is	0	2	4	6	8

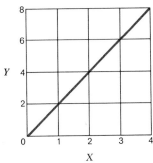

When the graph of a function is a straight line, we call it a *linear function.* When both variables appear in the first power, that is, they are neither squared nor cubed, etc., the function is linear. Therefore, $y = 3x + 2$, $y = 3x$, $y = .7x - 3$ are all linear functions.

9d The horizontal axis on a bivariate (two-variable) graph is often called the *x axis,* or the *abscissa;* the vertical axis is called the *y axis,* or the *ordinate.* Linear functions cross the y axis at the point where x is zero. This point is called the *y intercept.* In the graph shown in rule 9c, the y intercept is zero, but it need not always be.

9e When the independent variable (x) is multiplied by a constant, such as $y = 2x$, where the constant is 2, that constant indicates the slope of the line in a bivariate graph, and tells us how many units y increases for each unit increase in x. If the slope is positive, the line will run from lower left to upper right; if the slope is negative, the line will run from upper left to lower right.

Problems

1   Given $y = 3x + 2$: What is the independent variable? What is the dependent variable? What is the slope? What is the value of the y intercept (when $x = 0$, $y = ?$)?

2   Which of the following show a linear rather than curvilinear function?

   a $y = 6x$ b $m = 2n^2 + 1$
   c $y^2 = 4x - 3$ d $r = 4s + 5$

3   For each of the following pairs of equations choose the one in which the slope of the line, in relation to the abscissa, is the greater.

   a $y = 2x$ $y = 4x + 1$
   b $y = 6x - 1$ $y = 3x + 6$
   c $y = +4x - 5$ $y = +5x + 2$

V. Managing Linear Equations

Purpose   The purpose of this section is to describe basic rules for handling linear equations.

Rules

10a   The basic equality of any equation is not destroyed if the same number is added to each side of the equation or if the same number is subtracted from each side. Therefore, if $4x = 7$, $4x + 2 = 7 + 2$, and $4x - 2 = 7 - 2$.

A special case of this rule may be illustrated by the following problems. If $2x + 4 = 6$, then (subtracting 4 from both sides of the equation) $2x + 4 - 4 = 6 - 4$, or $2x = 6 - 4$. In effect we have transferred the 4 in the original equation ($2x + 4 = 6$) across the equals sign, changing its sign to minus. Again $3y - 2 = 4$, and (adding 2 to each side) $3y - 2 + 2 = 4 + 2$, or $3y = 4 + 2$. Once more we have, in effect, simply moved a quantity from one side of the equation to the other by changing its sign. It is generally true, then, that any term in an equation can be transposed from one side of the equals sign to the other if the sign of that term is changed.

10b The basic equality of any equation is not destroyed if each side of the equation is multiplied by the same number, or if each side is divided by the same number. Therefore, if $4x = 7$, then $2(4x) = 2(7)$, and $4x/2 = \frac{7}{2}$.

Problems

1 $3x = 8; \ 2(3x) =$

2 $4y - 5 = 12; \ (4y - 5)/2 =$

3 $3a = 4b + 1; \ 3a + 4 =$

4 $7m + 3 = 14; \ 7m =$

5 $a = y^2/x; \ ax =$

6 $NS_1S_2r = \Sigma xy; \ r =$

VI. Multiplying Binomials

Purpose This section describes multiplication of the binomial by another binomial.

Rules

11a To square a given value we merely multiply it by itself. Therefore, to square a binomial, such as $(x + y)$, we would multiply it by the same quantity, thus $(x + y)(x + y)$. To multiply one binomial by another, we first multiply each term in one by each term in the other and then collect terms:

$$
\begin{array}{l}
x + y \\
\underline{x + y} \\
(x)(x) + xy \\
 + xy + (y)(y) \\
\hline
x^2 + 2xy + y^2
\end{array}
\qquad
\begin{array}{l}
x - 2 \\
\underline{x - 2} \\
x^2 - 2x \\
 - 2x + 4 \\
\hline
x^2 - 4x + 4
\end{array}
$$

11b The quantities $(x + y)$ and $(x + y)$ are called the *factors* of $(x^2 + 2xy + y^2)$; that is, they are the quantities which multiplied together yield the latter value. In this case $(x + y)$ is also the square root, but a factor is not always a square root. When we multiply $(x + 1)(x + 2)$ and get $(x^2 + 3x + 2)$, neither $(x + 1)$ nor $(x + 2)$ is a square root.

Problems

1 $(x + y)^2 =$

2 $(x - 4)^2 =$

3 $(2x - y)^2 =$

4 What are the factors of $x^2 + 2xy + y^2$?

5 What are the factors of $x^2 + 5x + 6$?

Appendix **B**

Mathematical
Developments
of Procedures*

1 Development of the Procedure for Computing the Variance σ^2 and the Standard Deviation σ When Deviations Are Taken from a Point in the Distribution Other Than the Mean

Let GM be the guessed, or assumed, mean of the distribution. Then the assumed deviation x_i' of any given score X will be $X - GM = x_i'$, so $X = x_i' + GM$. (We denote this deviation score with a prime to distinguish it from a deviation from the actual mean of the distribution.)

Now let $g = \bar{X} - GM$, where $\bar{X}$ is the actual mean of the distribution. Then $\bar{X} = g + GM$. We have in this book symbolized the deviation of a score from its mean as $X - \bar{X} = x$.

So

$$X_i - \bar{X} = x_i' + GM - (g + GM)$$
$$= x_i' + GM - g - GM$$
$$= x_i' - g$$

thus

$$x_i = x_i' - g$$

and

$$x_i' = x_i + g$$

---

* It is assumed that the student has read the related chapters in the text before attempting these derivations. Pertinent symbols are defined in those chapters.

Now squaring, $x_i'^2 = x_i^2 + 2x_ig + g^2$, and summing all squared terms, we have

$$\Sigma x_i'^2 = \Sigma x_i^2 + 2\Sigma x_ig + \Sigma g^2$$

Now the term $2\Sigma x_ig$ is zero, since the sum of the deviations around the mean (Σx_i) is always zero, making this whole term zero. And since g is a constant, $\Sigma g^2 = Ng^2$. Our equation now becomes

$$\Sigma x_i'^2 = \Sigma x_i^2 + Ng^2$$

where N is the number of cases, and so

$$\Sigma x_i^2 = \Sigma x_i'^2 - Ng^2$$

Now dividing both sides by N, we have

$$\frac{\Sigma x_i^2}{N} = \frac{\Sigma x_i'^2}{N} - \frac{Ng^2}{N}$$

or

$$\frac{\Sigma x_i^2}{N} = \frac{\Sigma x_i'^2}{N} - g^2 \qquad\qquad \textbf{B1}$$

But $g = \bar{X} - \mathrm{GM}$, and since $\bar{X} = \Sigma X/N$, we have

$$g = \frac{\Sigma X}{N} - \mathrm{GM}$$

Now $x' = X - \mathrm{GM}$ and $\Sigma x' = \Sigma X - \Sigma \mathrm{GM}$, or $\Sigma x' = \Sigma X - N\mathrm{GM}$, and dividing both sides by N, we have

$$\frac{\Sigma x'}{N} = \frac{\Sigma X}{N} - \frac{N\mathrm{GM}}{N} = \bar{X} - \mathrm{GM} = g$$

thus

$$g = \frac{\Sigma x'}{N}$$

Now substituting this g value in Eq. B1,

$$\frac{\Sigma x_i^2}{N} = \frac{\Sigma x_i'^2}{N} - \left(\frac{\Sigma x'}{N}\right)^2$$

and since σ^2, the variance of a set of scores, is defined as $\Sigma x_i^2/N$, the variance also is

$$\sigma^2 = \frac{\Sigma x_i'^2}{N} - \left(\frac{\Sigma x'}{N}\right)^2$$

and the standard deviation is the square root of the variance, and so

$$\sigma = \sqrt{\frac{\Sigma x'^2}{N} - \left(\frac{\Sigma x'}{N}\right)^2}$$

We began by stating that x' was in score units. If we were dealing with grouped data in intervals, then $x' = id$, where the d indicates the deviation of an interval from the interval containing the guessed mean, and i is the score width of the interval. Then:

$$\frac{\Sigma x'}{N} = i\,\frac{\Sigma d}{N}$$

and

$$\frac{\Sigma x'^2}{N} = i^2\,\frac{\Sigma d^2}{N}$$

Therefore,

$$\frac{\Sigma x'^2}{N} - \left(\frac{\Sigma x'}{N}\right)^2 = i^2\,\frac{\Sigma d^2}{N} - \left(\frac{i\Sigma d}{N}\right)^2 = i^2\left[\frac{\Sigma d^2}{N} - \left(\frac{\Sigma d}{N}\right)^2\right]$$

And since the sum of all deviations of scores at any one deviation point is fd, where f is the frequency of scores at that point in the distribution, $\Sigma d^2 = \Sigma fd^2$ and $\Sigma d = \Sigma fd$. And so

$$\sigma^2 = i^2\left[\frac{\Sigma fd^2}{N} - \left(\frac{\Sigma fd}{N}\right)^2\right]$$

which can be rewritten

$$i^2\left[\frac{\Sigma fd^2 - \dfrac{(\Sigma fd)^2}{N}}{N}\right]$$

and

$$\sigma = i\sqrt{\frac{\Sigma fd^2}{N} - \left(\frac{\Sigma fd}{N}\right)^2} = \sqrt{\frac{i^2\left[\Sigma fd^2 - \dfrac{(\Sigma fd)^2}{N}\right]}{N}}$$

as found in Chap. 5.

2 Development of the Raw-score Formula for the Product-moment Correlation r_{xy} Beginning with the Basic z-score Formula

A group of scores X are to be correlated with a second group of scores Y.

$$r_{xy} = \frac{\Sigma z_x z_y}{N} \qquad z_x = \frac{X - \bar{X}}{\sigma_x} \qquad z_y = \frac{Y - \bar{Y}}{\sigma_y}$$

so

$$r_{xy} = \frac{\Sigma(X - \bar{X})(Y - \bar{Y})}{N\sigma_x\sigma_y}$$

$$\sigma_x = \sqrt{\frac{\Sigma X^2 - \frac{(\Sigma X)^2}{N}}{N}} \quad \text{and} \quad \sigma_y = \sqrt{\frac{\Sigma Y^2 - \frac{(\Sigma Y)^2}{N}}{N}}$$

Substituting, we have

$$r_{xy} = \frac{\Sigma(X - \bar{X})(Y - \bar{Y})}{N\sqrt{\frac{\left[\Sigma X^2 - \frac{(\Sigma X)^2}{N}\right]\left[\Sigma Y^2 - \frac{(\Sigma Y)^2}{N}\right]}{N \cdot N}}} \tag{B2}$$

Now let us deal only with the numerator of Eq. B2. For the development of the formula, we look at the numerator.

$$\Sigma(X - \bar{X})(Y - \bar{Y}) = \Sigma(XY - X\bar{Y} - \bar{X}Y + \bar{X}\bar{Y})$$
$$= \Sigma XY - \Sigma X\bar{Y} - \Sigma Y\bar{X} + \Sigma \bar{X}\bar{Y}$$

Now

$$\bar{X} = \frac{\Sigma X}{N} \quad \bar{Y} = \frac{\Sigma Y}{N} \quad \text{and} \quad \Sigma \bar{X}\bar{Y} = N\frac{\Sigma X\Sigma Y}{N \cdot N}$$

So, substituting, we have

$$\Sigma XY - \Sigma X\bar{Y} - \Sigma Y\bar{X} + \Sigma \bar{X}\bar{Y} = \Sigma XY - \frac{\Sigma X\Sigma Y}{N} - \frac{\Sigma Y\Sigma X}{N} + \frac{\Sigma X\Sigma Y}{N}$$

and collecting terms, we find that the numerator of Eq. B2 becomes

$$\Sigma XY - \frac{\Sigma X\Sigma Y}{N}$$

Now taking $N \cdot N$ out from under the radical in the denominator of Eq. B2, it becomes $1/N$, and we can cancel it with the N that is already outside the radical. And now with the new numerator and denominator, formula B2 becomes

$$r_{xy} = \frac{\Sigma XY - \frac{\Sigma X\Sigma Y}{N}}{\sqrt{\left[\Sigma X^2 - \frac{(\Sigma X)^2}{N}\right]\left[\Sigma Y^2 - \frac{(\Sigma Y)^2}{N}\right]}}$$

3 Development of the Equation for Predicting a Y Score Once an X Score Is Known

The formula for a predicted score Y' is $Y' = a + bX$, where $a = \bar{Y}$ when X is zero and $b =$ the increase in Y with a unit increase in X.   If raw scores are converted to deviation scores, the a value drops out, since the mean of both x and y distributions becomes zero.   So in deviation form the predicted score y' becomes $y' = bx$.

We can now set up the function

$$f = \frac{\Sigma(y - y')^2}{N} = \frac{\Sigma(y - bx)^2}{N}$$

where we have N deviations of the form $(y - y')$ or $(y - bx)$, where $y = Y - \bar{Y}$ and $x = X - \bar{X}$.   These values, when squared, added together, and divided by N, provide a variance of actual scores around the regression line.   This variance can be minimized by a particular choice of b, the value of which can be found by the calculus:

$$f = \frac{\Sigma(y - bx)^2}{N}$$

differentiating with respect to b (x and y held constant).   To illustrate with a general example, with $f = u^n$, the formulas for differentiation* show

$$df = nu^{n-1}\, du$$

Now if

$$f = (a - cx)^2$$
$$u = (a - cx)^2$$
$$du = (0 - c\, dx)$$
$$n = 2 \qquad n - 1 = 1$$

substituting in $df = nu^{n-1}\, du$, we have

$$df = 2(a - cx)(0 - c\, dx)$$

or

$$df = -2c(a - cx)\, dx$$

or

$$\frac{df}{dx} = -2c(a - cx)$$

---

* This procedure may be found in any elementary calculus book.   The student who is not familiar with the calculus is asked to exercise faith at this point.

With the above model the differentiation of the problem at hand is

$$f = \frac{1}{N} \Sigma(y - bx)^2$$

Referring to the above equation, $df = nu^{n-1} du$, placing the constant $1/N$ in evidence, since

$$d(cu) = c \, du$$
$$u = (y - bx)$$
$$du = (0 - x \, db)$$
$$n = 2 \qquad n - 1 = 1$$

Substituting we have

$$df = \frac{1}{N} \Sigma 2(y - bx)(0 - x \, db)$$

or

$$df = \frac{1}{N} \Sigma(-2x)(y - bx) \, db$$

and rearranging,

$$\frac{df}{db} = \frac{-2\Sigma x(y - bx)}{N}$$

which, set equal to zero and divided by -2, produces

$$\frac{\Sigma x(y - bx)}{N} = 0$$

or

$$\frac{\Sigma xy - b\Sigma x^2}{N} = 0$$

and putting each term in the denominator over N, we have

$$\frac{\Sigma xy}{N} - b \frac{\Sigma x^2}{N} = 0$$

Now, if

$$\frac{\Sigma x^2}{N} = \sigma_x{}^2$$

and if

$$z_x = \frac{X - \bar{X}}{\sigma_x} = \frac{x}{\sigma_x}$$

and

$$z_y = \frac{Y - \bar{Y}}{\sigma_y} = \frac{y}{\sigma_y}$$

and

$$r_{xy} = \frac{\Sigma z_x z_y}{N}$$

then

$$r_{xy} = \frac{\Sigma xy}{N\sigma_x \sigma_y}$$

and

$$\frac{\Sigma xy}{N} = r_{xy}\sigma_x \sigma_y$$

Thus,

$$r_{xy}\sigma_x \sigma_y - b\sigma_x^2 = 0$$

Now factoring,

$$\sigma_x(r_{xy}\sigma_y - b\sigma_x) = 0$$

and setting each factor equal to zero, we have

$$\sigma_x = 0 \quad \text{and} \quad r_{xy}\sigma_y - b\sigma_x = 0$$

and

$$b = r_{xy}\frac{\sigma_y}{\sigma_x}$$

Substituting this value for b in the formula $y' = bx$, we have

$$y' = r_{xy}\frac{\sigma_y}{\sigma_x}x$$

where y and x are deviation scores. Converting this formula to raw scores, $x = (X - \bar{X})$ and $y = (Y - \bar{Y})$, we have

$$Y' - \bar{Y} = r\frac{\sigma_y}{\sigma_x}(X - \bar{X})$$

$$Y' = r\frac{\sigma_y}{\sigma_x}(X - \bar{X}) + \bar{Y}$$

4 The Development of the Formula for the Standard Error of Estimate

The standard error of estimate s_{est} is the standard deviation of actual scores Y around their predicted scores Y' in a regression situation. We begin with the variance (standard deviation squared), sometimes called the *residual variance*. It is found like other variances by squaring the deviations around a point, summing them, and dividing by the number N of deviations involved, that is,

$$s_{est}^2 = \frac{\Sigma(Y - Y')^2}{N - 1}$$

Now if both actual and predicted scores are in deviation form, that is, $Y - \bar{Y} = y$ and $Y' - \bar{Y} = y'$, then

$$s_{est}^2 = \frac{\Sigma(y - y')^2}{N - 1}$$

We just saw in the previous derivation that $y' = r(s_y/s_x)x$, and so

$$s_{est}^2 = \frac{\Sigma\left(y - r\dfrac{s_y}{s_x}x\right)^2}{N - 1}$$

and squaring the numerator and putting each term over the denominator, we have

$$s_{est}^2 = \frac{\Sigma y^2}{N - 1} - \frac{\Sigma xy}{N - 1} 2r \frac{s_y}{s_x} + r^2 \frac{s_y^2}{s_x^2} \frac{\Sigma x^2}{N - 1}$$

But

$$\frac{\Sigma y^2}{N - 1} = \sigma_y^2 \quad \text{and} \quad \frac{\Sigma x^2}{N - 1} = \sigma_x^2 \quad \text{and} \quad \frac{\Sigma xy}{N - 1} = r\sigma_x\sigma_y$$

So substituting these values in the previous formula, we have

$$s_{est}^2 = s_y^2 - (rs_xs_y)2r\frac{s_y}{s_x} + r^2\frac{s_y^2}{s_x^2}(s_x^2)$$

$$= s_y^2 - 2r^2s_y^2 + r^2s_y^2$$

$$= s_y^2 - r^2s_y^2$$

$$= s_y^2(1 - r^2)$$

and the standard error then is

$$s_{est} = s_y \sqrt{1 - r^2}$$

Appendix C

Tables

Table I Squares and Square Roots of Numbers from 1 to 1,000

Suggestions for Expanding the Table

The student may increase the flexibility of this table (1) by using the Square column as the Number column and the Number column as the Square-root column and (2) by manipulating the decimal point in the terms in the Number and in the Square-root columns.

If I multiply 4×4 and get 16, then the number I began with, 4, is the square root of 16. Similarly, if I wish the square root of a number beyond 1,000, I may find it, at least to the significant figures necessary for work in this book, by looking in the column labeled Square. Then moving to the left I find the square root of this number in the column labeled Number. For example, suppose I want the square root of 1,300. I move down the Square column until I find a number as near as possible to 1,300. It is 1,296. To the left of 1,296 is 36, which is almost exactly the square root of 1,300. (The exact square root of 1,300 is 36.056. The more precise student may wish to make interpolations to arrive at the exact values; however, in the great majority of problems in this book interpolations will not alter the significant figures involved.)

The square root of 1,300 may also be found by manipulating the decimal point in the number and in its square root. The value of 1,300 is equal to 13×100, and so its square root must be equal to $\sqrt{13} \times \sqrt{100}$, or $\sqrt{13} \times 10$.

Our table contains the square root of 13; it is 3.6056.   And if we multiply this value by 10, we have 36.056, which is the square root of 1,300.

Here is another example.   What is the square root of 47,100?   This number is equal to 471 $\times$ 100, and its square root is $\sqrt{471} \times \sqrt{100}$, or 21.7025 $\times$ 10, or 217.025.

What is the square root of 4.21?   This number is equal to 421 $\times \frac{1}{100}$, and its square root is $\sqrt{421} \times 1/\sqrt{100}$, or 20.5183 $\times \frac{1}{10}$, or 2.05 retaining only two decimal places.

Some practice with the above suggestions should make it unnecessary for the student to have to compute square roots by the long method typically taught in high school mathematics classes.   However, in all cases the student should inspect his figures to see if his square root when multiplied by itself would reasonably be equal to the number for which the root was taken.

Table I   Squares and Square Roots of Numbers from 1 to 1,000*

Number	Square	Square root	Number	Square	Square root
1	1	1.0000	41	16 81	6.4031
2	4	1.4142	42	17 64	6.4807
3	9	1.7321	43	18 49	6.5574
4	16	2.0000	44	19 36	6.6332
5	25	2.2361	45	20 25	6.7082
6	36	2.4495	46	21 16	6.7823
7	49	2.6458	47	22 09	6.8557
8	64	2.8284	48	23 04	6.9282
9	81	3.0000	49	24 01	7.0000
10	1 00	3.1623	50	25 00	7.0711
11	1 21	3.3166	51	26 01	7.1414
12	1 44	3.4641	52	27 04	7.2111
13	1 69	3.6056	53	28 09	7.2801
14	1 96	3.7417	54	29 16	7.3485
15	2 25	3.8730	55	30 25	7.4162
16	2 56	4.0000	56	31 36	7.4833
17	2 89	4.1231	57	32 49	7.5498
18	3 24	4.2426	58	33 64	7.6158
19	3 61	4.3589	59	34 81	7.6811
20	4 00	4.4721	60	36 00	7.7460
21	4 41	4.5826	61	37 21	7.8102
22	4 84	4.6904	62	38 44	7.8740
23	5 29	4.7958	63	39 69	7.9373
24	5 76	4.8990	64	40 96	8.0000
25	6 25	5.0000	65	42 25	8.0623
26	6 76	5.0990	66	43 56	8.1240
27	7 29	5.1962	67	44 89	8.1854
28	7 84	5.2915	68	46 24	8.2462
29	8 41	5.3852	69	47 61	8.3066
30	9 00	5.4772	70	49 00	8.3666
31	9 61	5.5678	71	50 41	8.4261
32	10 24	5.6569	72	51 84	8.4853
33	10 89	5.7446	73	53 29	8.5440
34	11 56	5.8310	74	54 76	8.6023
35	12 25	5.9161	75	56 25	8.6603
36	12 96	6.0000	76	57 76	8.7178
37	13 69	6.0828	77	59 29	8.7750
38	14 44	6.1644	78	60 84	8.8318
39	15 21	6.2450	79	62 41	8.8882
40	16 00	6.3246	80	64 00	8.9443

* By permission from H. Sorenson, "Statistics for Students of Psychology and Education," copyright 1936, McGraw-Hill Book Company, New York.

Table I   Squares and Square Roots of Numbers from 1 to 1,000* (Continued)

Number	Square	Square root	Number	Square	Square root
81	65 61	9.0000	121	1 46 41	11.0000
82	67 24	9.0554	122	1 48 84	11.0454
83	68 89	9.1104	123	1 51 29	11.0905
84	70 56	9.1652	124	1 53 76	11.1355
85	72 25	9.2195	125	1 56 25	11.1803
86	73 96	9.2736	126	1 58 76	11.2250
87	75 69	9.3274	127	1 61 29	11.2694
88	77 44	9.3808	128	1 63 84	11.3137
89	79 21	9.4340	129	1 66 41	11.3578
90	81 00	9.4868	130	1 69 00	11.4018
91	82 81	9.5394	131	1 71 61	11.4455
92	84 64	9.5917	132	1 74 24	11.4891
93	86 49	9.6437	133	1 76 89	11.5326
94	88 36	9.6954	134	1 79 56	11.5758
95	90 25	9.7468	135	1 82 25	11.6190
96	92 16	9.7980	136	1 84 96	11.6619
97	94 09	9.8489	137	1 87 69	11.7047
98	96 04	9.8995	138	1 90 44	11.7473
99	98 01	9.9499	139	1 93 21	11.7898
100	1 00 00	10.0000	140	1 96 00	11.8322
101	1 02 01	10.0499	141	1 98 81	11.8743
102	1 04 04	10.0995	142	2 01 64	11.9164
103	1 06 09	10.1489	143	2 04 49	11.9583
104	1 08 16	10.1980	144	2 07 36	12.0000
105	1 10 25	10.2470	145	2 10 25	12.0416
106	1 12 36	10.2956	146	2 13 16	12.0830
107	1 14 49	10.3441	147	2 16 09	12.1244
108	1 16 64	10.3923	148	2 19 04	12.1655
109	1 18 81	10.4403	149	2 22 01	12.2066
110	1 21 00	10.4881	150	2 25 00	12.2474
111	1 23 21	10.5357	151	2 28 01	12.2882
112	1 25 44	10.5830	152	2 31 04	12.3288
113	1 27 69	10.6301	153	2 34 09	12.3693
114	1 29 96	10.6771	154	2 37 16	12.4097
115	1 32 25	10.7238	155	2 40 25	12.4499
116	1 34 56	10.7703	156	2 43 36	12.4900
117	1 36 89	10.8167	157	2 46 49	12.5300
118	1 39 24	10.8628	158	2 49 64	12.5698
119	1 41 61	10.9087	159	2 52 81	12.6095
120	1 44 00	10.9545	160	2 56 00	12.6491

* By permission from H. Sorenson, "Statistics for Students of Psychology and Education," copyright 1936, McGraw-Hill Book Company, New York.

Table I   Squares and Square Roots of Numbers from 1 to 1,000* (Continued)

Number	Square	Square root	Number	Square	Square root
161	2 59 21	12.6886	201	4 04 01	14.1774
162	2 62 44	12.7279	202	4 08 04	14.2127
163	2 65 69	12.7671	203	4 12 09	14.2478
164	2 68 96	12.8062	204	4 16 16	14.2829
165	2 72 25	12.8452	205	4 20 25	14.3178
166	2 75 56	12.8841	206	4 24 36	14.3527
167	2 78 89	12.9228	207	4 28 49	14.3875
168	2 82 24	12.9615	208	4 32 64	14.4222
169	2 85 61	13.0000	209	4 36 81	14.4568
170	2 89 00	13.0384	210	4 41 00	14.4914
171	2 92 41	13.0767	211	4 45 21	14.5258
172	2 95 84	13.1149	212	4 49 44	14.5602
173	2 99 29	13.1529	213	4 53 69	14.5945
174	3 02 76	13.1909	214	4 57 96	14.6287
175	3 06 25	13.2288	215	4 62 25	14.6629
176	3 09 76	13.2665	216	4 66 56	14.6969
177	3 13 29	13.3041	217	4 70 89	14.7309
178	3 16 84	13.3417	218	4 75 24	14.7648
179	3 20 41	13.3791	219	4 79 61	14.7986
180	3 24 00	13.4164	220	4 84 00	14.8324
181	3 27 61	13.4536	221	4 88 41	14.8661
182	3 31 24	13.4907	222	4 92 84	14.8997
183	3 34 89	13.5277	223	4 97 29	14.9332
184	3 38 56	13.5647	224	5 01 76	14.9666
185	3 42 25	13.6015	225	5 06 25	15.0000
186	3 45 96	13.6382	226	5 10 76	15.0333
187	3 49 69	13.6748	227	5 15 29	15.0665
188	3 53 44	13.7113	228	5 19 84	15.0997
189	3 57 21	13.7477	229	5 24 41	15.1327
190	3 61 00	13.7840	230	5 29 00	15.1658
191	3 64 81	13.8203	231	5 33 61	15.1987
192	3 68 64	13.8564	232	5 38 24	15.2315
193	3 72 49	13.8924	233	5 42 89	15.2643
194	3 76 36	13.9284	234	5 47 56	15.2971
195	3 80 25	13.9642	235	5 52 25	15.3297
196	3 84 16	14.0000	236	5 56 96	15.3623
197	3 88 09	14.0357	237	5 61 69	15.3948
198	3 92 04	14.0712	238	5 66 44	15.4272
199	3 96 01	14.1067	239	5 71 21	15.4596
200	4 00 00	14.1421	240	5 76 00	15.4919

* By permission from H. Sorenson, "Statistics for Students of Psychology and Education," copyright 1936, McGraw-Hill Book Company, New York.

Table I Squares and Square Roots of Numbers from 1 to 1,000* (Continued)

Number	Square	Square root	Number	Square	Square root
241	5 80 81	15.5242	281	7 89 61	16.7631
242	5 85 64	15.5563	282	7 95 24	16.7929
243	5 90 49	15.5885	283	8 00 89	16.8226
244	5 95 36	15.6205	284	8 06 56	16.8523
245	6 00 25	15.6525	285	8 12 25	16.8819
246	6 05 16	15.6844	286	8 17 96	16.9115
247	6 10 09	15.7162	287	8 23 69	16.9411
248	6 15 04	15.7480	288	8 29 44	16.9706
249	6 20 01	15.7797	289	8 35 21	17.0000
250	6 25 00	15.8114	290	8 41 00	17.0294
251	6 30 01	15.8430	291	8 46 81	17.0587
252	6 35 04	15.8745	292	8 52 64	17.0880
253	6 40 09	15.9060	293	8 58 49	17.1172
254	6 45 16	15.9374	294	8 64 36	17.1464
255	6 50 25	15.9687	295	8 70 25	17.1756
256	6 55 36	16.0000	296	8 76 16	17.2047
257	6 60 49	16.0312	297	8 82 09	17.2337
258	6 65 64	16.0624	298	8 88 04	17.2627
259	6 70 81	16.0935	299	8 94 01	17.2916
260	6 76 00	16.1245	300	9 00 00	17.3205
261	6 81 21	16.1555	301	9 06 01	17.3494
262	6 86 44	16.1864	302	9 12 04	17.3781
263	6 91 69	16.2173	303	9 18 09	17.4069
264	6 96 96	16.2481	304	9 24 16	17.4356
265	7 02 25	16.2788	305	9 30 25	17.4642
266	7 07 56	16.3095	306	9 36 36	17.4929
267	7 12 89	16.3401	307	9 42 49	17.5214
268	7 18 24	16.3707	308	9 48 64	17.5499
269	7 23 61	16.4012	309	9 54 81	17.5784
270	7 29 00	16.4317	310	9 61 00	17.6068
271	7 34 41	16.4621	311	9 67 21	17.6352
272	7 39 84	16.4924	312	9 73 44	17.6635
273	7 45 29	16.5227	313	9 79 69	17.6918
274	7 50 76	16.5529	314	9 85 96	17.7200
275	7 56 25	16.5831	315	9 92 25	17.7482
276	7 61 76	16.6132	316	9 98 56	17.7764
277	7 67 29	16.6433	317	10 04 89	17.8045
278	7 72 84	16.6733	318	10 11 24	17.8326
279	7 78 41	16.7033	319	10 17 61	17.8606
280	7 84 00	16.7332	320	10 24 00	17.8885

* By permission from H. Sorenson, "Statistics for Students of Psychology and Education," copyright 1936, McGraw-Hill Book Company, New York.

Table I   Squares and Square Roots of Numbers from 1 to 1,000* (Continued)

Number	Square	Square root	Number	Square	Square root
321	10 30 41	17.9165	361	13 03 21	19.0000
322	10 36 84	17.9444	362	13 10 44	19.0263
323	10 43 29	17.9722	363	13 17 69	19.0526
324	10 49 76	18.0000	364	13 24 96	19.0788
325	10 56 25	18.0278	365	13 32 25	19.1050
326	10 62 76	18.0555	366	13 39 56	19.1311
327	10 69 29	18.0831	367	13 46 89	19.1572
328	10 75 84	18.1108	368	13 54 24	19.1833
329	10 82 41	18.1384	369	13 61 61	19.2094
330	10 89 00	18.1659	370	13 69 00	19.2354
331	10 95 61	18.1934	371	13 76 41	19.2614
332	11 02 24	18.2209	372	13 83 84	19.2873
333	11 08 89	18.2483	373	13 91 29	19.3132
334	11 15 56	18.2757	374	13 98 76	19.3391
335	11 22 25	18.3030	375	14 06 25	19.3649
336	11 28 96	18.3303	376	14 13 76	19.3907
337	11 35 69	18.3576	377	14 21 29	19.4165
338	11 42 44	18.3848	378	14 28 84	19.4422
339	11 49 21	18.4120	379	14 36 41	19.4679
340	11 56 00	18.4391	380	14 44 00	19.4936
341	11 62 81	18.4662	381	14 51 61	19.5192
342	11 69 64	18.4932	382	14 59 24	19.5448
343	11 76 49	18.5203	383	14 66 89	19.5704
344	11 83 36	18.5472	384	14 74 56	19.5959
345	11 90 25	18.5742	385	14 82 25	19.6214
346	11 97 16	18.6011	386	14 89 96	19.6469
347	12 04 09	18.6279	387	14 97 69	19.6723
348	12 11 04	18.6548	388	15 05 44	19.6977
349	12 18 01	18.6815	389	15 13 21	19.7231
350	12 25 00	18.7083	390	15 21 00	19.7484
351	12 32 01	18.7350	391	15 28 81	19.7737
352	12 39 04	18.7617	392	15 36 64	19.7990
353	12 46 09	18.7883	393	15 44 49	19.8242
354	12 53 16	18.8149	394	15 52 36	19.8494
355	12 60 25	18.8414	395	15 60 25	19.8746
356	12 67 36	18.8680	396	15 68 16	19.8997
357	12 74 49	18.8944	397	15 76 09	19.9249
358	12 81 64	18.9209	398	15 84 04	19.9499
359	12 88 81	18.9473	399	15 92 01	19.9750
360	12 96 00	18.9737	400	16 00 00	20.0000

* By permission from H. Sorenson, "Statistics for Students of Psychology and Education," copyright 1936, McGraw-Hill Book Company, New York.

Table I Squares and Square Roots of Numbers from 1 to 1,000* (Continued)

Number	Square	Square root	Number	Square	Square root
401	16 08 01	20.0250	441	19 44 81	21.0000
402	16 16 04	20.0499	442	19 53 64	21.0238
403	16 24 09	20.0749	443	19 62 49	21.0476
404	16 32 16	20.0998	444	19 71 36	21.0713
405	16 40 25	20.1246	445	19 80 25	21.0950
406	16 48 36	20.1494	446	19 89 16	21.1187
407	16 56 49	20.1742	447	19 98 09	21.1424
408	16 64 64	20.1990	448	20 07 04	21.1660
409	16 72 81	20.2237	449	20 16 01	21.1896
410	16 81 00	20.2485	450	20 25 00	21.2132
411	16 89 21	20.2731	451	20 34 01	21.2368
412	16 97 44	20.2978	452	20 43 04	21.2603
413	17 05 69	20.3224	453	20 52 09	21.2838
414	17 13 96	20.3470	454	20 61 16	21.3073
415	17 22 25	20.3715	455	20 70 25	21.3307
416	17 30 56	20.3961	456	20 79 36	21.3542
417	17 38 89	20.4206	457	20 88 49	21.3776
418	17 47 24	20.4450	458	20 97 64	21.4009
419	17 55 61	20.4695	459	21 06 81	21.4243
420	17 64 00	20.4939	460	21 16 00	21.4476
421	17 72 41	20.5183	461	21 25 21	21.4709
422	17 80 84	20.5426	462	21 34 44	21.4942
423	17 89 29	20.5670	463	21 43 69	21.5174
424	17 97 76	20.5913	464	21 52 96	21.5407
425	18 06 25	20.6155	465	21 62 25	21.5639
426	18 14 76	20.6398	466	21 71 56	21.5870
427	18 23 29	20.6640	467	21 80 89	21.6102
428	18 31 84	20.6882	468	21 90 24	21.6333
429	18 40 41	20.7123	469	21 99 61	21.6564
430	18 49 00	20.7364	470	22 09 00	21.6795
431	18 57 61	20.7605	471	22 18 41	21.7025
432	18 66 24	20.7846	472	22 27 84	21.7256
433	18 74 89	20.8087	473	22 37 29	21.7486
434	18 83 56	20.8327	474	22 46 76	21.7715
435	18 92 25	20.8567	475	22 56 25	21.7945
436	19 00 96	20.8806	476	22 65 76	21.8174
437	19 09 69	20.9045	477	22 75 29	21.8403
438	19 18 44	20.9284	478	22 84 84	21.8632
439	19 27 21	20.9523	479	22 94 41	21.8861
440	19 36 00	20.9762	480	23 04 00	21.9089

* By permission from H. Sorenson, "Statistics for Students of Psychology and Education," copyright 1936, McGraw-Hill Book Company, New York.

Table I   Squares and Square Roots of Numbers from 1 to 1,000* (Continued)

Number	Square	Square root	Number	Square	Square root
481	23 13 61	21.9317	521	27 14 41	22.8254
482	23 23 24	21.9545	522	27 24 84	22.8473
483	23 32 89	21.9773	523	27 35 29	22.8692
484	23 42 56	22.0000	524	27 45 76	22.8910
485	23 52 25	22.0227	525	27 56 25	22.9129
486	23 61 96	22.0454	526	27 66 76	22.9347
487	23 71 69	22.0681	527	27 77 29	22.9565
488	23 81 44	22.0907	528	27 87 84	22.9783
489	23 91 21	22.1133	529	27 98 41	23.0000
490	24 01 00	22.1359	530	28 09 00	23.0217
491	24 10 81	22.1585	531	28 19 61	23.0434
492	24 20 64	22.1811	532	28 30 24	23.0651
493	24 30 49	22.2036	533	28 40 89	23.0868
494	24 40 36	22.2261	534	28 51 56	23.1084
495	24 50 25	22.2486	535	28 62 25	23.1301
496	24 60 16	22.2711	536	28 72 96	23.1517
497	24 70 09	22.2935	537	28 83 69	23.1733
498	24 80 04	22.3159	538	28 94 44	23.1948
499	24 90 01	22.3383	539	29 05 21	23.2164
500	25 00 00	22.3607	540	29 16 00	23.2379
501	25 10 01	22.3830	541	29 26 81	23.2594
502	25 20 04	22.4054	542	29 37 64	23.2809
503	25 30 09	22.4277	543	29 48 49	23.3024
504	25 40 16	22.4499	544	29 59 36	23.3238
505	25 50 25	22.4722	545	29 70 25	23.3452
506	25 60 36	22.4944	546	29 81 16	23.3666
507	25 70 49	22.5167	547	29 92 09	23.3880
508	25 80 64	22.5389	548	30 03 04	23.4094
509	25 90 81	22.5610	549	30 14 01	23.4307
510	26 01 00	22.5832	550	30 25 00	23.4521
511	26 11 21	22.6053	551	30 36 01	23.4734
512	26 21 44	22.6274	552	30 47 04	23.4947
513	26 31 69	22.6495	553	30 58 09	23.5160
514	26 41 96	22.6716	554	30 69 16	23.5372
515	26 52 25	22.6936	555	30 80 25	23.5584
516	26 62 56	22.7156	556	30 91 36	23.5797
517	26 72 89	22.7376	557	31 02 49	23.6008
518	26 83 24	22.7596	558	31 13 64	23.6220
519	26 93 61	22.7816	559	31 24 81	23.6432
520	27 04 00	22.8035	560	31 36 00	23.6643

* By permission from H. Sorenson, "Statistics for Students of Psychology and Education," copyright 1936, McGraw-Hill Book Company, New York.

Table I Squares and Square Roots of Numbers from 1 to 1,000* (Continued)

Number	Square	Square root	Number	Square	Square root
561	31 47 21	23.6854	601	36 12 01	24.5153
562	31 58 44	23.7065	602	36 24 04	24.5357
563	31 69 69	23.7276	603	36 36 09	24.5561
564	31 80 96	23.7487	604	36 48 16	24.5764
565	31 92 25	23.7697	605	36 60 25	24.5967
566	32 03 56	23.7908	606	36 72 36	24.6171
567	32 14 89	23.8118	607	36 84 49	24.6374
568	32 26 24	23.8328	608	36 96 64	24.6577
569	32 37 61	23.8537	609	37 08 81	24.6779
570	32 49 00	23.8747	610	37 21 00	24.6982
571	32 60 41	23.8956	611	37 33 21	24.7184
572	32 71 84	23.9165	612	37 45 44	24.7385
573	32 83 29	23.9374	613	37 57 69	24.7588
574	32 94 76	23.9583	614	37 69 96	24.7790
575	33 06 25	23.9792	615	37 82 25	24.7992
576	33 17 76	24.0000	616	37 94 56	24.8193
577	33 29 29	24.0208	617	38 06 89	24.8395
578	33 40 84	24.0416	618	38 19 24	24.8596
579	33 52 41	24.0624	619	38 31 61	24.8797
580	33 64 00	24.0832	620	38 44 00	24.8998
581	33 75 61	24.1039	621	38 56 41	24.9199
582	33 87 24	24.1247	622	38 68 84	24.9399
583	33 98 89	24.1454	623	38 81 29	24.9600
584	34 10 56	24.1661	624	38 93 76	24.9800
585	34 22 25	24.1868	625	39 06 25	25.0000
586	34 33 96	24.2074	626	39 18 76	25.0200
587	34 45 69	24.2281	627	39 31 29	25.0400
588	34 57 44	24.2487	628	39 43 84	25.0599
589	34 69 21	24.2693	629	39 56 41	25.0799
590	34 81 00	24.2899	630	39 69 00	25.0998
591	34 92 81	24.3105	631	39 81 61	25.1197
592	35 04 64	24.3311	632	39 94 24	25.1396
593	35 16 49	24.3516	633	40 06 89	25.1595
594	35 28 36	24.3721	634	40 19 56	25.1794
595	35 40 25	24.3926	635	40 32 25	25.1992
596	35 52 16	24.4131	636	40 44 96	25.2190
597	35 64 09	24.4336	637	40 57 69	25.2389
598	35 76 04	24.4540	638	40 70 44	25.2587
599	35 88 01	24.4745	639	40 83 21	25.2784
600	36 00 00	24.4949	640	40 96 00	25.2982

* By permission from H. Sorenson, "Statistics for Students of Psychology and Education," copyright 1936, McGraw-Hill Book Company, New York.

Table I   Squares and Square Roots of Numbers from 1 to 1,000* (Continued)

Number	Square	Square root	Number	Square	Square root
641	41 08 81	25.3180	681	46 37 61	26.0960
642	41 21 64	25.3377	682	46 51 24	26.1151
643	41 34 49	25.3574	683	46 64 89	26.1343
644	41 47 36	25.3772	684	46 78 56	26.1534
645	41 60 25	25.3969	685	46 92 25	26.1725
646	41 73 16	25.4165	686	47 05 96	26.1916
647	41 86 09	25.4362	687	47 19 69	26.2107
648	41 99 04	25.4558	688	47 33 44	26.2298
649	42 12 01	25.4755	689	47 47 21	26.2488
650	42 25 00	25.4951	690	47 61 00	26.2679
651	42 38 01	25.5147	691	47 74 81	26.2869
652	42 51 04	25.5343	692	47 88 64	26.3059
653	42 64 09	25.5539	693	48 02 49	26.3249
654	42 77 16	25.5734	694	48 16 36	26.3439
655	42 90 25	25.5930	695	48 30 25	26.3629
656	43 03 36	25.6125	696	48 44 16	26.3818
657	43 16 49	25.6320	697	48 58 09	26.4008
658	43 29 64	25.6515	698	48 72 04	26.4197
659	43 42 81	25.6710	699	48 86 01	26.4386
660	43 56 00	25.6905	700	49 00 00	26.4575
661	43 69 21	25.7099	701	49 14 01	26.4764
662	43 82 44	25.7294	702	49 28 04	26.4953
663	43 95 69	25.7488	703	49 42 09	26.5141
664	44 08 96	25.7682	704	49 56 16	26.5330
665	44 22 25	25.7876	705	49 70 25	26.5518
666	44 35 56	25.8070	706	49 84 36	26.5707
667	44 48 89	25.8263	707	49 98 49	26.5895
668	44 62 24	25.8457	708	50 12 64	26.6083
669	44 75 61	25.8650	709	50 26 81	26.6271
670	44 89 00	25.8844	710	50 41 00	26.6458
671	45 02 41	25.9037	711	50 55 21	26.6646
672	45 15 84	25.9230	712	50 69 44	26.6833
673	45 29 29	25.9422	713	50 83 69	26.7021
674	45 42 76	25.9615	714	50 97 96	26.7208
675	45 56 25	25.9808	715	51 12 25	26.7395
676	45 69 76	26.0000	716	51 26 56	26.7582
677	45 83 29	26.0192	717	51 40 89	26.7769
678	45 96 84	26.0384	718	51 55 24	26.7955
679	46 10 41	26.0576	719	51 69 61	26.8142
680	46 24 00	26.0768	720	51 84 00	26.8328

* By permission from H. Sorenson, "Statistics for Students of Psychology and Education," copyright 1936, McGraw-Hill Book Company, New York.

Table I   Squares and Square Roots of Numbers from 1 to 1,000* (Continued)

Number	Square	Square root	Number	Square	Square root
721	51 98 41	26.8514	761	57 91 21	27.5862
722	52 12 84	26.8701	762	58 06 44	27.6043
723	52 27 29	26.8887	763	58 21 69	27.6225
724	52 41 76	26.9072	764	58 36 96	27.6405
725	52 56 25	26.9258	765	58 52 25	27.6586
726	52 70 76	26.9444	766	58 67 56	27.6767
727	52 85 29	26.9629	767	58 82 89	27.6948
728	52 99 84	26.9815	768	58 98 24	27.7128
729	53 14 41	27.0000	769	59 13 61	27.7308
730	53 29 00	27.0185	770	59 29 00	27.7489
731	53 43 61	27.0370	771	59 44 41	27.7669
732	53 58 24	27.0555	772	59 59 84	27.7849
733	53 72 89	27.0740	773	59 75 29	27.8029
734	53 87 56	27.0924	774	59 90 76	27.8209
735	54 02 25	27.1109	775	60 06 25	27.8388
736	54 16 96	27.1293	776	60 21 76	27.8568
737	54 31 69	27.1477	777	60 37 29	27.8747
738	54 46 44	27.1662	778	60 52 84	27.8927
739	54 61 27	27.1846	779	60 68 41	27.9106
740	54 76 00	27.2029	780	60 84 00	27.9285
741	54 90 81	27.2213	781	60 99 61	27.9464
742	55 05 64	27.2397	782	61 15 24	27.9643
743	55 20 49	27.2580	783	61 30 89	27.9821
744	55 35 36	27.2764	784	61 46 56	28.0000
745	55 50 25	27.2947	785	61 62 25	28.0179
746	55 65 16	27.3130	786	61 77 96	28.0357
747	55 80 09	27.3313	787	61 93 69	28.0535
748	55 95 04	27.3496	788	62 09 44	28.0713
749	56 10 01	27.3679	789	62 25 21	28.0891
750	56 25 00	27.3861	790	62 41 00	28.1069
751	56 40 01	27.4044	791	62 56 81	28.1247
752	56 55 04	27.4226	792	62 72 64	28.1425
753	56 70 09	27.4408	793	62 88 49	28.1603
754	56 85 16	27.4591	794	63 04 36	28.1780
755	57 00 25	27.4773	795	63 20 25	28.1957
756	57 15 36	27.4955	796	63 36 16	28.2135
757	57 30 49	27.5136	797	63 52 09	28.2312
758	57 45 64	27.5318	798	63 68 04	28.2489
759	57 60 81	27.5500	799	63 84 01	28.2666
760	57 76 00	27.5681	800	64 00 00	28.2843

* By permission from H. Sorenson, "Statistics for Students of Psychology and Education," copyright 1936, McGraw-Hill Book Company, New York.

Table I   Squares and Square Roots of Numbers from 1 to 1,000* (Continued)

Number	Square	Square root	Number	Square	Square root
801	64 16 01	28.3019	841	70 72 81	29.0000
802	64 32 04	28.3196	842	70 89 64	29.0172
803	64 48 09	28.3373	843	71 06 49	29.0345
804	64 64 16	28.3549	844	71 23 36	29.0517
805	64 80 25	28.3725	845	71 40 25	29.0689
806	64 96 36	28.3901	846	71 57 16	29.0861
807	65 12 49	28.4077	847	71 74 09	29.1033
808	65 28 64	28.4253	848	71 91 04	29.1204
809	65 44 81	28.4429	849	72 08 01	29.1376
810	65 61 00	28.4605	850	72 25 00	29.1548
811	65 77 21	28.4781	851	72 42 01	29.1719
812	65 93 44	28.4956	852	72 59 04	29.1890
813	66 09 69	28.5132	853	72 76 09	29.2062
814	66 25 96	28.5307	854	72 93 16	29.2233
815	66 42 25	28.5482	855	73 10 25	29.2404
816	66 58 56	28.5657	856	73 27 36	29.2575
817	66 74 89	28.5832	857	73 44 49	29.2746
818	66 91 24	28.6007	858	73 61 64	29.2916
819	67 07 61	28.6082	859	73 78 81	29.3087
820	67 24 00	28.6356	860	73 96 00	29.3258
821	67 40 41	28.6531	861	74 13 21	29.3428
822	67 56 84	28.6705	862	74 30 44	29.3598
823	67 73 29	28.6880	863	74 47 69	29.3769
824	67 89 76	28.7054	864	74 64 96	29.3939
825	68 06 25	28.7228	865	74 82 25	29.4109
826	68 22 76	28.7402	866	74 99 56	29.4279
827	68 39 29	28.7576	867	75 16 89	29.4449
828	68 55 84	28.7750	868	75 34 24	29.4618
829	68 72 41	28.7924	869	75 51 61	29.4788
830	68 89 00	28.8097	870	75 69 00	29.4958
831	69 05 61	28.8271	871	75 86 41	29.5127
832	69 22 24	28.8444	872	76 03 84	29.5296
833	69 38 89	28.8617	873	76 21 29	29.5466
834	69 55 56	28.8791	874	76 38 76	29.5635
835	69 72 25	28.8964	875	76 56 25	29.5804
836	69 88 96	28.9137	876	76 73 76	29.5973
837	70 05 69	28.9310	877	76 91 29	29.6142
838	70 22 44	28.9482	878	77 08 84	29.6311
839	70 39 21	28.9655	879	77 26 41	29.6479
840	70 56 00	28.9828	880	77 44 00	29.6648

* By permission from H. Sorenson, "Statistics for Students of Psychology and Education," copyright 1936, McGraw-Hill Book Company, New York.

Table I Squares and Square Roots of Numbers from 1 to 1,000* (Continued)

Number	Square	Square root	Number	Square	Square root
881	77 61 61	29.6816	921	84 82 41	30.3480
882	77 79 24	29.6985	922	85 00 84	30.3645
883	77 96 89	29.7153	923	85 19 29	30.3809
884	78 14 56	29.7321	924	85 37 76	30.3974
885	78 32 25	29.7489	925	85 56 25	30.4138
886	78 49 96	29.7658	926	85 74 76	30.4302
887	78 67 69	29.7825	927	85 93 29	30.4467
888	78 85 44	29.7993	928	86 11 84	30.4631
889	79 03 21	29.8161	929	86 30 41	30.4795
890	79 21 00	29.8329	930	86 49 00	30.4959
891	79 38 81	29.8496	931	86 67 61	30.5123
892	79 56 64	29.8664	932	86 86 24	30.5287
893	79 74 49	29.8831	933	87 04 89	30.5450
894	79 92 36	29.8998	934	87 23 56	30.5614
895	80 10 25	29.9166	935	87 42 25	30.5778
896	80 28 16	29.9333	936	87 60 96	30.5941
897	80 46 09	29.9500	937	87 79 69	30.6105
898	80 64 04	29.9666	938	87 98 44	30.6268
899	80 82 01	29.9833	939	88 17 21	30.6431
900	81 00 00	30.0000	940	88 36 00	30.6594
901	81 18 01	30.0167	941	88 54 81	30.6757
902	81 36 04	30.0333	942	88 73 64	30.6920
903	81 54 09	30.0500	943	88 92 49	30.7083
904	81 72 16	30.0666	944	89 11 36	30.7246
905	81 90 25	30.0832	945	89 30 25	30.7409
906	82 08 36	30.0998	946	89 49 16	30.7571
907	82 26 49	30.1164	947	89 68 09	30.7734
908	82 44 64	30.1330	948	89 87 04	30.7896
909	82 62 81	30.1496	949	90 06 01	30.8058
910	82 81 00	30.1662	950	90 25 00	30.8221
911	82 99 21	30.1828	951	90 44 01	30.8383
912	83 17 44	30.1993	952	90 63 04	30.8545
913	83 35 69	30.2159	953	90 82 09	30.8707
914	83 53 96	30.2324	954	91 01 16	30.8869
915	83 72 25	30.2490	955	91 20 25	30.9031
916	83 90 56	30.2655	956	91 39 36	30.9192
917	84 08 89	30.2820	957	91 58 49	30.9354
918	84 27 24	30.2985	958	91 77 64	30.9516
919	84 45 61	30.3150	959	91 96 81	30.9677
920	84 64 00	30.3315	960	92 16 00	30.9839

* By permission from H. Sorenson, "Statistics for Students of Psychology and Education," copyright 1936, McGraw-Hill Book Company, New York.

Table I   Squares and Square Roots of Numbers from 1 to 1,000* (Continued)

Number	Square	Square root	Number	Square	Square root
961	92 35 21	31.0000	981	96 23 61	31.3209
962	92 54 44	31.0161	982	96 43 24	31.3369
963	92 73 69	31.0322	983	96 62 89	31.3528
964	92 92 96	31.0483	984	96 82 56	31.3688
965	93 12 25	31.0644	985	97 02 25	31.3847
966	93 31 56	31.0805	986	97 21 96	31.4006
967	93 50 89	31.0966	987	97 41 69	31.4166
968	93 70 24	31.1127	988	97 61 44	31.4325
969	93 89 61	31.1288	989	97 81 21	31.4484
970	94 09 00	31.1448	990	98 01 00	31.4643
971	94 28 41	31.1609	991	98 20 81	31.4802
972	94 47 84	31.1769	992	98 40 64	31.4960
973	94 67 29	31.1929	993	98 60 49	31.5119
974	94 86 76	31.2090	994	98 80 36	31.5278
975	95 06 25	31.2250	995	99 00 25	31.5436
976	95 25 76	31.2410	996	99 20 16	31.5595
977	95 45 29	31.2570	997	99 40 09	31.5753
978	95 64 84	31.2730	998	99 60 04	31.5911
979	95 84 41	31.2890	999	99 80 01	31.6070
980	96 04 00	31.3050	1,000	100 00 00	31.6228

* By permission from H. Sorenson, "Statistics for Students of Psychology and Education," copyright 1936, McGraw-Hill Book Company, New York.

Table II Areas under the Normal Curve*

z or $\dfrac{x}{\sigma}$	Area Between Mean and z	Area Beyond z	z or $\dfrac{x}{\sigma}$	Area Between Mean and z	Area Beyond z
1	2	3	1	2	3
0.00	.0000	.5000	0.35	.1368	.3632
0.01	.0040	.4960	0.36	.1406	.3594
0.02	.0080	.4920	0.37	.1443	.3557
0.03	.0120	.4880	0.38	.1480	.3520
0.04	.0160	.4840	0.39	.1517	.3483
0.05	.0199	.4801	0.40	.1554	.3446
0.06	.0239	.4761	0.41	.1591	.3409
0.07	.0279	.4721	0.42	.1628	.3372
0.08	.0319	.4681	0.43	.1664	.3336
0.09	.0359	.4641	0.44	.1700	.3300
0.10	.0398	.4602	0.45	.1736	.3264
0.11	.0438	.4562	0.46	.1772	.3228
0.12	.0478	.4522	0.47	.1808	.3192
0.13	.0517	.4483	0.48	.1844	.3156
0.14	.0557	.4443	0.49	.1879	.3121
0.15	.0596	.4404	0.50	.1915	.3085
0.16	.0636	.4364	0.51	.1950	.3050
0.17	.0675	.4325	0.52	.1985	.3015
0.18	.0714	.4286	0.53	.2019	.2981
0.19	.0753	.4247	0.54	.2054	.2946
0.20	.0793	.4207	0.55	.2088	.2912
0.21	.0832	.4168	0.56	.2123	.2877
0.22	.0871	.4129	0.57	.2157	.2843
0.23	.0910	.4090	0.58	.2190	.2810
0.24	.0948	.4052	0.59	.2224	.2776
0.25	.0987	.4013	0.60	.2257	.2743
0.26	.1026	.3974	0.61	.2291	.2709
0.27	.1064	.3936	0.62	.2324	.2676
0.28	.1103	.3897	0.63	.2357	.2643
0.29	.1141	.3859	0.64	.2389	.2611
0.30	.1179	.3821	0.65	.2422	.2578
0.31	.1217	.3783	0.66	.2454	.2546
0.32	.1255	.3745	0.67	.2486	.2514
0.33	.1293	.3707	0.68	.2517	.2483
0.34	.1331	.3669	0.69	.2549	.2451

* Reprinted from Robert B. Clarke, Arthur P. Coladarci, John Caffrey, "Statistical Reasoning and Procedures," Charles E. Merrill Books, Inc., Columbus, Ohio, 1965.

Table II   Areas under the Normal Curve (Continued)

z or $\dfrac{x}{\sigma}$	Area Between Mean and z	Area Beyond z	z or $\dfrac{x}{\sigma}$	Area Between Mean and z	Area Beyond z
1	2	3	1	2	3
0.70	.2580	.2420	1.05	.3531	.1469
0.71	.2611	.2389	1.06	.3554	.1446
0.72	.2642	.2358	1.07	.3577	.1423
0.73	.2673	.2327	1.08	.3599	.1401
0.74	.2704	.2296	1.09	.3621	.1379
0.75	.2734	.2266	1.10	.3643	.1357
0.76	.2764	.2236	1.11	.3665	.1335
0.77	.2794	.2206	1.12	.3686	.1314
0.78	.2823	.2177	1.13	.3708	.1292
0.79	.2852	.2148	1.14	.3729	.1271
0.80	.2881	.2119	1.15	.3749	.1251
0.81	.2910	.2090	1.16	.3770	.1230
0.82	.2939	.2061	1.17	.3790	.1210
0.83	.2967	.2033	1.18	.3810	.1190
0.84	.2995	.2005	1.19	.3830	.1170
0.85	.3023	.1977	1.20	.3849	.1151
0.86	.3051	.1949	1.21	.3869	.1131
0.87	.3078	.1922	1.22	.3888	.1112
0.88	.3106	.1894	1.23	.3907	.1093
0.89	.3133	.1867	1.24	.3925	.1075
0.90	.3159	.1841	1.25	.3944	.1056
0.91	.3186	.1814	1.26	.3962	.1038
0.92	.3212	.1788	1.27	.3980	.1020
0.93	.3238	.1762	1.28	.3997	.1003
0.94	.3264	.1736	1.29	.4015	.0985
0.95	.3289	.1711	1.30	.4032	.0968
0.96	.3315	.1685	1.31	.4049	.0951
0.97	.3340	.1660	1.32	.4066	.0934
0.98	.3365	.1635	1.33	.4082	.0918
0.99	.3389	.1611	1.34	.4099	.0901
1.00	.3413	.1587	1.35	.4115	.0885
1.01	.3438	.1562	1.36	.4131	.0869
1.02	.3461	.1539	1.37	.4147	.0853
1.03	.3485	.1515	1.38	.4162	.0838
1.04	.3508	.1492	1.39	.4177	.0823

Table II Areas under the Normal Curve (Continued)

z or $\frac{x}{\sigma}$	Area Between Mean and z	Area Beyond z	z or $\frac{x}{\sigma}$	Area Between Mean and z	Area Beyond z
1	2	3	1	2	3
1.40	.4192	.0808	1.75	.4599	.0401
1.41	.4207	.0793	1.76	.4608	.0392
1.42	.4222	.0778	1.77	.4616	.0384
1.43	.4236	.0764	1.78	.4625	.0375
1.44	.4251	.0749	1.79	.4633	.0367
1.45	.4265	.0735	1.80	.4641	.0359
1.46	.4279	.0721	1.81	.4649	.0351
1.47	.4292	.0708	1.82	.4656	.0344
1.48	.4306	.0694	1.83	.4664	.0336
1.49	.4319	.0681	1.84	.4671	.0329
1.50	.4332	.0668	1.85	.4678	.0322
1.51	.4345	.0655	1.86	.4686	.0314
1.52	.4357	.0643	1.87	.4693	.0307
1.53	.4370	.0630	1.88	.4699	.0301
1.54	.4382	.0618	1.89	.4706	.0294
1.55	.4394	.0606	1.90	.4713	.0287
1.56	.4406	.0594	1.91	.4719	.0281
1.57	.4418	.0582	1.92	.4726	.0274
1.58	.4429	.0571	1.93	.4732	.0268
1.59	.4441	.0559	1.94	.4738	.0262
1.60	.4452	.0548	1.95	.4744	.0256
1.61	.4463	.0537	1.96	.4750	.0250
1.62	.4474	.0526	1.97	.4756	.0244
1.63	.4484	.0516	1.98	.4761	.0239
1.64	.4495	.0505	1.99	.4767	.0233
1.65	.4505	.0495	2.00	.4772	.0228
1.66	.4515	.0485	2.01	.4778	.0222
1.67	.4525	.0475	2.02	.4783	.0217
1.68	.4535	.0465	2.03	.4788	.0212
1.69	.4545	.0455	2.04	.4793	.0207
1.70	.4554	.0446	2.05	.4798	.0202
1.71	.4564	.0436	2.06	.4803	.0197
1.72	.4573	.0427	2.07	.4808	.0192
1.73	.4582	.0418	2.08	.4812	.0188
1.74	.4591	.0409	2.09	.4817	.0183

Table II   Areas under the Normal Curve (Continued)

z or $\dfrac{x}{\sigma}$ 1	Area Between Mean and z 2	Area Beyond z 3	z or $\dfrac{x}{\sigma}$ 1	Area Between Mean and z 2	Area Beyond z 3
2.10	.4821	.0179	2.45	.4929	.0071
2.11	.4826	.0174	2.46	.4931	.0069
2.12	.4830	.0170	2.47	.4932	.0068
2.13	.4834	.0166	2.48	.4934	.0066
2.14	.4838	.0162	2.49	.4936	.0064
2.15	.4842	.0158	2.50	.4938	.0062
2.16	.4846	.0154	2.51	.4940	.0060
2.17	.4850	.0150	2.52	.4941	.0059
2.18	.4854	.0146	2.53	.4943	.0057
2.19	.4857	.0143	2.54	.4945	.0055
2.20	.4861	.0139	2.55	.4946	.0054
2.21	.4864	.0136	2.56	.4948	.0052
2.22	.4868	.0132	2.57	.4949	.0051
2.23	.4871	.0129	2.58	.4951	.0049
2.24	.4875	.0125	2.59	.4952	.0048
2.25	.4878	.0122	2.60	.4953	.0047
2.26	.4881	.0119	2.61	.4955	.0045
2.27	.4884	.0116	2.62	.4956	.0044
2.28	.4887	.0113	2.63	.4957	.0043
2.29	.4890	.0110	2.64	.4959	.0041
2.30	.4893	.0107	2.65	.4960	.0040
2.31	.4896	.0104	2.66	.4961	.0039
2.32	.4898	.0102	2.67	.4962	.0038
2.33	.4901	.0099	2.68	.4963	.0037
2.34	.4904	.0096	2.69	.4964	.0036
2.35	.4906	.0094	2.70	.4965	.0035
2.36	.4909	.0091	2.71	.4966	.0034
2.37	.4911	.0089	2.72	.4967	.0033
2.38	.4913	.0087	2.73	.4968	.0032
2.39	.4916	.0084	2.74	.4969	.0031
2.40	.4918	.0082	2.75	.4970	.0030
2.41	.4920	.0080	2.76	.4971	.0029
2.42	.4922	.0078	2.77	.4972	.0028
2.43	.4925	.0075	2.78	.4973	.0027
2.44	.4927	.0073	2.79	.4974	.0026

Table II Areas under the Normal Curve (Continued)

z or $\dfrac{x}{\sigma}$ 1	Area Between Mean and z 2	Area Beyond z 3	z or $\dfrac{x}{\sigma}$ 1	Area Between Mean and z 2	Area Beyond z 3
2.80	.4974	.0026	3.15	.4992	.0008
2.81	.4975	.0025	3.16	.4992	.0008
2.82	.4976	.0024	3.17	.4992	.0008
2.83	.4977	.0023	3.18	.4993	.0007
2.84	.4977	.0023	3.19	.4993	.0007
2.85	.4978	.0022	3.20	.4993	.0007
2.86	.4979	.0021	3.21	.4993	.0007
2.87	.4979	.0021	3.22	.4994	.0006
2.88	.4980	.0020	3.23	.4994	.0006
2.89	.4981	.0019	3.24	.4994	.0006
2.90	.4981	.0019	3.30	.4995	.0005
2.91	.4982	.0018	3.40	.4997	.0003
2.92	.4982	.0018	3.50	.4998	.0002
2.93	.4983	.0017	3.60	.4998	.0002
2.94	.4984	.0016	3.70	.4999	.0001
2.95	.4984	.0016			
2.96	.4985	.0015			
2.97	.4985	.0015			
2.98	.4986	.0014			
2.99	.4986	.0014			
3.00	.4987	.0013			
3.01	.4987	.0013			
3.02	.4987	.0013			
3.03	.4988	.0012			
3.04	.4988	.0012			
3.05	.4989	.0011			
3.06	.4989	.0011			
3.07	.4989	.0011			
3.08	.4990	.0010			
3.09	.4990	.0010			
3.10	.4990	.0010			
3.11	.4991	.0009			
3.12	.4991	.0009			
3.13	.4991	.0009			
3.14	.4992	.0008			

Table III   Distribution of t^*

Probability

n	.1	.05	.02	.01	.001
1	6.314	12.706	31.821	63.657	636.619
2	2.920	4.303	6.965	9.925	31.598
3	2.353	3.182	4.541	5.841	12.924
4	2.132	2.776	3.747	4.604	8.610
5	2.015	2.571	3.365	4.032	6.869
6	1.943	2.447	3.143	3.707	5.959
7	1.895	2.365	2.998	3.499	5.408
8	1.860	2.306	2.896	3.355	5.041
9	1.833	2.262	2.821	3.250	4.781
10	1.812	2.228	2.764	3.169	4.587
11	1.796	2.201	2.718	3.106	4.437
12	1.782	2.179	2.681	3.055	4.318
13	1.771	2.160	2.650	3.012	4.221
14	1.761	2.145	2.624	2.977	4.140
15	1.753	2.131	2.602	2.947	4.073
16	1.746	2.120	2.583	2.921	4.015
17	1.740	2.110	2.567	2.898	3.965
18	1.734	2.101	2.552	2.878	3.922
19	1.729	2.093	2.539	2.861	3.883
20	1.725	2.086	2.528	2.845	3.850
21	1.721	2.080	2.518	2.831	3.819
22	1.717	2.074	2.508	2.819	3.792
23	1.714	2.069	2.500	2.807	3.767
24	1.711	2.064	2.492	2.797	3.745
25	1.708	2.060	2.485	2.787	3.725
26	1.706	2.056	2.479	2.779	3.707
27	1.703	2.052	2.473	2.771	3.690
28	1.701	2.048	2.467	2.763	3.674
29	1.699	2.045	2.462	2.756	3.659
30	1.697	2.042	2.457	2.750	3.646

* Table III is taken from Table III of Fisher and Yates, "Statistical Tables for Biological, Agricultural and Medical Research," published by Oliver and Boyd Ltd., Edinburgh and London, 1953; by permission of the authors and publishers.

Table IVa   Variance Ratio F, 5 Per Cent Points*†

n_2 \ n_1	1	2	3	4	5	6	8	12	24	∞
1	161.4	199.5	215.7	224.6	230.2	234.0	238.9	243.9	249.0	254.3
2	18.51	19.00	19.16	19.25	19.30	19.33	19.37	19.41	19.45	19.50
3	10.13	9.55	9.28	9.12	9.01	8.94	8.84	8.74	8.64	8.53
4	7.71	6.94	6.59	6.39	6.26	6.16	6.04	5.91	5.77	5.63
5	6.61	5.79	5.41	5.19	5.05	4.95	4.82	4.68	4.53	4.36
6	5.99	5.14	4.76	4.53	4.39	4.28	4.15	4.00	3.84	3.67
7	5.59	4.74	4.35	4.12	3.97	3.87	3.73	3.57	3.41	3.23
8	5.32	4.46	4.07	3.84	3.69	3.58	3.44	3.28	3.12	2.93
9	5.12	4.26	3.86	3.63	3.48	3.37	3.23	3.07	2.90	2.71
10	4.96	4.10	3.71	3.48	3.33	3.22	3.07	2.91	2.74	2.54
11	4.84	3.98	3.59	3.36	3.20	3.09	2.95	2.79	2.61	2.40
12	4.75	3.88	3.49	3.26	3.11	3.00	2.85	2.69	2.50	2.30
13	4.67	3.80	3.41	3.18	3.02	2.92	2.77	2.60	2.42	2.21
14	4.60	3.74	3.34	3.11	2.96	2.85	2.70	2.53	2.35	2.13
15	4.54	3.68	3.29	3.06	2.90	2.79	2.64	2.48	2.29	2.07
16	4.49	3.63	3.24	3.01	2.85	2.74	2.59	2.42	2.24	2.01
17	4.45	3.59	3.20	2.96	2.81	2.70	2.55	2.38	2.19	1.96
18	4.41	3.55	3.16	2.93	2.77	2.66	2.51	2.34	2.15	1.92
19	4.38	3.52	3.13	2.90	2.74	2.63	2.48	2.31	2.11	1.88
20	4.35	3.49	3.10	2.87	2.71	2.60	2.45	2.28	2.08	1.84
21	4.32	3.47	3.07	2.84	2.68	2.57	2.42	2.25	2.05	1.81
22	4.30	3.44	3.05	2.82	2.66	2.55	2.40	2.23	2.03	1.78
23	4.28	3.42	3.03	2.80	2.64	2.53	2.38	2.20	2.00	1.76
24	4.26	3.40	3.01	2.78	2.62	2.51	2.36	2.18	1.98	1.73
25	4.24	3.38	2.99	2.76	2.60	2.49	2.34	2.16	1.96	1.71
26	4.22	3.37	2.98	2.74	2.59	2.47	2.32	2.15	1.95	1.69
27	4.21	3.35	2.96	2.73	2.57	2.46	2.30	2.13	1.93	1.67
28	4.20	3.34	2.95	2.71	2.56	2.44	2.29	2.12	1.91	1.65
29	4.18	3.33	2.93	2.70	2.54	2.43	2.28	2.10	1.90	1.64
30	4.17	3.32	2.92	2.69	2.53	2.42	2.27	2.09	1.89	1.62
40	4.08	3.23	2.84	2.61	2.45	2.34	2.18	2.00	1.79	1.51
60	4.00	3.15	2.76	2.52	2.37	2.25	2.10	1.92	1.70	1.39
120	3.92	3.07	2.68	2.45	2.29	2.17	2.02	1.83	1.61	1.25
∞	3.84	2.99	2.60	2.37	2.21	2.10	1.94	1.75	1.52	1.00

* Lower 5 per cent points are found by interchange of n_1 and n_2; that is, n_1 must always correspond with the greater mean square.

† Table IVa is taken from Table V of Fisher and Yates, "Statistical Tables for Biological, Agricultural and Medical Research," published by Oliver and Boyd Ltd., Edinburgh and London, 1953; by permission of the authors and publishers.

Table IVb   Variance Ratio F, 1 Per Cent Points*†

n_2 \ n_1	1	2	3	4	5	6	8	12	24	∞
1	4052	4999	5403	5625	5764	5859	5982	6106	6234	6366
2	98.50	99.00	99.17	99.25	99.30	99.33	99.37	99.42	99.46	99.50
3	34.12	30.82	29.46	28.71	28.24	27.91	27.49	27.05	26.60	26.12
4	21.20	18.00	16.69	15.98	15.52	15.21	14.80	14.37	13.93	13.46
5	16.26	13.27	12.06	11.39	10.97	10.67	10.29	9.89	9.47	9.02
6	13.74	10.92	9.78	9.15	8.75	8.47	8.10	7.72	7.31	6.88
7	12.25	9.55	8.45	7.85	7.46	7.19	6.84	6.47	6.07	5.65
8	11.26	8.65	7.59	7.01	6.63	6.37	6.03	5.67	5.28	4.86
9	10.56	8.02	6.99	6.42	6.06	5.80	5.47	5.11	4.73	4.31
10	10.04	7.56	6.55	5.99	5.64	5.39	5.06	4.71	4.33	3.91
11	9.65	7.20	6.22	5.67	5.32	5.07	4.74	4.40	4.02	3.60
12	9.33	6.93	5.95	5.41	5.06	4.82	4.50	4.16	3.78	3.36
13	9.07	6.70	5.74	5.20	4.86	4.62	4.30	3.96	3.59	3.16
14	8.86	6.51	5.56	5.03	4.69	4.46	4.14	3.80	3.43	3.00
15	8.68	6.36	5.42	4.89	4.56	4.32	4.00	3.67	3.29	2.87
16	8.53	6.23	5.29	4.77	4.44	4.20	3.89	3.55	3.18	2.75
17	8.40	6.11	5.18	4.67	4.34	4.10	3.79	3.45	3.08	2.65
18	8.28	6.01	5.09	4.58	4.25	4.01	3.71	3.37	3.00	2.57
19	8.18	5.93	5.01	4.50	4.17	3.94	3.63	3.30	2.92	2.49
20	8.10	5.85	4.94	4.43	4.10	3.87	3.56	3.23	2.86	2.42
21	8.02	5.78	4.87	4.37	4.04	3.81	3.51	3.17	2.80	2.36
22	7.94	5.72	4.82	4.31	3.99	3.76	3.45	3.12	2.75	2.31
23	7.88	5.66	4.76	4.26	3.94	3.71	3.41	3.07	2.70	2.26
24	7.82	5.61	4.72	4.22	3.90	3.67	3.36	3.03	2.66	2.21
25	7.77	5.57	4.68	4.18	3.86	3.63	3.32	2.99	2.62	2.17
26	7.72	5.53	4.64	4.14	3.82	3.59	3.29	2.96	2.58	2.13
27	7.68	5.49	4.60	4.11	3.78	3.56	3.26	2.93	2.55	2.10
28	7.64	5.45	4.57	4.07	3.75	3.53	3.23	2.90	2.52	2.06
29	7.60	5.42	4.54	4.04	3.73	3.50	3.20	2.87	2.49	2.03
30	7.56	5.39	4.51	4.02	3.70	3.47	3.17	2.84	2.47	2.01
40	7.31	5.18	4.31	3.83	3.51	3.29	2.99	2.66	2.29	1.80
60	7.08	4.98	4.13	3.65	3.34	3.12	2.82	2.50	2.12	1.60
120	6.85	4.79	3.95	3.48	3.17	2.96	2.66	2.34	1.95	1.38
∞	6.64	4.60	3.78	3.32	3.02	2.80	2.51	2.18	1.79	1.00

* Lower 1 per cent points are found by interchange of n_1 and n_2; that is, n_1 must always correspond with the greater mean square.

† Table IVb is taken from Table V of Fisher and Yates, "Statistical Tables for Biological, Agricultural and Medical Research," published by Oliver and Boyd Ltd., Edinburgh and London, 1953; by permission of the authors and publishers.

Table V Distribution of χ^2*†

Probability

n	.50	.30	.20	.10	.05	.02	.01	.001
1	.455	1.074	1.642	2.706	3.841	5.412	6.635	10.827
2	1.386	2.408	3.219	4.605	5.991	7.824	9.210	13.815
3	2.366	3.665	4.642	6.251	7.815	9.837	11.345	16.266
4	3.357	4.878	5.989	7.779	9.488	11.668	13.277	18.467
5	4.351	6.064	7.289	9.236	11.070	13.388	15.086	20.515
6	5.348	7.231	8.558	10.645	12.592	15.033	16.812	22.457
7	6.346	8.383	9.803	12.017	14.067	16.622	18.475	24.322
8	7.344	9.524	11.030	13.362	15.507	18.168	20.090	26.125
9	8.343	10.656	12.242	14.684	16.919	19.679	21.666	27.877
10	9.342	11.781	13.442	15.987	18.307	21.161	23.209	29.588
11	10.341	12.899	14.631	17.275	19.675	22.618	24.725	31.264
12	11.340	14.011	15.812	18.549	21.026	24.054	26.217	32.909
13	12.340	15.119	16.985	19.812	22.362	25.472	27.688	34.528
14	13.339	16.222	18.151	21.064	23.685	26.873	29.141	36.123
15	14.339	17.322	19.311	22.307	24.996	28.259	30.578	37.697
16	15.338	18.418	20.465	23.542	26.296	29.633	32.000	39.252
17	16.338	19.511	21.615	24.769	27.587	30.995	33.409	40.790
18	17.338	20.601	22.760	25.989	28.869	32.346	34.805	42.312
19	18.338	21.689	23.900	27.204	30.144	33.687	36.191	43.820
20	19.337	22.775	25.038	28.412	31.410	35.020	37.566	45.315
21	20.337	23.858	26.171	29.615	32.671	36.343	38.932	46.797
22	21.337	24.939	27.301	30.813	33.924	37.659	40.289	48.268
23	22.337	26.018	28.429	32.007	35.172	38.968	41.638	49.728
24	23.337	27.096	29.553	33.196	36.415	40.270	42.980	51.179
25	24.337	28.172	30.675	34.382	37.652	41.566	44.314	52.620
26	25.336	29.246	31.795	35.563	38.885	42.856	45.642	54.052
27	26.336	30.319	32.912	36.741	40.113	44.140	46.963	55.476
28	27.336	31.391	34.027	37.916	41.337	45.419	48.278	56.893
29	28.336	32.461	35.139	39.087	42.557	46.693	49.588	58.302
30	29.336	33.530	36.250	40.256	43.773	47.962	50.892	59.703

* For larger values of n, the expression $\sqrt{2\chi^2} - \sqrt{2n-1}$ may be used as a normal deviate with unit variance, remembering that the probability for χ^2 corresponds with that of a single tail of the normal curve.

† Table V is taken from Table IV of Fisher and Yates, "Statistical Tables for Biological, Agricultural and Medical Research," published by Oliver and Boyd Ltd., Edinburgh and London, 1953; by permission of the authors and publishers.

Appendix **D**

**Answers to
Practice
Problems**

Chapter 2

Page 14
1 IQ point, 5, 14, 78–82, 77.5–82.5
2 7, 15, 109.5
Page 24
1a .5–4.5   b 55.5–58.5
  c 3.45–4.05   d 1.245–1.505
2a 3 points, 10; 2 points, 15   b 5 points, 14
  c 1.5 points, 15   d .3 point, 15

Chapter 3

Page 32
1a X is 13.0, Y is 12.5
2a No
Page 34
1 10.5
2 Mary 53, Elizabeth 53; they have equal means.
3 53 words per minute
Page 40
1 63.44
2 Is your answer equal to the answer to Prob. 1?

Chapter 4

Page 51
1a 16th percentile, percentile rank   b 32d percentile, percentile rank
2a 32.5   b 25.3
3a 19.75   b 24.36   c 27.05
4   82d (81.5)

Chapter 5

Page 66
1 2.48
2 .62
Page 69
1a 3.46   b 3.61
Page 72
1a 11.34   b 11.44

Chapter 6

Page 80
1a 84 per cent   b 98 per cent
2 64 and 72 inches
Page 84
1a .75   b 77 per cent, 23 per cent
2a −.75   b 77 per cent, 23 per cent   c 54 per cent
3 Nonsense syllables
Page 86

1	z	T	% below
	1.10	61	86
	.80	58	79
	.10	51	54
	−1.00	40	16
	−1.20	38	12
	−2.00	30	2

Chapter 7

Page 95
1a Positive, moderate   b Positive, moderate
  c Positive, low   d Negative, low
  e Negative, low   f Positive, high

Page 99
1a .92   b   Coefficients are equal (except for roundings).
Page 101
1b Curvilinear

2a r^2 $\sqrt{1 - r^2}$ $(1 - \sqrt{1 - r^2})100$

r^2	$\sqrt{1-r^2}$	$(1-\sqrt{1-r^2})100$
.04	.98	2
.36	.80	20
.64	.60	40
1.00	.00	100

  b   Positively accelerating, curvilinear
  c   Negatively accelerating, curvilinear
  d   Positively accelerating, curvilinear
Page 103
1a Homoscedasticity
  b   Satisfactory
  c   Linearity and homoscedasticity
  d   Satisfactory
  e   Curvilinearity
Page 106
1a 2.3

  b r is .97, s_{IQ} is 8.54, s_{GPA} is .48.   Substitute these values into the formula
      for b, then proceed with usual prediction procedure.   You should again
      get a predicted GPA of 2.3.
Page 109
1a 10.6 per cent   b   30.9 per cent, .6 per cent
2   26.43

Chapter 8

Page 122
1   .125, .375, .375, .125
2   .004, .031, .273
Page 125
1a .15 per cent   b   <.01 per cent
2   12.1 per cent
Page 132
1   3.50, no, not likely
2   3.80, no, not likely
Page 137
1   from 59.75 to 62.25
2   from 16.22 to 18.98

Chapter 9

Page 144
1a Probably not, 4 out of 20 with this great a difference
 b no
2a 2.714
Page 146
1a 1.00   **b** 1.00
Page 151
1a *F* is 1.398, nonsignificant
 b *t* is .575, nonsignificant
Page 155
1 *t* is .20, nonsignificant
2 *t* is .46, nonsignificant

Chapter 10

Page 169
1 *F* is 3.45, nonsignificant
2 Should be equal except for roundings.

Chapter 11

Page 184
1 1.24, nonsignificant
2 5.09, nonsignificant
3 3.96, nonsignificant
Page 188
1 .28, nonsignificant
Page 191
1 1.38, nonsignificant
2 1.30, nonsignificant

Appendix A

I

1a 107	**b** 8	**c** 17
d 30	**e** $ax + 2ay$	**f** $i^2\Sigma fd^2 - i^2 \dfrac{(\Sigma fd)^2}{N}$
2a Unequal	**b** Unequal	**c** Unequal
d Equal	**e** Equal	

3a .583   b $\dfrac{ax}{by}$ c $\dfrac{\Sigma X^2}{N^2}$

d 2.67   e $\dfrac{xb}{ya}$ f 1.42

g $\dfrac{bzx - ay}{yb}$

II

1a 4
b $X_3 = 100,\ X_1 = 105$
c 105.5
d(1) X_2 is more than X_1
(2) X_3 is less than X_1
(3) $(X_1 + X_2)$ is more than $(X_3 + X_4)$
(4) X_1 is not equal to X_2
(5) $A = X_1^2 + X_2^2 + \cdots + X_n^2$, or the sum of the squared X scores

2a Incorrect   b Correct
c Correct   d Correct

3a The average is the sum of all scores divided by the number of scores.
b If we subtract a constant from each score, add up all the scores after this subtraction, and divide this sum by the number of scores we have, the result will be the average minus the constant.
c If we multiply each score by a constant, add up the resulting products, and divide by the number of scores we have, the result is the mean multiplied by the constant.
d If we subtract the average from each score, summate the resulting differences, and divide them by the number of scores we have, the result will be zero.
e The value of $X_1 + X_2 + X_3 + X_4$ is not equal to the value of $X_5 + X_6 + X_7 + X_8$.

4a $\bar{X} = \dfrac{\displaystyle\sum_{i=1}^{10} X_i}{N}$

b $\dfrac{X_1}{X_5} + \dfrac{X_2}{X_5} + \dfrac{X_3}{X_5} + \dfrac{X_4}{X_5} = \dfrac{X_1 + X_2 + X_3 + X_4}{X_5} = \dfrac{\displaystyle\sum_{i=1}^{4} X_i}{X_5}$

c $\displaystyle\sum_{i=1}^{4} X_i^2 - \dfrac{\left(\displaystyle\sum_{i=1}^{4} X_i\right)^2}{N}$

III

1	-3	**2**	-2
3	-9	**4**	-17
5	-12	**6**	28
7	3	**8**	-6

IV

1 $X, y, 3, 2$
2a Linear   b Curvilinear
  c Curvilinear   d Linear
3a $y = 4x + 1$ b $y = 6x - 1$
  c $y = +5x + 2$

V

1	16	**2**	6
3	$4b + 5$	**4**	11
5	y^2	**6**	$\dfrac{\Sigma xy}{Ns_1 s_2}$

VI

1 $x^2 + 2xy + y^2$ **2** $x^2 - 8x + 16$
3 $4x^2 - 4xy + y^2$ **4** $(x + y)(x + y)$
5 $(x + 3)(x + 2)$

Index

Alienation, coefficient of, 100
Analysis of variance (*see* Variance, analysis
   of)
Array, 102
Average, choosing appropriate, 42–43
   mean, 33–40
      combining from several samples, 40–41
      computed from grouped data, 36–40
      computed from ungrouped data, 33–34
      of proportions, 123
      of a sampling distribution, 127
   median, 28–32
   mode, 27–28
   types of, 27
   uses of, 27

Bell-shaped curve, 75

Bimodal distribution, 8
Binomial distribution (*see* Probability)
Bivariate graph, 22–23

Central-limits theorem, 126
Chi square, 174–184
   assumptions in, 183–184
   contingency table in, 178
   degrees of freedom in (*see* Degrees of
      freedom)
   test of independence, 178
   Yates' correction for small cells, 181–
      183
Confidence levels, 129–130
Correlation, assumptions in, 102–103
   computation of, with raw scores, 98–99
      with z scores, 97

Correlation, defined, 92
  interpretation of, 100–101, 109
  limits of coefficient of, 92
  Pearson product-moment, 96
    derivation of raw-score procedure,
      206–211
  of ranked data, 110–113
  scatter diagram in, 93–95
Cumulative frequency, 20–21
Cumulative percentage, 21

Decile, 54
Decoid, 55
Degrees of freedom, 145
  in analysis of variance, 169
  in chi square, 177, 180–181
  in a *t* distribution, 135
  in a *t* test, 150, 154
Descriptive methods, 2
Dispersion, 59
Distribution, bimodal, 8
  frequency (*see* Frequency distribution)
  sampling, 127
  skewed, 78
  Student's, 148
  t, 133, 134
    degrees of freedom with, 135, 154

Errors, type I, 130–131
  type II, 130–131

F test, in analysis of variance, 168
  for homogeneity of variance in *t* test, 150
Fiducial limits, 137
Forecasting efficiency, index of, 101
Frequency, 10
Frequency distribution, construction pro-
    cedure, 9
  defined, 8–9
Frequency polygon, construction of, 16
  smoothing of, 16–18

Graphic representation of data, 15
Grouping, defined, 12
  errors of, 19–20
  procedure for, 13

Histogram, 15–16
Homoscedasticity, 103
  (*See also* Correlation, assumptions in)

Inferential procedures, 2
Interval, step, 10
Interval estimate, 137

Leptokurtosis, 78
Limits, central, theorem of, 126
  real, 11
    in grouped data, 13
    in histograms, 15

Mean (*see* Average)
Median (*see* Average)
Median test, 189–192
Mode (*see* Average)

Nonparametric tests, 173
Normal curve, 18, 76
  areas of the, 78–80
  deviations from the, 78
  formulas for, 77–78
Null hypothesis, 130

Ogive, 21

Parameter, 2
  defined, 3
Parametric tests, 173
Pascal's triangle (*see* Probability)
Percentile, computation of, 51–52
  with zero frequency intervals, 52
Percentile rank, 47
Platykurtosis, 78
Population, 2
Prediction equation (*see under* Regression)
Probability, areas under the normal curve
    and, 124–125
  binomial expansion and, 120–121
    mean of the binomial distribution and,
      123

Probability, binomial expansion and, standard deviation of the binomial distribution and, 123
   computed from Pascal's triangle, 121–122
   defined, 119

Quartile, 54
Quartile deviation, 62–64
Quartoid, 55

Randomization, 2
Range, 61
Real limits (*see* Limits)
Regression coefficient, 104
Regression effect, 110
Regression equation, 104, 106
Regression line, 104
rho (*see* Correlation, of ranked data)
Root-mean-squared deviation, 65

Samples, defined, 2
   random, 2
Sampling distribution and standard error of the mean, 127
Scatter around a mean, 59
Scatter diagram (*see* Correlation)
Series, continuous, 4
   discrete, 3
Sign test, 186–188
Skewness, 78
Standard deviation, grouped data as means of indicating, calculation of, 70–72
   derivation of procedure for, 205–206
   of proportions, 123
   sample versus population, 68–69
   of a sampling distribution (*see* Standard error)
   ungrouped data calculations for, 65–69
Standard error, 72
   of the difference, 144

Standard error, of estimate, 101, 107–109
   derivation of procedure, 211
   of the mean, 87–88, 127
   estimated from sample data, 132
Standard scores, T scores, 80–85
   z scores, 85–87
Statistics, 2
   defined, 3
Student's distribution, 148

t distribution (*see* Distribution, t)
T scores (*see* Standard scores)
t test, 141–151
   with correlated observations, 152–155
   homogeneity of variance in, 150
   large samples, 148–149
   one- or two-tailed test, 156
   sample size and sampling distribution in, 147
   small samples, 149
   unequal variances, 151–152
Type I, type II errors (*see* Errors)

Variability, among groups, 59
   within groups, 60
   within individuals, 60
Variance, 66
   analysis of, assumptions in, 170
      grand mean, 162
      partitioning of variance, 162–163
      sum of squares in, 162
         among groups, 163–167
         within groups, 163–166
         total, 167
   among groups, 163–166
   homogeneity in t test, 150
   pooled, in t test, 145

Yates' correction (*see* Chi square)

z scores (*see* Standard scores)